SYLVIA PANTALEO

Exploring Student Response to Contemporary Picturebooks

UNIVERSITY OF TORONTO PRESS
Toronto   Buffalo   London

© University of Toronto Press Incorporated 2008
Toronto Buffalo London
www.utppublishing.com
Printed in Canada

ISBN 978-0-8020-9799-6

Printed on acid-free paper

Library and Archives Canada Cataloguing in Publication

Pantaleo, Sylvia, 1957–
Exploring student response to contemporary picturebooks / Sylvia Pantaleo.

Includes bibliographical references and index.
ISBN 978-0-8020-9799-6

1. Picture books for children – Educational aspects.   2. Children's literature
– History and criticism.   3. School children – Books and reading.
4. Children – Books and reading.   I. Title.

LB1044.9.P49P35 2008   372.41'2   C2008-903525-9

This book has been published with the help of a grant from the Canadian
Federation for the Humanities and Social Sciences, through the Aid to
Scholarly Publications Programme, using funds provided by the Social
Sciences and Humanities Research Council of Canada.

University of Toronto Press acknowledges the financial assistance to
its publishing program of the Canada Council for the Arts and the
Ontario Arts Council.

University of Toronto Press acknowledges the financial support for its
publishing activities of the Government of Canada through the
Book Publishing Industry Development Program (BPIDP).

To Paul, my soul mate

Contents

Acknowledgments

My sincere appreciation to the Grades 1 and 5 teachers and students who participated in my research. I also thank my research assistant, Adele Vernon, who assisted me with data analysis. An Elva Knight award from the International Reading Association in 2002 funded one year of my research with Grade 1 students. A three-year grant from the Social Sciences and Humanities Research Council of Canada funded my research with older elementary school students.

This book contains some material and ideas that were originally published in various academic journals (those Pantaleo publications in the reference list marked with an asterisk). The following journals and organizations kindly granted me permission to use my material in this publication: *Journal of Children's Literature*, *The Dragon Lode*, *The Reading Teacher*, *Journal of Early Childhood Literacy*, *Journal of Research in Childhood Education*, Springer Science and Business Media (*Children's Literature in Education* and *Early Childhood Education Journal*), *Australian Journal of Language and Literacy*, *Language Arts*, *Changing English*, *Literacy* (United Kingdom Literacy Association), and *English in Australia*.

EXPLORING STUDENT RESPONSE
TO CONTEMPORARY PICTUREBOOKS

Introduction

Many books have been written on the subject of children's literature. Although this book addresses the nature of picturebooks, it differs in focus and intent from other texts such as *Pictures on the Page* (Graham, 1990), *The Picture Book Comes of Age* (Schwarcz & Schwarcz, 1991), *Looking at Pictures in Picturebooks* (Doonan, 1993), *From Picturebook to Literary Theory* (Stephens & Watson, 1994), *Reading Contemporary Picturebooks: Picturing Text* (Lewis, 2001), and *How Picturebooks Work* (Nikolajeva & Scott, 2001), which are devoted specifically to a discussion of picturebooks. Data gathered over four years is used here to describe children's interpretations of and responses to a selection of contemporary picturebooks. This research augments the literature on the nature of elementary students' literary understanding; contributes to the scholarly work on children's responses to literature by describing how the students responded to postmodern picturebooks, specifically books with Radical Change characteristics (Dresang, 1999) and metafictive devices (Waugh, 1984); and extends the research on the social nature of intertextuality. Note: 'picturebook' is spelled here as one word to emphasize the ecological relationship in this type of book between the words and pictures (Lewis, 2001).

This work details the experiences of children in Grades 1 and 5 as they read a selection of contemporary picturebooks with Radical Change characteristics (Dresang, 1999) and/or metafictive devices (Waugh, 1984). My research was among the earliest to use Dresang's Radical Change characteristics (1999) as a framework for examining some of the changes in contemporary children's literature with elementary students. Further, although many researchers and theorists have written about metafiction, few recent studies have explored students' literary understandings of and responses to picturebooks with metafictive devices.

Some brief definitions may be appropriate here. According to Waugh, metafiction is 'fictional writing which self-consciously and systematically draws attention to its status as an artefact in order to pose questions about the relationship between fiction and reality' (1984, p. 2). The common element of the various metafictive devices is their power to distance readers from text, often frustrating traditional reading expectations and practices and positioning 'readers in more active interpretive roles' (McCallum, 1996, p. 398).

Eliza Dresang's Radical Change theory (1999) recognizes how temporal and spatial relationships in society 'have resulted in historically manifested narrative forms' in literature (Holquist, 1996, p. 109). Briefly, Radical Change theory proposes that history works on literature through changing forms and formats, changing perspectives, and changing boundaries. Metafiction, Radical Change, and their application to my research will be more thoroughly discussed in the chapters that follow.

Data gathered over four years is used to discuss the children's interpretations of and responses to the picturebooks. Overall, the objectives of *Exploring Student Response to Contemporary Picturebooks* include the following:

- to contextualize the research in several theoretical frameworks (e.g., Radical Change, postmodernism, intertextuality, and social constructivism);
- to describe Eliza Dresang's Radical Change theory (1999) as a context for understanding the changes in contemporary literature for children and young adults;
- to examine how literature reflects broader social and cultural characteristics;
- to describe the research designs and methods used in the four research projects;
- to discuss the oral and written responses of Grades 1 and 5 children to a selection of contemporary picturebooks with Radical Change characteristics or metafictive devices;
- to examine how Grade 5 students used their knowledge of Radical Change characteristics to create their own stories/books; and
- to discuss the educational significance and pedagogical implications of using literature, such as that used in the studies, in classrooms.

Chapter 1 describes the semiotic relationship between the visual and verbal texts in picturebooks, and the theoretical frameworks that situate the children's literature used in the studies. The interrelationships among postmodern fiction, metafiction, and Radical Change characteristics are examined, and brief discussions about theories and research associated with response to literature are presented. Other topics in chapter 1 include reading aloud to children, literature discussion groups, teacher influence on student response to literature, and the social and intertextual nature of talk in the classroom. These topics are integral to contextualizing the research in the relevant scholarly literature and to understanding and interpreting the findings.

Chapter 2 provides contextual information about the Grade 1 research sites and participants, the qualitative investigative procedures used in the research, and the analyses of the multiple sources of data. This chapter also includes an analysis of the children's responses to various Radical Change characteristics in two of the picturebooks used during the studies, *The Three Pigs* (Wiesner, 2001) and *Voices in the Park* (Browne, 1998).

Chapter 3 looks at the Grade 1 children's oral responses to various metafictive devices in three other picturebooks used in the studies: *Willy the Dreamer* (Browne, 1997); *Tuesday* (Wiesner, 1991); and *Shortcut* (Macaulay, 1995). The active role of the reader in understanding and interpreting these sophisticated picturebooks is discussed, and the concept of interthinking (Mercer, 2000) is used to frame a discussion about the small-group and whole-class read-aloud sessions.

Contextual information about the Grade 5 research site and participants, the qualitative investigative procedures, and the analyses of the multiple sources of data are provided in chapter 4. Data about the Grade 5 students' favourite picturebooks is followed by an examination of the themes that emerged from the students' small-group discussions of and written responses to some of the picturebooks read during the research: *Zoom* (Banyai, 1995) and *Re-Zoom* (Banyai, 1995); *The Three Pigs* (Wiesner, 2001); *The Stinky Cheese Man and Other Fairly Stupid Tales* (Scieszka, 1992); *Who's Afraid of the Big Bad Book?* (Child, 2002); and *Black and White* (Macaulay, 1990). A final section describes the students' perspectives on what they learned about reading picturebooks by reading the literature in the studies.

Chapter 5 includes a detailed analysis of the stories written by three Grade 5 children, and focuses specifically on the Radical Change characteristics they incorporated into their work. A general discussion of the students' stories considers both group and gender similarities and differences. The chapter concludes with a discussion of the intertextual nature of both the students' work and of the literature used during the research. In all of the research classrooms, membership in particular 'social/textual' communities (Kress, 2003) affected the students' oral and written responses about the literature.

An examination of some of the broader implications of students reading, viewing, discussing, and creating print and digital texts in school that reflect changing ways of communicating and representing in their world takes place in chapter 6. Dewey's term 'collateral learning' (1938) is used to emphasize the importance of developing life-long attitudes toward connecting, interacting, and accessing an increasing diversity of symbolic representations.

In all, this book shows how the literature used in my research not only provided the children with pleasurable reading experiences, but also taught the students literary and artistic codes and conventions, critical thinking skills, visual literacy skills, and interpretive strategies. Like children's book authors and illustrators such as David Wiesner, Anthony Browne, David Macaulay, Chris Van Allsburg, Peter Sis, and Jon Scieszka, I have the utmost respect for children and for their abilities as readers. The work presented here demonstrates how children are most capable of interpreting, and in the case of the Grade 5 students, producing sophisticated visual and narrative devices in picturebooks.

1 Contextualizing Contemporary Picturebooks and Response to Literature

Text and Image in Picturebooks

Margaret Meek (1988) has written of the private lessons that readers give themselves by reading, reminding us that texts are not 'neutral substances' and that reading does not happen in a vacuum (pp. 5 & 6). On a questionnaire that I distributed near the conclusion of my research, I asked the Grade 5 children, 'What have you learned about reading picturebooks by reading the picturebooks in the study?' All of the students described more than one lesson that they had learned. Over three-quarters of the fifty-eight students explained that they had learned to 'read the illustrations' – to look carefully at and to study the pictures. Many students explained that they had learned about the importance of looking for hidden items or details in illustrations. In David Macaulay's words, the children had learned 'that it is essential to see, not merely to look' (1991, p. 419). The second most frequent answer, provided by over two-thirds of the students, was that they had learned the importance of careful reading, of taking their time when reading picturebooks. These two recurring and interrelated ideas reflected the nature of the sophisticated literature used in my research. The students less frequently explained that they had learned about the importance of rereading (text and pictures), and of recognizing the relationships between text and illustrations (e.g., synergistic, contradictory).

The students' answers reflect their understanding of the semiotic relationship that exists between the visual and verbal texts in picturebooks. Indeed, picturebooks can be described as multimodal texts, as they contain two semiotic modes, image and writing (Kress, 2003), that are used and combined in multiple ways. The illustrations and the words work together to convey a message, and both sign systems are necessary for constructing meaning (except in wordless picturebooks). Siegel's concept of transmediation, 'a special case of semiosis in the sense that learners use one sign system to mediate another,' (1995, p. 461) seems to accurately describe the synergistic relationship between text and illustrations in picturebooks. Synergy can be defined as 'the simultaneous action of separate agencies which together, have greater total effect than the sum of their individual effects' (Guralnik, 1976, p. 1444). In picturebooks, the 'total effect' depends on the text, the illustrations, and the reciprocity between these two sign systems where 'we adjust our interpretation of the pictures in terms of the words and our interpretation of the words in terms of the pictures' (Sipe, 1998, p. 103).

The synergistic nature of picturebooks has been described in a variety of ways by academics. Marantz identified picturebooks as 'visual-verbal' entities (1977, p. 150); that are not 'literary works' but 'art objects to be experienced' (p. 151). Galda and Cullinan wrote that picturebooks 'tell a story or develop an understanding of a concept through a unique combination of text and art' (2002, p. 11). Doonan used the term 'composite text' to describe the 'work that is made from the union of what the words say and what the pictures show. Properly speaking, it exists nowhere but in the reader/beholder's head' (1993, p. 83).

Many scholars have also written about the visual images in children's literature (Doonan, 1993; Graham, 1990; Lewis, 2001; Nikolajeva & Scott, 2000, 2001; Nodelman, 1988; Sipe, 1998; Styles & Arizpe, 2001). Indeed, several schemes have been proposed to describe the perceived interaction of pictures and words in picturebooks. Agosto differentiated between *parallel storytelling*, where the text and illustrations simultaneously tell the same story, and *interdependent storytelling*, where 'both forms of media [must be considered] concurrently in order to comprehend' the book's story (1999, p. 267). Golden described five different types of visual–verbal relationships: 'text and picture are symmetrical; text depends on picture for clarification; illustration enhances, elaborates text; text carries primary narrative, illustration is selective; and illustration carries primary narrative, text is selective' (1990, p. 104). Congruency, elaboration, specification, amplification, extension, complementation, alternation, deviation, and counterpoint are terms used by Schwarcz (1982) to explain the interaction of text and pictures. Doonan used some of the same vocabulary as Schwarcz in her description of the possible relationships between the visual and verbal texts in picturebooks (elaborate, amplify, extend, complement, contradict, and deviate) (1993, p. 18), as did Nikolajeva and Scott (2001), who criticized many of the existing typologies that describe the relationships between words and pictures.

Other individuals have used a single term or concept in their discussion of the interaction between illustrations and text in picturebooks. For example, Sipe (1998) uses the word 'synergy' to describe the relationship, and Mitchell (1994) coined the term 'imagetext' (p. 9) to avoid the use of a binary theory that looks at the relation of pictures and discourse. He describes imagetexts as 'composite synthetic works (or concepts) that combine image and text' (p. 89). According to Mitchell's definition, picturebooks are thus imagetexts. Lewis (2001) critiqued many of the categorization schemes and suggested an alternative way of looking at picturebooks. He discussed the 'ecology' of the picturebook, in which pictures and words 'interact ecologically, [so] that the book acts as a miniature ecosystem' (p. 48). An ecological perspective emphasizes 'the interdependence or interanimation of word and image' (Lewis, p. 48). In many contemporary picturebooks, this interdependence has become increasingly sophisticated and complex.

Reading pictures is a multifaceted and sometimes personal act that requires focus and sophistication. Children often look at illustrations more closely and 'see' more details in pictures (Kiefer, 1995) than 'skipping and scanning' adults (Meek, 1988, p. 19). Several individuals have explored how children read images in text (Arizpe & Styles, 2003; Kiefer, 1995; Styles & Arizpe, 2001; Walsh, 2000, 2003). For example, Arizpe and Styles (2003) used three multilayered picturebooks to investigate how children aged four to eleven read visual texts. They found that the children who participated in individual and group interviews about the literature were sophisticated readers of visual texts, able to 'read colours, borders, body language, framing devices, covers, endpapers, visual metaphors and visual jokes' (p. 224). Walsh (2003) found that the images in picturebooks evoked a variety of responses in her research participants, some for whom English was a second language. Kiefer's work (1995) revealed how the illustrations in picturebooks influenced children's oral, written, visual, and representative responses. Drawing on Halliday's work (1969) on the functions of language, she developed a taxonomy to describe the children's verbal responses to various picturebooks, which reflected the developmental differences she observed and recorded in the children's responses (1995, p. 25). Not only can the text not be separated from the image in picturebooks, but the complexity of their relationship belies their apparent simplicity.

Contemporary Picturebooks, Postmodernism, Metafiction, and Radical Change

Picturebooks can be read (and looked at) as reflective of the culture and history from which they've emerged. Lewis wrote that 'the diversity of the picturebook is the outcome of its flexibility' (2001, p. 62). He noted that throughout its history, social and cultural changes have impacted the ecology of the picturebook. Bader described a picturebook as a 'social, cultural, historical document' (1976, p. 1) Although she was not writing specifically about picturebooks, Kristeva emphasized that 'texts cannot be separated from the larger cultural or social textuality out of which they are constructed' (Allen, 2000, p. 36). Bakhtin's (1981) term 'chronotope' is useful for understanding how literature reflects the time and space relationships in our world. Chronotopes are particular combinations of time and space that can be used 'as a means for studying the relation between any text and its times, and thus a fundamental tool for a broader social and historical analysis' (Holquist, 1990, p. 113). They can also be the products of the writer's imagination: 'Out of the actual chronotopes of our world (which serve as the source of representation) emerge the reflected and *created* chronotopes of the world represented in the work' (Bakhtin, 1981, p. 253).

Today's children and youth live in a multimedia world characterized by fragmentation, juxtaposition of differing forms, and a diversity of symbolic representations. With respect to children's literature, a growing range of print texts is available to readers. Various conceptual and theoretical frameworks have been proposed to explain the changes that have emerged in contemporary children's literature. Several scholars have noted how the changes in current children's and young-adult literature reflect the broader historical, social, and cultural movement referred to as postmodernism (Coles & Hall, 2001; Goldstone, 1998, 2001/2002; Lewis, 2001; McCallum, 1996; Yearwood, 2002). Although Coles and Hall cautioned that 'postmodernism and its meaning is a contested terrain,' they believe that one undisputed feature of postmodernism is 'its rejection of unity, homogeneity, totality and closure' (2001, p. 114). In other words, the beginning, middle, and end story structure has given way to intricacies of text and image that can challenge and confound readers' expectations.

Lewis identified several key features that characterize life in the postmodern world: indeterminacy, fragmentation, decanonization, irony, hybridization, and performance and participation (2001, pp. 88–91). Because writers and illustrators have been exposed to 'the same postmodernizing influences as everyone else ... it would be reasonable to suppose that such influences might find their way into books' (p. 99). Two of the postmodern characteristics identified by Goldstone, 'greater power given to the reader/viewer encouraging cocreation with the author or artist' and 'nonlinearity' (2001/2002, p. 363), are most in evidence in the picturebooks chosen for the four studies discussed here. Nikolajeva wrote that 'an ever-growing segment of contemporary children's literature is transgressing its own boundaries ... exhibiting the most prominent features of postmodernism, such as genre eclecticism, disintegration of traditional narrative structures, polyphony, intersubjectivity and metafiction' (1998, p. 222). The next sections will examine definitions of metafiction and use the example of *The Three Pigs* (Weisner, 2001) to explore a variety of metafictive devices.

Metafiction

Although metafictive devices have been used since the beginning of literary publishing, they are most reflective of the trends in contemporary literature. Lewis wrote that 'one can see why metafictive devices are essential to the postmodernist enterprise, with its sustained attack on all manifestations of authoritative order and unity' (2001, p. 94). Metafiction draws the attention of readers to how texts work and to how meaning is created through the use of a number of specific devices (see appendix A). This list is neither exhaustive nor definitive, but it does illustrate the range of techniques that comprises metafiction.

In *Metafiction: The Theory and Practice of Self-conscious Fiction*, Waugh (1984) discussed the metafictional novel and described various techniques authors use to create metafictional texts. The work of Lodge (1992), Goldstone, (1998), Lewis (1990, 2001), Trites (1994), Stephens and Watson (1994), Nikolajeva and Scott (2001), and McCallum (1996), reveals one common aspect of metafiction: its self-referentiality or self-consciousness. McCallum wrote that it is necessary to consider 'the specific strategies through which metafictions play with literary and cultural codes and conventions' (1996, p. 400). In picturebooks, metafictive devices can be employed in both the verbal and the visual text. Illustrations can reveal, sometimes independently of and sometimes in conjunction with the words, how the fictional reality of the story is constructed, and thereby comment on how our world is constructed.

Generally, metafictive techniques are used in combination, and the synergy of multiple devices serves to amplify the fictional status and self-conscious nature of a text. Further, the devices are not mutually exclusive: there is overlap among many of the techniques, and several of the specific devices identified in appendix A could be subsumed by some of the more general metafictive techniques described in the literature such as 'boundary-breaking' (Lewis, 1990), 'unstable text' (Fish, 1994), and 'nontraditional ways of using plot, character, and setting' (Anstey, 2002, p. 447). The devices have in common their ability to create distance between readers and the text and to give readers an active role to play in interpreting both the text and illustrations.

Little research has actually explored students' literary understandings of and responses to books with metafictive characteristics (e.g., McClay, 2000; Pantaleo, 2002, 2004b, 2004d, 2005b). Further, although some research has focused on primary grade students' responses to literature (e.g., Barone, 1990; Commeyras & Sumner, 1996; Hickman, 1981; Labbo, 1996; Many & Wiseman, 1992; Sipe & Bauer, 2001), few studies have examined the responses of Grade 1 children (e.g., Kiefer, 1993; McGee, 1992; Sipe, 2000). My work with Grade 1 students addressed two gaps in the literature as it included an exploration of the children's responses to and understandings of metafictive devices in several picturebooks.

METAFICTIVE DEVICES IN *THE THREE PIGS*

David Wiesner's 2002 Caldecott Medal winner *The Three Pigs* (2001) was one of the picturebooks that I used with both the Grade 1 and Grade 5 students. A synopsis of *The Three Pigs* is followed by a description of the metafictive devices apparent in this sophisticated and clever picturebook.

The first two pages of Wiesner's book are similar to traditional versions of *The Three Little Pigs*: the pigs set out into the world to seek their fortune, and each builds a house. However, on the third page when the wolf is huffing and puffing at the straw house, the force of the wolf's blowing causes the first pig to tumble out of the storyboard and exclaim, '*Hey! He blew me right out of the story!*' (unpaginated). The text of the original story continues but there is no pig 'in the story' for the wolf to devour. The first pig comes across the storyboard with the second pig in his stick house and informs him that '*it's safe out here*' (unpaginated). The second pig walks out of his storyboard and he too avoids getting eaten up. The illustrations and text contradict each other, as there is no pork dinner for the bewildered wolf. When the third pig exits the story, the adventure begins. The pigs construct a paper airplane from one of the pages of the story (a page with an illustration of the wolf, who looks most distressed). The three pigs fly through white space. '*Wheeeeeee!*' the third pig exclaims, as they become airborne. After the pigs crash their storyboard airplane, one sticks his snout out at the reader and says, '*I think ... someone's out there*' (unpaginated). The pigs explore other storyboards and enter *Hey Diddle Diddle*, as well as a medieval tale about a dragon and a knight. The cat from *Hey Diddle Diddle* and the dragon from the second story join the trio as they proceed on their adventure. Finally, the pigs decide to return 'home' and literally 'pick up' the original tale just as the wolf threatens to blow down the brick house. Imagine the wolf's surprise when the dragon pokes his head out of the third pig's door. The dragon's head bumps some of the words in the text, and letters go askew. The pigs collect enough letters to end the tale with '*And they all lived happily ever aft*' (unpaginated).

Wiesner's *The Three Pigs* is parodic in nature; it 'reminds us of something known, then gives fresh pleasure by duplicating form that contrasts to new and humorous meaning' (Lukens, 1999, p. 224). The story contains pictures within pictures and stories within stories, and its intertextual nature is most evident in the way that Wiesner introduces these other stories, and characters from other stories, to the book. The mixing of genres includes the original tale about the three pigs, the new story the pigs create as they romp through the book, the stories depicted in the storyboards on several pages, the nursery rhyme *Hey Diddle Diddle*, and the medieval narrative of the dragon and the knight. The new story continues to evolve as characters leave their original stories (and consequently change those stories) to join the three pigs. Several of the discrete stories eventually intertwine and relate to one another. Readers must be attentive and make sense of the multiple layers of visual and textual information. For example, when the dragon and the pigs exit the dragon's story, several storyboards appear on this and the subsequent page.

The Three Pigs contains many digressions, gaps, and disruptions, and there is no 'secondary story world' for readers to get lost in. Disruptions of traditional time and space relationships in stories and narratives are plentiful as the pigs deconstruct the original tale, choose particular storyboards to enter, and create a nonlinear and nonsequential story as they go about their adventure. Readers must follow the pigs' excursions as they exit and enter stories, changing the original tales and creating new tales. Readers must also remain attentive to the multiple stories. Subsequent events are not easy to predict, given the multiple disruptions and intertextual (and intratextual) connections.

Typographic experimentation in *The Three Pigs* has Wiesner using four different font styles and several sizes of text. One font is used for the 'original tale,' but when the first pig gets blown out of the story on the third page, a second font is introduced. The text format also changes as the first pig's spoken words are conveyed in speech balloons. Wiesner uses speech balloons and the same font for the articulations of the other two pigs, the cat, and the dragon. A third font (large and purple) is employed for the text of *Hey Diddle Diddle*. A fourth text font is used for the dragon and knight story. It varies in size on different pages and is an appropriate typographic style for a medieval tale. Wiesner has explained that computer programs also allowed to him to manipulate the text to 'be put in perspective or bent and twisted' (Silvey, 2001, p. 49).

One pig actually enters the 'reader's space' when he peers out of the page and states, '*I think … someone's out there*' (unpaginated), demonstrating his awareness that someone is reading the book. The pigs become commentators on their own story when the third pig points to his house in one of the storyboards and says, '*It's my place. Notice the brickwork. I did it myself*' (unpaginated). On this same page one of the other pigs communicates his desire to end this extratextual excursion: '*You know what? Let's go home*' (unpaginated).

The Three Pigs contains a remarkable mixing of genres, language and speech styles, and ways of telling the story. The pigs speak in 'people prose' (Purves, 1994); their articulations authentically reflect the rhythm and style of conversational language. No narrative connects the snippets of conversation; readers must do this 'reading work' themselves. When the dragon exits his narrative, he too speaks in 'people prose,' but his vocabulary and syntax appropriately reflect his medieval story world. He thanks the pigs for assisting him: '*Many thanks for rescuing me, O brave and noble swine*' (unpaginated).

Wiesner employs a pastiche of illustrative styles in *The Three Pigs*. Several illustrative media (watercolours, gouache, coloured inks, pencil, and coloured pencil) are used (unpaginated), and when the pigs enter the nursery rhyme and the dragon story, their colouring and texture change appropriately for each new context. When the pigs exit the original story and the other stories they have entered, their skin texture becomes fuzzy and life-like, and the character of the illustrations is transformed. Wiesner has commented on the different styles he used for each story and the illustrative traditions he emulated in his artwork:

> The art of the first story, created in pen line and paint, was inspired by Arthur Rackham and Leslie Brooke, the creator of the Johnny Crow books. When the pigs came out of that story, I needed another style … In the dragon story, I acknowledge the line work of Howard Pyle, the father of children's book illustration in America. (Silvey, 2001, p. 49)

One unusual design and layout feature of *The Three Pigs* is Wiesner's use of white space when the pigs exit the traditional tale. The pigs construct an airplane from one of the storyboards and they fly off into the space of two mostly white double-page spreads (openings eight and nine). In his original layout for the picturebook, Wiesner 'had a double-page spread, all white space, all unprinted as the pigs flew right out of the field of vision' (Silvey, 2001, p. 49). However, he was advised to revise his initial layout; the production director believed that many libraries and bookstores would interpret the white pages as a 'mistake,' and return the copies of the book.

Indeterminacy is demonstrated in *The Three Pigs* when, at the end of the book, the original tale has been changed as the cat and the dragon join the three pigs in their story. It is not known how the cat's and the dragon's departure from their stories will affect the trajectory of those texts. Wiesner's entertaining variation on the tale of the three little pigs gives readers a workout as they attempt to follow the multiple story lines and visual gymnastics the author's imagination has created.

Radical Change

Eliza Dresang's Radical Change theory (1999) includes many of the characteristics of postmodern society discussed previously, but she does not use postmodernism as a context in which to frame her theory. Rather, Dresang proposes that 'connectivity, interactivity and access in the digital world explain the fundamental changes taking place' in contemporary children's and young-adult literature (p. 14). Like postmodernism, Radical Change is a historical phenomenon (Pantaleo, 2004a).

Clear distinctions exist in the interrelationships among postmodern fiction, metafiction, and Radical Change characteristics. Postmodern fictions reflect larger trends in our culture and society and are characterized by features such as those identified by Lewis (2001), Goldstone (2001/2002), and Nikolajeva (1998). Many postmodern fictions are inherently metafictive. Radical Change theory also explains how changes in society such as the digital world are reflected in contemporary literature. In academic discourse, some scholars (e.g., Goldstone, 1998; McCallum, 1996; Trites, 1994) have referred to several of Dresang's type one and type two Radical Change characteristics as metafictive devices (see appendix B for a list of picturebooks with Radical Change and/or metafictive devices). However, as Lewis notes, it is important to distinguish between postmodernism, a 'cultural and intellectual' (2001, p. 88) phenomenon, and metafiction, 'an approach, or set of devices, for undermining expectations or for exposing the fictional nature of fictions.' Postmodernism and Radical Change theory are historical phenomena, whereas metafiction is 'an a-historical notion' (p. 94).

Dresang believes that contemporary children's and young-adult literature 'are changing in step with positive changes in the digital world' (1999, p. 14). In *Radical Change: Books for Youth in a Digital Age* (1999), Dresang explains that the fundamental changes in contemporary handheld books – changing forms and formats, changing perspectives, and changing boundaries – reflect the underlying principles of the digital age: interactivity, connectivity, and access. However, Dresang emphasizes that the framework she developed from her Radical Change theory for understanding, appreciating, and evaluating the three types of changes in contemporary literature 'is *not* limited to the digital age' (p. 28). She goes on to identify several selections of children's and young-adult literature from the late 1960s and early 1970s that exhibit Radical Change characteristics.

Type one Radical Change, changing forms and formats, incorporates one or more of the following characteristics: 'graphics in new forms and formats, words and pictures reaching new levels of synergy, non-linear organization and format, nonsequential organization and format, multiple layers of meaning [and] interactive formats' (p. 19). Type two Radical Change, changing perspectives, includes 'multiple perspectives, visual and verbal, previously unheard voices, [and] youth who speak for themselves' (p. 24). Books that incorporate type three Radical Change, changing boundaries, incorporate characteristics such as 'subjects previously hidden, settings previously overlooked, characters portrayed in new complex ways, new types of communities, [and] unresolved endings' (p. 26). The three types of Radical Change and their characteristics are not mutually exclusive. Indeed, a synergistic relationship exists among several of the Radical Change characteristics. Many books contain more than one type of Radical Change, and as Dresang notes, a reader's perspective should be taken into account when considering the exact subcategory of each type of Radical Change (p. 41).

Dresang describes her Radical Change framework as proposing that 'connectivity, interactivity and access in the digital world explain the fundamental changes taking place in the body of literature for young readers' (p. 14). According to Dresang, the principles of connectivity and interactivity apply to both readers and books. The changing forms and formats of many contemporary picturebooks, such as those used in my research projects, require that readers to make connections between the 'hypertext-like links' in the books, and among the multiple perspectives, narratives, and layers of meaning. Connectivity also refers to the increased sense of community created by the books, as the forms and formats encourage sharing among readers.

Since the publication of *Radical Change*, Dresang has expanded her ideas to include information behaviour (2005). In a chapter in *Theories of Information Behavior: A Researcher's Guide* (Fisher, Erdelez & McKechnie, 2005), Dresang discussed how the digital principles of interactivity, connectivity, and access explain not only the technology of the book, but also describe many aspects of contemporary information behaviour in both handheld and electronic resources (pp. 298–302).

In the following sections, a description of some of Dresang's Radical Change characteristics will be followed by illustrative examples from *The Three Pigs* (Wiesner, 2001).

TYPE ONE RADICAL CHANGE – CHANGING FORMS AND FORMATS

Graphics in New Forms and Formats. Dresang (1999) uses the term 'graphic' to describe a 'digitally-influenced book ... if it is visually unusual or outstanding' (p. 82). Some of the features that exemplify this particular characteristic include the use of colour to communicate meanings or to 'take the place of words,' or 'pictures, maps, or graphs [that] play a predominant part in a book that might be expected to have mostly words' (p. 82). In some graphic books, the design or placement of words on a page can represent sounds or transmit meaning, or text may be superimposed on an illustration, 'appearing simultaneously as both words and picture' (p. 82). Although a book does not need to have colour or illustrations to be categorized as graphic, Dresang explains that something in the book must be 'visually striking' (p. 83).

The Three Pigs fits Dresang's notion of a digitally influenced book. Wiesner uses colour to communicate meaning in the various stories in the book (bright watercolours for the nursery rhyme, sepia for the medieval tale), and transmits meaning by the design and placement of words on the pages. Four different fonts and several sizes of text appear in the book, and Wiesner varies the placement and appearance of text, such as when the dragon's head collides with the text and the letters are scattered.

Words and Pictures Reaching New Levels of Synergy. Categories that describe the various text and image interactions in picturebooks have been developed by researchers including Nikolajeva and Scott (2001) and Lewis (2001). Lewis critiques many of the existing categorization schemes, and suggests an alternative way of looking at picturebooks, an ecological perspective that emphasizes 'the interdependence or interanimation of word and image' (p. 48). Similarly, Sipe (1998) uses the term 'synergy' to describe the relationship between text and illustration and to underscore the simultaneity effect of the two sign systems. Siegel's (1995) concept of transmediation most accurately describes the synergistic relationship between text and illustrations in *The Three Pigs*. When the pigs exit the original story and the other stories they enter, their skin texture transforms, their eyes become realistic (each pig has a different eye colour – green, blue, and brown), and their personalities change. No words describe these transformations – readers must 'read the illustrations' to notice the changes.

Nonlinear and Nonsequential Organization and Format. The European North American linear narrative format of beginning, middle, and end is simply one discursive structure of stories (McCabe, 1997). Clearly, the plot trajectory in many contemporary picturebooks is not direct, chronological, or continuous. Disruptions or interruptions create a sequence of events that does not follow a chronological, causal, or logical order. Readers observe the interactivity of the pigs with other characters and other stories as the pigs deconstruct the original tale, choose particular storyboards to enter, and create a nonlinear sequential story as they go about their adventure.

Multiple Layers of Meaning. A multilayered reading experience is created through the use of literary devices such as time switches and stories within stories (verbal and/or visual layering). According to Dresang, 'two aspects distinguish these techniques as Radical Change: the nonlinearity and the complexity with which they are employed' (1999, p. 116).

The Three Pigs provides a multilayered reading experience by including many intertextual connections, nonlinear and complex time switches, and verbal and visual layering of stories – pictures within pictures and stories within stories. For instance, Wiesner uses of speech balloons for the pigs, the dragon, and the cat. The speech balloons are part of the illustrations, but they also form the text.

Interactive Formats. Picturebooks have always required that readers be interactive as they move back and forth between the visual and verbal text. However, 'radically changed forms and formats demand a greater degree of attentiveness and interaction ... children must decide whether to "point and click" here or there with their eyes and their minds' (Dresang, 1999, p. 114). The nature of many texts with Radical Change characteristics requires that readers make complex decisions whether to continue with the 'main' narrative or visual text, or to pursue another textual or illustrative path. One example of an interactive format is the inclusion of parallel stories. The second narrative may be told entirely through illustrations (e.g., *Something From Nothing*, Gilman, 1992), or with words. Other interactive formats can include a voice (or voices) that comment on the story, and texts that require reading of more than one set of words (e.g., speech bubbles). In *The Three Pigs*, readers must remain attentive to the multiple stories, and subsequent events are not easily predicted due to the multiple disruptions and intertextual and intratextual connections (see appendix J for other interactive features).

TYPE TWO RADICAL CHANGE – CHANGING PERSPECTIVES

Multiple Perspectives, Visual and Verbal. Multiple perspectives can be created through multiple voices in one book, many voices in many books, one character who speaks from a range of life stances, or through pictures (Dresang 1999, p. 126). Picturebooks can include multiple visual perspectives as well. Prior to the digital age, most picturebooks were illustrated with mid-range illustrations but in many contemporary picturebooks readers view scenes from below, above, 'to the side or the midst of the action' (p. 139).

The Three Pigs provides a postmodern and playful perspective on existing literature. Several voices are heard throughout the story (the narrator, the pigs, the dragon, and the cat), and most of these verbal perspectives are also portrayed visually. Wiesner not only introduces multiple visual perspectives (the storyboards and other stories), but illustrates scenes from various points of view. Readers observe the action from front, side, underneath, behind (when the pigs are flying on the paper airplane), and bird's-eye views.

Wiesner conveys verbal perspectives by integrating several language forms into this picturebook. Storybook language is used for the 'original tale' and the dragon's story, *Hey Diddle Diddle* introduces nursery rhyme language, and the pigs themselves speak in people prose.

TYPE THREE RADICAL CHANGE – CHANGING BOUNDARIES

Unresolved Endings. An unresolved ending is one of five characteristics of type three Radical Change. Authors may choose to leave the conclusions of their work open to interpretation and the lack of closure and uncertainty in these books can be unsettling for some readers. In some books, the open endings force readers to 'reconsider the meaning of the entire story' (Dresang, 1999, p. 232). For example, at the end of *The Three Pigs*, the dragon and the cat from *Hey Diddle Diddle* have become part of the original tale. It is unclear how these creatures' departure from their own original texts, and their presence in pigs' story has affected and will affect the three texts.

An appreciation of the nature of picturebooks and an understanding the conceptual foundations of postmodernism, metafiction, and Radical Change will enhance reader comprehension and interpretation of the data analysis in my subsequent chapters. I use several of Dresang's Radical Change characteristics as a framework to discuss the Grade 1 students' oral responses to and interpretations of *The Three Pigs* (Wiesner, 2001) and *Voices in the Park* (Browne, 1998) in chapter 3. I also use Dresang's Radical Change characteristics to analyse the stories written by the Grade 5 students who participated in my research. Further, I incorporate the principles of interactivity and connectivity throughout the discussions of the Grades 1 and 5 students' oral and written responses.

Response to Literature

The students who participated in my research spent a significant amount of time talking about the picturebooks used in the studies. Oral communication or sign language contributes to the way we construct knowledge and understanding. Like Louise Rosenblatt (1976), I believe that readers should be involved actively in constructing meaning when they read, and that they should have opportunities to talk about, write about, or represent their responses. While I acknowledge that the classroom context, no matter how democratic and caring, frames students' oral, written, visual, or representational responses, my teaching and research experiences have revealed that elementary and middle school students' responses to literature can provide teachers with a window into, or at least a glimpse of, students' reading transactions.

The phrase 'response to literature' is overused by researchers, theorists, and practitioners. The expression is often used as an umbrella term 'to refer to any aspect of literature and its teaching' (Squire, 1990, p. 13). Purves and Rippere explain the complexity of 'response to literature' as

> mental, emotional, intellectual, sensory, physical. It encompasses the cognitive, affective, perceptual and psychomotor activities that the reader … performs as he reads or after he has read. Yet most teachers know that, in the classroom, a student's response will be like an iceberg: only a small part will become apparent to the teacher or even to the student himself. (1968, p. xiii)

Squire reminds reader-oriented reader-response theorists (Rosenblatt, 1991) that, 'the text itself imposes rigorous limits on the nature and direction' of a reader's response (Squire, p. 14). Further, Squire emphasizes that readers cannot be given 'a predetermined response' (p. 14).

Reader-response theories attempt to explain the location of meaning during the reading event. Although reader-response theorists differ in their specific underlying orientations and explanations of the roles and activities of readers, texts, and contexts in the reading process, all agree that readers are actively involved in the construction of meaning (Tompkins, 1980). Thus, readers' responses are integral to their understandings and interpretations of texts.

Louise Rosenblatt's transactional theory (1976) emphasizes the dynamic role of the reader during the reading event, while it recognizes the roles of the text and the context. Rosenblatt (1985) adopted Dewey's term 'transaction' to describe the reciprocal relationship between reader and text. In reading, both reader and text act upon each other, and mutually contribute to and define the relationship. Readers selectively attend to the various symbolizations that are brought into their awareness by the signs on the page. Rosenblatt (1981) explained how readers choose and organize particular elements or memories, stimulated or guided by the marks or squiggles on a page: 'As the reader's eyes move along the page, the newly evoked symbolizations are tested for whether they can be fitted into the tentative meanings already constructed for the preceding portion of the text' (Rosenblatt, 1994, p. 1064).

Rosenblatt asserted that during the transaction between text and reader, a 'poem' or new experience is evoked. She described the particularity of the evocation and of the diversity of reader response, as each reader brings a unique repertoire of literary and life experiences to each reading event. A reader's 'linguistic-experiential reservoir reflects' her or his 'cultural, social, and personal history' (Rosenblatt, 1994, p. 1064). Rosenblatt's ecological consideration of the literary transaction also allows for the social and cultural contexts of the reading event. The poem, the lived-through work, is what readers respond to 'as it is being called forth during the transaction, and as it is reflected on, interpreted, evaluated, analyzed, criticized afterward' (Rosenblatt, 1986, p. 124). For Rosenblatt, response occurs both during and after the reading event because even as we are generating and engaged with the evocation, 'we are reacting to it; this may affect our choices as we proceed with reading' (1994, p. 1070). 'Interpretation can be understood as the effort to report, analyze and explain the evocation' or meaning (p. 1071). Rosenblatt (1978) believes that readers can make various defensible interpretations of their evocations, and points out that some interpretations are more valid than others.

Rosenblatt also distinguishes aesthetic from efferent reading and views these two stances as poles on a continuum. In aesthetic reading, the reader 'adopts an attitude of readiness to attend to what is being lived through during the reading event' (1988, p. 74) and focuses on both the private and public aspects of meaning. Rosenblatt emphasizes that both public and private meanings have cognitive and affective associations. In efferent reading, 'the process of making meaning out of a text involves selective attention to what is to be retained' as residue after the reading and focuses mainly on the public referents of meaning (1981, p. 6). 'The distinction between aesthetic and nonaesthetic reading, then, derives ultimately from what the reader does, the stance that he adopts and the activities he carries out in relation to the text' (1978, p. 27). Rosenblatt believes that any text can be read from either a predominantly aesthetic or efferent stance, with most reading events falling somewhere along the aesthetic/efferent continuum. Further, the synergistic relationship among reader, textual, and contextual factors affects the stance a reader adopts toward any one text. Rosenblatt also asserts that there are no purely aesthetic nor purely efferent readings, and that readers' stances may fluctuate as they read.

Iser's reception theory also recognizes the active role of readers in the construction of meaning and the plurality of meaning of text. For Iser, reading is always 'the process of anticipation and retrospection' (1980, p. 50). A reader's wandering viewpoint that travels inside the text involves the reader in the processes 'of continually forming and modifying both expectations of what is to come and interpretations of what has previously been read' (Thomson, 1984, p. 21). Omissions or gaps in texts engage readers in the construction of meaning as they invite readers to establish their own connections by bringing in life and literary experiences. The textual indeterminacies also limit interpretations as readers must fill in gaps with information that is consistent with events and characters in the text.

Readers should always be involved actively in the construction of meaning, and the picturebooks used in my studies with the Grades 1 and 5 students require a high degree of reader participation. Picturebooks have generally required readers to fill in gaps and generate predictions on multiple levels as they move back and forth between text and artwork. However, the picturebooks used in my research demand a high level of sophistication and complexity with respect to gap-filling (Iser, 1978) and predicting. These picturebooks are writerly texts that require readers to be actively involved in 'producing' the text. Barthes (1975) describes writerly or scriptible texts as those that require readers to draw inferences, generate connections, fill in gaps, make interpretations, and formulate hypotheses. Writerly texts achieve plurality of meaning because each reader brings a unique repertoire of literary and life experiences to each reading event. The Grade 1 inter-active read-aloud sessions and the Grade 5 small-group peer-led dis-cussions provided the children with opportunities to share their understandings and interpretations of these writerly picturebooks, and to use oral language to think together.

Interthinking and the Social Nature of Response

Neil Mercer has coined the term 'interthinking' to link the cognitive and social functions of group talk. He defined interthinking as the 'joint, coordinated intellectual activity which people regularly accom-plish using language' (2000, p. 16). Essentially, interthinking means using talk to think collectively, to engage with others' ideas through oral language. Dawes writes that 'the most useful medium for inter-thinking is talk, because talk allows rapid reflection and response. Speaking and listening is the child's primary access to the minds of other people' (2001, p. 126). Vygotsky (1978) also stressed the funda-mental role of language in social contexts in developing human cogni-tion. 'Language plays a crucial role in a socially formed mind because it is our primary avenue of communication and mental contact with others, serves as the major means by which social experience is repre-sented psychologically and is an indispensable tool for thought' (Berk & Winsler, 1995, p. 12).

The social constructivist perspective is consistent with Vygotsky's sociocultural theory of cognitive development in its explanation of the social construction of understanding by individuals in specific con-texts (Schwandt, 1998). In the personal sense, individuals construct meaning as new information interacts with existing knowledge. In the larger sense, 'while knowledge is personally constructed, the con-structed knowledge is socially mediated as a result of cultural experi-ences and interactions with others in that culture' (McRobbie & Tobin, 1997, p. 194). Social constructivism provides a theoretical paradigm for understanding how people construct particular ways of knowing, thinking, and communicating about the world.

Children quickly learn the 'rules' for speaking at school. Classroom talk is multifaceted and shaped by a number of individual, social, and cultural factors that operate synergistically. The whole of a teacher's behaviour, her tone of voice, gestures, stance, and the way she 'receives' children's articulations of any kind, communicates expectations about what and how language can and should be used in the classroom (Barnes, 1992, p. 33). A teacher's pattern of oral communication also signals expectations with respect to thinking and behaviour. Further, 'the communication pattern of any classroom is the outcome of a history of mutual interpretation by teacher and pupils, in each case based upon previous experiences which they bring to the lessons' (Barnes, 1992, p. 33). 'Talk itself creates its own context' (Mercer, 1995, p. 68); the intertextual history of talk – what we say, how we say it, and how others receive it – creates the foundation for subsequent talk.

In my research, I wanted the children to be engaged in and experience pleasure and enjoyment from the interactive read-aloud sessions and the small-group discussions. The teachers and I worked to create an interpretive community (Fish, 1980) of individuals who engaged collaboratively in the construction and interpretation of meaning. The discussion transcripts in the following chapters demonstrate that the peer and adult exchanges afforded the students with opportunities for scaffolding interpretations, extending understandings, exploring significances, and constructing storylines.

Reading Aloud to Children, Student Discussions, and Teacher Influence

Practitioners, researchers, and theorists agree that reading aloud to children is highly beneficial (Galda, Ash, & Cullinan, 2000; Teale, 2003; Yaden, Rowe, & MacGillivray, 2000). Gordon Wells's seminal research (1986) documented the power of reading stories to children and many researchers have examined the talk of teachers and students during read-aloud sessions and literature discussions (Martinez & Roser, 2003). Reading aloud can develop children's literacy skills, promote interest in reading, increase knowledge about concepts about print, facilitate language development, increase reading achievement, provide opportunities for social interaction, and improve writing abilities (Galda et al., 2000). Several researchers have noted the multiple benefits of using an interactive format when reading aloud to children (Barrentine, 1996; Copenhaver, 2001; Sipe, 2000a, 2001; Wasik & Bond, 2001). Barrentine wrote that 'instruction and conversation are woven' during interactive readings (1996, p. 38). Sipe's grounded theory on young children's literary understanding was developed in a classroom where the teacher used an interactive read-aloud format (2001). Sipe subsequently applied his theory to data gathered in other classrooms where primary-grade children were encouraged to respond to stories in an interactive manner (2001). I also chose to use an interactive read-aloud format with the Grade 1 students who participated in my research.

Researchers who examined children's comprehension of stories when read aloud in whole-class, small-group, and one-to-one settings (Morrow, 1987, 1988; Morrow & Smith, 1990) found that 'reading to children in small groups offer[ed] as much interaction as one-to-one readings and appear[ed] to lead to greater gains in comprehension than whole-class or even one-to one readings' (Morrow & Gambrell, 2000, p. 571). How children's questions and comments develop over time as they listen to stories, and how the changes in children's responses indicate internalization of the interactive behaviour of the adult who is reading the story (Morrow & Gambrell) have also been documented. A teacher's stance toward reading, literature, and response invites students to adopt reciprocal stances (Beach, 1993). Indeed, numerous studies have documented how teachers influence students' oral and written responses to literature (Eeds & Wells, 1989; Hickman, 1983, 1984; Hynds, 1992; Marshall, 1987; Pantaleo, 1995; Purves, 1973; Villaume & Worden, 1993).

Hickman's research (1983, 1984) with elementary students (Grades K–5) found that 'the teacher's own response behavior was mirrored again and again in children's comments, questions, and approaches' (1983, p. 13). Many and Wiseman (1992) described how various teaching approaches to literature affected the content of Grade 3 students' written responses. Children who received instruction that focused on their literary experiences, their reactions and thoughts to stories, wrote responses 'indicating more involvement in the story world, described similarities between characters and real people, and treated literature more as an aesthetic experience than a lesson or an object to be studied' (p. 265). Efferent responses, which focused on literary analysis, were most frequently written by children who had received instruction on identifying and critiquing 'literary elements' through an 'analysis of character development, problems and solutions, and themes as developed in both text and illustrations' (p. 269).

Other studies have also explored the role of the teacher in literature discussions (e.g., Almasi, 1995; Battle, 1995; Maloch, 2002, 2004; McGee, 1992; Roser & Martinez, 1985; Short, Kauffman, Kaser, Kahn, & Crawford, 1999), the nature of teacher talk in literature discussions, and the influence of teacher talk on student talk and behaviour. Eeds and Wells maintained that 'grand conversations' about literature were possible when teachers were fellow participants in discussion groups and shared their own personal transactions with texts and acknowledging that their ideas, interpretations, and opinions were possibilities, not definitive answers (1989, p. 28). Villaume and Worden wrote that the 'ways students engage in literature discussions with adults and peers set the foundation for the way students think about literature as they read independently' (1993, p. 463). According to Hynds, teachers' questions 'not only affect students' literary responses and interpretation processes; they affect the stances students take toward texts and toward reading in general' (1992, p. 92).

The purposes and goals of literature discussion groups should be considered when examining teacher participation. 'Instead of arguing for or against teacher presence in literature circles,' Kauffman, Short, Crawford, Kahn, and Kaser 'believe that discussions with and without teachers offer different, but equally valuable, potentials for social interaction and the negotiation of meaning' (1996, p. 373). Many factors influence student response during literature discussions; to examine one, such as teacher participation, in isolation, is complicated by the multifaceted nature of each, as well as the synergy among individual, textual, contextual, and social factors.

Research that examined primary grade students' discussions of children's literature (e.g., Barone, 1990; Commeyras & Sumner, 1996; Hickman, 1981; Jewell & Pratt, 1999; Labbo, 1996; Many & Wiseman, 1992; Pantaleo, 2002, 2003a, 2003b, 2004a, 2004b, 2004c, 2004d, 2005a; Sipe & Bauer, 2001) has suggested that 'young children are capable of producing elaborate and sophisticated responses to literature, especially when supported with instruction' (Morrow & Gambrell, 2000, p. 575). McGee (1992) studied grand conversations of Grade 1 students and found that the children responded in personal and interpretative ways, and focused on text-specific elements, character, and story events. Her analysis revealed a continuum of text-bound and reader-bound statements. Kiefer (1993, 1995), like McGee, developed a descriptive framework to describe children's oral responses to literature. She found that both primary and intermediate students responded to picturebooks in meaningful ways using four different functions of language. Sipe (2000a, 2001) has also examined the oral responses of primary grade children in several classrooms. His analyses of transcripts of read-aloud sessions and picturebook discussions have revealed the complex nature of young children's literary understanding. The Grade 1 students in my studies, several of whom were not meeting grade-level expectations in language arts, most capably dealt with the Radical Change characteristics and metafictive devices in the picturebooks.

Little research has explored immigrants' children's responses to picturebooks. Colledge (2005) noted, understandably, how many of the culturally specific intertextualities in the picturebooks she used in her research were not grasped by the young Bengali-speaking children she was working with. However, the picturebooks provided the students with 'a bridge between the known and the culturally unfamiliar' (p. 24). The children made close observations about setting and characters from the visual features in the literature, indicating a level of interpretation that went 'largely unnoticed by their teachers,' who encouraged the children to focus mainly on the written text (p. 29). Walsh (2000 & 2003) has also researched second language learners' responses to picturebooks. She (2003) found that aside from the expected differences in English language proficiency, the children 'made the same range of comments' as native speaker of English (p. 129), articulated predictions and inferences, made evaluative comments, and empathized with characters.

Similarly, Coulthard's (2003) research with bilingual children demonstrated how, despite different cultural traditions, the children were emotionally engaged and reached deep levels of meaning after reading two contemporary picturebooks. Coulthard described how sophisticated picturebooks by Anthony Browne provided the children with 'intellectual challenge,' and both stimulated and provided ways for the children to demonstrate thinking (p. 189). Picturebooks, such as the detailed visual texts Coulthard used in her research, 'can overcome the barrier of words for those who do not yet speak or read English, providing more equal access to the world of the story' (p. 189). Browne's picturebooks facilitated language learning and inspired the children to talk in a way that pushed 'their language to the outer limits' (p. 189).

Older elementary students' responses to literature including their participation in literature discussion groups have also been studied (Marshall, 2000). Research has focused on peer-led discussions, in which small groups of students work together to collaboratively construct meaning and interpret text. Students select the topics to talk about, share the responsibility for turn taking, and negotiate the rules and conventions for the discussion (Almasi, O'Flahavan, & Ayra, 2001). The factors that affect peer discussions have been described, along with the cognitive, affective, and social benefits and cautions (Evans, 1996, 2002; Leal, 1993) associated with this type of discussion format. Almasi, Garas, Cho, Ma, Shanahan, and Augustino wrote that 'providing readers with the opportunity to explain, clarify, and co-construct their understanding of text via peer discussion enhances student engagement with text (Almasi, McKeown & Beck, 1996), higher order thinking skills, and reading comprehension (Almasi, 1995; Morrow & Gambrell, 2000)' (2004, p. 5). Almasi et al. found that primary grade students who participated in peer discussions, when compared to those in a control condition, 'became more accepting of students in their classrooms in varied contexts' (2004, p. 24). Evans, who examined Grade 5 students' 'perceptions of their experiences participating in peer-led literature discussion groups' (p. 47), identified intersections 'between gender and bossiness' and 'potential intersections between bossiness, race and class' (2002, p. 67). The research findings on peer-led discussions, like those on teacher-led discussions, underscore the complexity of student response in the classroom.

The Social Nature of Intertextuality

The types of interactions that took place during the read-aloud sessions in the Grade 1 classrooms and the small-group and whole-class discussions in the Grade 5 classrooms that I studied influenced the students' repertoires of literary and life experiences (Rosenblatt, 1981). Through multiple experiences with literature, readers construct schemata or cognitive representations of story elements, discourses, and genres, and grow in their understanding that every text is 'itself the intertext of another text' (Barthes, 1975, p. 77). The reader is an elemental component of intertextuality, as 'what is produced at the moment of reading is due to the cross-fertilization of ... all the texts which the reader brings to it' (Still & Worton, 1990, pp. 1–2). Thus, the students' intertextual histories were constantly changing as they listened to, talked about, and responded to each picturebook. Changes in individual functioning subsequently influenced the next read-aloud and discussion sessions, and these social experiences shaped individual thinking. The children's membership in a particular 'social/textual community' (Kress, 2003b, p. 159) affected their conversations about the literature, as well as their visual and written responses, resonating with past research that has emphasized the social nature of intertextuality (Bloome & Egan-Robertson, 1993; Cairney, 1992; Oyler & Barry, 1996). The students' experiences during my research created a particular type of 'literacy club' (Smith, 1988) with specific values and knowledge that included the structural, discursive, linguistic, literary, and visual features of literature with Radical Change characteristics. The shared intertextual histories were most evident as the studies progressed; during the read-aloud sessions with the Grade 1 students and the discussions with the Grade 5 students, the children frequently made connections to previously read picturebooks.

Two examples illustrate the shared intertextual histories of the students. During an art class near the end of the Grade 5 study in 2003, Max (all student names are pseudonyms) painted a large green balloon with a black string attached and wrote the caption, 'This is not a balloon.' One of the transparencies that I had shared with the students before I read Anthony Browne's *Willy the Dreamer* (1997) was a piece of artwork by Magritte called 'The Treason of the Picture,' a painting of a pipe with the text *'Ceci n'est pas une pipe.'* Max's painting was displayed on the wall of Ms H.'s Grade 5 classroom and the students found his artwork very humorous. Like Browne, Max had transformed Magritte's sign, and the members of this particular interpretive community (Fish, 1980) understood the intertextual significance of Max's painting.

In David Wiesner's *The Three Pigs* (2001), one pig enters the 'reader's space' when he peers out of the page and says, *'I think ... someone's out there'* (unpaginated). The pig may be speaking to his brothers, to himself, or to readers. Regardless, the children in Ms P.'s Grade 1 class were absolutely astonished by the pig's statement. Their incredulous looks and laughter indicated a lack of experience with this type of narrative device. At this point in the whole-class read-aloud session, all of the children started talking: they remarked that the pig was looking at them, the person beside them, or their friends. Interestingly, a few days later when pairs of children were presenting mini puppet plays to their classmates, Kathy turned her puppet to the audience and had it say, 'Hey, I think someone's out there.' The children burst into laughter – they completely understood and appreciated this intertextual reference.

Consistent with a 'theory of literacy as social practice' (Barton & Hamilton, 2000, p. 7), these examples emphasize how Max's visual representation and Kathy's oral comments were embedded in a specific context of social interactions and activities that were generated as they engaged with particular kinds of texts. Johnston wrote that 'children grow into the intellectual life around them' and 'that intellectual life is fundamentally social' (2004, p. 65). The students' membership in a particular classroom community and the purposes and expectations associated with 'a kind of textual practice' (Dyson, 2001, p. 381) influenced the children's conversations, writing, and representations. The picturebooks provided the students with much aesthetic pleasure, and enjoyment of literature is the essential constituent to becoming a lifelong reader. Further, the students developed and demonstrated a sense of agency as a result of their recognition and application of the sophisticated literary devices they learned about through reading and discussing the picturebooks.

2 Grade 1 Children, Three Porcines, and Four Voices

In this chapter I describe Grade 1 students' understandings of and responses to the Radical Change characteristics in *The Three Pigs* (Wiesner, 2001) and *Voices in the Park* (Browne, 1998), two of the picturebooks that I read to the participants in my research. I acted both as researcher and teacher in my studies, as I worked directly with the classroom teachers and the Grade 1 students. An understanding of the contexts and the qualitative methodological procedures of my research will provide readers with a framework for understanding the discussions of the interpretations of my findings that follow.

Research Site and Participants

Year One

The first study took place in a Grade 1 classroom in an elementary school of approximately 300 students in a midsize city in eastern Ontario, Canada. The student population came from predominantly lower socioeconomic class families, and several families were recent immigrants to Canada. Of the twenty-three children in Ms P.'s Grade 1 class who participated in the study, English was not the language spoken at home for eight children: two had very limited proficiency in English, one was somewhat proficient in English, and the other five were quite proficient in English. Four girls and eleven boys were of European-Canadian ethnicity, one girl and one boy were South Asian, two boys were Asian, one boy was from Libya, one boy was from Saudi Arabia, one boy was from Cambodia, and one boy was from Chile. When asked to describe the children's literacy skills at the beginning of the year, Ms P., who was in her seventh year of teaching, believed that, in general, the students' skills were below average. The work of seven students remained below provincial standards for Grade 1 in both reading and writing at the end of the year.

The students participated in guided reading groups and numerous whole-class reading and writing activities in Language Arts and other curricular areas. Ms P. read aloud at least one book (fiction, nonfiction, or poetry) daily, and the students often completed follow-up writing activities related to the selections. According to Ms P., the students' enjoyment of listening to stories had been evident from the beginning of the school year. She described the large-group story discussions as 'limited in depth' and dominated by a few students. Ms P. believed that some students' limited vocabularies inhibited their contributions to the story discussions.

Year Two

During the second year of my research, I worked in an elementary school (Grades K–7) of approximately 155 students in a city in western British Columbia, Canada. The school was located in a predominantly commercial area of the inner city, and the school's population consisted primarily of students from families of lower socio-economic status.

In Mrs W.'s Grade 1 class, English was not the language spoken at home for two of the twenty children. Of the nineteen participants, two girls and one boy were of First Nations ancestry, one boy was from Romania, one girl was from Uruguay, one girl was of African-Canadian ethnicity, and thirteen children were from Euro-Canadian families. Mrs W., who was a trained Reading Recovery teacher and in her sixteenth year of teaching, believed that most of the children's literacy skills were within the average range for beginning Grade 1. There were two notable exceptions: two boys were significantly delayed and below the British Columbia Grade 1 provincial standards for both reading and writing. Three students demonstrated significant delays in speech and language and received weekly in-school therapy from a speech and language pathologist.

At the beginning of the Grade 1 year the children were involved in many language and literacy activities including guided reading, shared reading, independent reading, teacher read-alouds, buddy reading with Grade 4 students, shared writing, interactive writing, journal writing, modelled writing, morning message, working with words, and response-based activities. Mrs W. noted that overall, her class was responsive to teacher read-alouds and demonstrated much interest in rhythmic poems and songs.

Research Methods

Year One

The primary purpose of my study with Ms P.'s Grade 1 students was to explore the nature of their literary understanding by examining their verbal, written, and visual arts responses to picturebooks. Although some past research has examined children's literary understanding, these studies often focused on the traditional or central elements of narrative (Baumann & Bergeron, 1993). Limited research exists on storybook reading with young children, in which literary understanding is conceptualized in a broader and richer way.

I spent time in Ms P.'s Grade 1 classroom during January 2001 in order to develop a rapport with the children. Data collection took place between February and May. Of the nineteen boys and five girls in the Grade 1 classroom, all but one of the students' parents gave informed consent for their children to participate in the study. With input from Ms P., the research participants were organized into heterogeneous groups of three or four students. The membership of each small group fluctuated throughout the study for pragmatic reasons (student absences or participation in other programs).

The following picturebooks were read with and to the children: *Willy the Dreamer* (Browne, 1997); *Snowflake Bentley* (Martin, 1998); *Safari* (Bateman, 1998); *Something From Nothing* (Gilman, 1992); *Shortcut* (Macaulay, 1995); *The Empty Pot* (Demi, 1990); *Voices in the Park* (Browne, 1998); *The Three Pigs* (Wiesner, 2001); and *Tuesday* (Wiesner, 1991). The nine books represented a variety of types of picturebooks – storybook, nonfiction, informational narrative, wordless – and covered a range of complexity and sophistication of presentation of verbal and visual text (see appendix C for annotations of the literature used in the four studies).

The children were pulled out of regular classroom activities once a week for approximately twenty-five minutes for the small-group read-aloud sessions that took place in a vacant room in the school. The students were encouraged to talk to one another or to me at any point during the read-aloud sessions (Barrentine, 1996). Many benefits have been identified with the use an interactive format when reading aloud to children. Research on effective reading instruction has found that effective teachers engaged in an interactive style that encouraged active student involvement (Taylor, Peterson, Pearson & Rodriguez, 2002). Effective teachers also 'posed more "open" questions, to which multiple responses' were appropriate (Allington, 2002, p. 744). I approached my study without a predetermined set of questions to ask the children. Rather, I asked questions that were appropriate, and that were natural extensions of the talk surrounding each book. I expanded on the children's comments, articulated topic-continuing replies, and asked questions during the sessions that encouraged student consideration and discussion of unexplored textual and illustrative aspects. Each small-group read-aloud session was audio-recorded.

After I had read the story to each small group, I reread the book to the entire class and again, student participation was encouraged. Understandably, the children's small-group read-aloud experiences influenced both their articulations and my questions during the whole-class read-aloud sessions. Ms P. took field notes and recorded students' comments, facial expressions, and body language as I read each book to the class. Again, all of the whole-class read-aloud sessions were audio-recorded.

The students completed an independent writing activity after the small-group read-aloud sessions for the first five books. Unfortunately, neither Ms P. nor I were able to assist the children with their writing – she was often working with a guided reading group, and I was conducting another small-group session. We found that some students copied each other's ideas or rushed through their work. For the last four books, we changed our procedures so that the children wrote their responses after the whole-class read-aloud sessions. We were able to remind the children before they began writing to think about what they were feeling, thinking, wondering, questioning, or imagining as they listened to and talked about the story. Finally, after each whole-class read-aloud session, the students completed a drama, visual arts, and/or writing activity that was designed to extend their reading experiences of the literature. For example, for *The Three Pigs* (Wiesner, 2001), the children were instructed to copy Wiesner's idea and blow the pigs into a different story (Pantaleo, 2002).

At the completion of the study, I interviewed each student. The children were asked to identify their favourite picturebook(s) that I had read aloud and to provide reasons for their selections. I also asked the students to share their opinions about participating in the small-group read-aloud sessions.

Year Two

My research in year two extended the previous study with Grade 1 children as I focused specifically on the students' responses to and interpretations of contemporary books with metafictive devices. Again, I spent time in Mrs W.'s Grade 1 classroom prior to beginning the study in September 2002. Of the parents or guardians of the nine boys and eleven girls in Mrs W.'s class, all but one gave informed consent for their children to participate in the study. During the nine-week study, the children listened to me read the following eight picturebooks: *Willy the Dreamer* (Browne, 1997); *Something From Nothing* (Gilman, 1992); *Tuesday* (Wiesner, 1991); *The Three Pigs* (Wiesner, 2001); *The True Story of the Three Little Pigs* (Scieszka, 1989); *Shortcut* (Macaulay, 1995); *Voices in the Park* (Browne, 1998); and *A Day at Damp Camp* (Lyon, 1996). I selected these books because I believe that each of them contains at least one metafictive device (see appendix A).

The children participated in both small-group and whole-class interactive read-aloud sessions. For the small-group read-aloud sessions, the students were organized into heterogeneous groups of three or four students, and group membership changed for each picturebook. Again, the children were pulled out of regular classroom activities once a week for approximately twenty-five minutes to participate in the sessions. After I read the story to each small group, I reread the book to the entire class, and student participation was encouraged. All read-aloud sessions were audio-recorded and Mrs W. took field notes during each session.

Following each whole-class read-aloud session, the children were asked to visually represent their responses to the picturebook. Mrs W. and I reminded the students to think about their feelings, questions, and imaginings as they listened to and talked about the story before they began their pictures. The children received minimal direction to complete their drawings, and no whole-class discussion took place about what the children 'might' draw. All of the children immediately began to draw their visual representations once they returned to their desks from the carpeted area where the whole-class read-alouds

occurred. As the children worked on their pictures, Mrs W. and I circulated around the room, and talked with the students about their
work. Since the study took place at the beginning of the school year,
the children dictated their accompanying sentences to either Mrs W. or
myself. The children informed us when their drawings were complete
or nearly complete and they were ready to dictate their sentences. If
necessary, we verbally prompted the children with 'Tell me about your
picture,' or 'What do you want to say about your picture?'

At the completion of the study, the children were interviewed individually about their favourite picturebooks and about their participation in the read-aloud sessions.

Data Analysis

Year One

My research data included the transcriptions of the small-group and
whole-class read-aloud sessions, drama response sessions, and my
weekly meetings with Ms P. Other data included photocopies of the
children's work, the observational field notes of Ms P., and my
research journal. For each book used in the study six small-group read-
aloud sessions and one whole-class read-aloud session were held. Due
to technical problems, one small-group read-aloud session of *Tuesday*
(Wiesner, 1991), half of a small-group read-aloud of *Voices in the Park*
(Browne, 1998), and the whole class discussion of *The Empty Pot* (Demi,
1990) were not audio-recorded. Approximately 210 minutes of audiotape was produced for each book.

I had no predetermined categorization schemes to apply to the data,
but generated them based on my interpretation of the data. Like Sipe
(2000a), I used the conversational turn 'everything said by one speaker
before another began to speak' (Sinclair & Coulthard, 1975, p. 231), as
the unit of analysis when I examined the students' responses to and
understandings of some aspects of the publisher's peritext such as the
dust jacket, cover, endpages, frontispiece, and title page (Pantaleo,
2003a), and when I focused on the textual associations made by the
children during the read-aloud sessions (Pantaleo, 2004c). My own conversational turns were not included in either analysis of data. I read
over the transcriptions of the small-group and whole-class read-aloud
sessions many times, and data analysis was recursive in nature: initial

codes were often revised based on subsequent readings of the transcripts. However, I was aware that by organizing children's responses into distinct categories regardless of the category labels, I minimized the complex and synergistic nature of students' literary understanding, and failed to capture the richness of the read-aloud discussions.

The transcripts of the small group read-aloud sessions were also analysed deductively. I searched for examples in the transcripts that both reflected and illustrated the Grade 1 students' understandings of and responses to various metafictive devices and Radical Change characteristics (Dresang, 1999) in the literature.

During both studies with the Grade 1 children, the talk about the picturebooks was influenced by the membership of each small group, the nature of each book's text and illustrations, and the questions and comments of the participants and myself. Although each group's conversations varied in scope and substance, the transcript excerpts included here, taken from the small-group read-aloud sessions, are representative of the students' talk.

I also analysed some of the children's written responses (Pantaleo, 2002). Again, data analysis was iterative in nature. The initial categories that emerged from my analysis of the students' written work were tentative and further study resulted in revisions to the conceptual categories. Finally, the student interview data was analysed by tallying the number of selections for each picturebook. I generated categories to describe the students' reasons for their book selections by using the same analysis procedures that I employed for the children's written responses.

Year Two

For each book used in this portion of the study, I held five small-group and one whole-class read-aloud sessions, which resulted in approximately 200 minutes of audiotape. I read the transcripts of the read-aloud sessions several times to search for examples that both reflected and illustrated the children's responses to and interpretations of various metafictive devices (Pantaleo, 2005b). Some of my other research findings from this study, including an analysis of the children's oral responses to and interpretations of *The Three Pigs* (Wiesner, 2001), *A Day at Damp Camp* (Lyon, 1996), and *Tuesday* (Wiesner, 1991), as well as an analysis of the written and visual texts created by Mrs

W.'s students after the whole-class read-aloud session, can be found in Pantaleo, 2003b, 2004a, and 2005a. Finally, the same procedures used in year one to analyse the student interview data about their favourite picturebooks were used in year two.

In the remainder of this chapter, I discuss the Grade 1 students' oral responses to *The Three Pigs* (Wiesner, 2001) and *Voices in the Park* (Browne, 1998).

The Three Pigs

The children in both research classrooms exuded confidence in their 'knowledge' of the trajectory of the story once they heard the title of the book and viewed the illustration of the three pigs on the dust jacket. In the two excerpts below, the children share their enthusiasm for and knowledge about the story. The 'S' comments are my own.

Ms P.'s Grade 1
S: The title is The Three Pigs.
Kathy: Oh, I know what it is! The pigs and the big bad wolf.
Robert: It's like the three little pigs and the big bad wolf!
Changwei: I know this story!
Mrs W.'s Grade 1
Blane: The Three Pigs.
Anita: Oh, The Three Pigs.
Bishop: It's those pigs that build a house and the fox comes along and he huffs and he puffs.
Anita: Hey, I've read that story. I've got that story.
Blane: I think it's the book that I've got.
S: You have the book, Blane?
Blane: Yeah, I have The Three Pigs.
Anita: I love that book.
S: You love that book, do you?
Anita: Yes, and the wolf he huffs and ...
All: And he puffs and he blows your house down!

For most children, the title page reconfirmed their prediction that the story would be the traditional tale as three pigs, one carrying straw, one carrying sticks, and a third hauling a cart of bricks, are depicted on the title page.

Ms P.'s Grade 1
Peter: Oh, this is The Three Little Pigs!
Chris: Yeah, I was right. It is The Three Little Pigs.
Omar: And the big bad wolf. Someone puts up a straw house, and the wolf blowed everything.
Peter: This guy [pointing to the pig with the bricks], his house can't be blowed down. And he saves his brothers.
Mrs W.'s Grade 1
S: Let's look at the title page. It says The Three Pigs ...
Sue: Oh, it looks like it is about the pigs.
Cassandra: Yeah, it's that one.
S: Why do you do say that, Cassandra?
Cassandra: Because one pig is carrying straw, one's carrying bricks, and one's carrying sticks.
Sue: And they're off to make their houses.
Marnie: Of course! [When viewing the dust jacket, Marnie had shared her predictions that Wiesner's book would be similar to the traditional tale of The Three Little Pigs.]

The children were knowledgeable about different versions of the classic tale. Ivan commented, 'In one version, he blows the one with sticks and the one with straw down and eats the pigs up. But the guy with the brick house is the one who lives.' Ali replied, 'I've got a tape of the story and all the pigs live.' Ethan explained that 'One time I read a book, and instead of it being the big bad wolf and the three little pigs, it was the three little wolves and the big bad pig.'

Radical Change Characteristics

David Wiesner's Caldecott Medal winner exhibits all of the characteristics of type one Radical Change (changing forms and formats), and the multiple visual and verbal perspectives of type two Radical Change (changing perspectives) (Dresang, 1999). It is important to remember that neither the three types of Radical Change nor the characteristics of each type are mutually exclusive. A synergistic relationship exists among many of the Radical Change characteristics and, as Dresang notes, the reader's perspective should be taken into account when considering the exact subcategory of each type of Radical Change (p. 41). The Grade 1 children's understandings of and responses to several Radical Change characteristics evident in *The Three Pigs* are discussed below.

TYPE ONE RADICAL CHANGE – CHANGING FORMS AND FORMATS

Graphics in New Forms and Formats. In *The Three Pigs*, colour is used to communicate meaning or to 'take the place of words,' the design or placement of words on a page represents sounds or transmits meaning, and text is superimposed on illustrations, 'appearing simultaneously as both words and picture' (Dresang, 1999, p. 82).

Wiesner transmits meaning by the design and placement of words on the pages. Although the Grade 1 children did not comment on the different fonts used in Wiesner's picturebook, several students remarked on the speech balloons. Six children in Ms P.'s class and two children in Mrs W.'s class used speech balloons in their visual responses to *The Three Pigs*. Further, as a follow-up activity to the story in Ms P.'s Grade 1 class, the children were instructed to copy Wiesner's idea and blow the pigs into a different story. Although we did not discuss the use of speech balloons, fifteen children included them in their artwork, in addition to the text they wrote under each illustration.

During the small-group read-aloud sessions of *The Three Pigs*, the children referred to the speech balloons as 'word clouds,' 'word bubbles,' 'thinking bubbles,' 'brain bubbles,' and 'those thinking things.' They often pointed at specific balloons for me to read. The excerpt below expresses the surprise of a group of students in Ms P.'s class when no speech balloon appears for one of the pigs on the page where the dragon has left its story (text from the book is in quotation marks):

S: *And this pig said,* 'Don't mention it.' *And this pig says,* 'Look who's here. Welcome!' *And the cat goes,* 'Hey diddle diddle!'
Brianna: *Hey, where's the other pig? Why isn't he talking?*
Ryan: *Where is his bubble?*
S: *He didn't say anything this time. You're right; there is no speech balloon for him.*

Placement of text communicates meaning near the end of the book when the dragon sticks his head out of the door of the third pig's brick house and collides with the text. The children explained how 'the words came apart' when the 'dragon knocked them with his horns.' Letters go awry, and the pigs and the dragon collect enough to form the words 'And they all lived happily ever aft.'

Mrs W.'s Grade 1
Bishop: They're putting the words on.
S: Lookit, that's right. They've got a basket here. What are they collecting?
Bishop: Letters.
S: Now why are they collecting the letters?
Anita: To get them back in order.
S: To get them back in order.
Blane: We can't just stick in a, b, c, d ... we need words.

In Ms P.'s class, each small group predicted that the jumbled letters would be used for alphabet soup. The following excerpt is representative of the children's construction of this part of the narrative:

S: 'The wolf huffed ... But no matter how ... could not blow ...' What happened?
Tom: The dragon came out and then he bowed down his head.
S: What did the dragon do?
Tom: He opened the door and the wolf was so scared of the dragon.
José: I think the wolf blew a few letters out of the words.
Frank: No, I think the dragon got it with his horns.
S: Got it with his head when he opened the door?
José: I think the wolf might have blown a few of them, and then the dragon knocked the rest of them out.
Tom: They grabbed all the letters.
S: Yes. 'OK, that's enough!' the pig says. This pig says, 'Come inside, everyone. Soup's on!' The cat says,' I think we're going to like it here.'
Frank: Oh no!
S: What do you think is going to happen, Frank?
Frank: I think the dragon and the cat are going to stay.
José: I think the dragon is going to eat the words.
Tom: No.
José: Yeah, it looks like he's going to eat the words.
S: He's collecting them in a basket.
Tom: To get them for the soup.

S: To catch them for soup? Because he said, 'Soup's on'?
José: Yeah, he's probably going to catch them and then put them in the soup,
   and they're going to have alphabet soup.

The final illustration depicts one pig placing the letters 'e' and 'r' to finish the word 'after.' The letters are not straight – they have been 'placed' manually (pigually). When asked to explain this typographic phenomenon, the children provided a number of explanations including 'Because the dragon ruined them,' 'Because the dragon collected them and tried to put them back,' 'They [the pigs] don't know how to print them,' 'Because the dragon tried to put them up, and they keeped falling,' and 'The dragon is bumping them with the horn.' Thus, the children understood and interpreted Wiesner's varying placements and styles of typography.

Words and Pictures Reaching New Levels of Synergy. Illustrators use several techniques to achieve synergy between text and images in picturebooks. In some books, words and pictures cannot be separated as they are 'integrated in form and format' (Dresang, 1999, p. 90). The term synergy is used by some to describe the relationship between pictures and words in all picturebooks since 'both the text and the illustration sequence would be incomplete without the other' (Sipe, 1998, p. 98). Dresang (1999) writes that words and pictures in many contemporary picturebooks are reaching new levels of synergy.

When the pigs leave their own original story, and when they enter the nursery rhyme and the dragon story, their colouring and texture change appropriately for each new context. No text describes these transformations; readers must interpret the significance of these changes. The following excerpts are typical of the children's interpretations of the transformations:

Ms P.'s Grade 1
Peter: He's got hair you can feel on him. But here [points to part of pig] it is
   still part of him that's cartoonish. But then this [points to part of pig] is
   the real part. And the pig …
Omar: Wait, that's another pig.
S: Actually that's …
Ali: That's him! Look, wait. Inside the book it's cartoon, and out of the book
   it's not.

Mrs W.'s Grade 1

S: 'Hey! He blew me right out of the story!' *So what happened to this pig?*
Kirstin: *He blewed right out of the story and now he has to go back in.*
S: *The wolf blew so hard, right Kirstin, that he blew the pig right out of the storyboard. Those are called storyboards. And what happened to him, Dom? Look at his skin now, what's happening?*
Dom: *It's getting hairier.*
S: *That's right, it's like its got hair on it, but in the book …*
Russell: *He doesn't.*
S: *That's right. Why?*
Russell: *Because he's a fairy tale.*
S: *And out here?*
Russell: *He's real and he has hair.*
Kirstin: *Hey, look at what I noticed. Right there, there's no hair [points to part of pig still in storyboard] and on the rest of him [points to part of pig out of storyboard] there's hair.*
S: *Because what has happened?*
Kirstin: *His feet are in the page, but the rest isn't.*

When the pigs enter *Hey Diddle Diddle* and the dragon story, they are depicted in the same illustrative style used in each narrative world (e.g., in the medieval tale the pigs have no colour). The double-page spread of *Hey Diddle Diddle* shows the pigs both entering and exiting the nursery rhyme. The following two excerpts are typical of the children's remarks about the pigs' transformations:

Mrs W.'s Grade 1

S: *He's pulling in . . .*
Hannah: *Hey! Baa baa black sheep.*
S: *Good guess.*
Sebastian: *Hey little little the cat in the fiddle.*
Jeffrey: *The cow jumped over the moon.*
S: *See, you can read!*
All: *The little dog laughed to see such sport and the dish ran away with the spoon.*
S: *Very good. So what have they pulled in? What do you call this?*
Natalie: *A new story.*
S: *Exactly, they pulled in a new story. This is a nursery rhyme. Hey diddle diddle, the cat and the fiddle, the cow jumped over the moon. The*

little dog laughed to see such sport and the dish ran away with the spoon. *Now what happened to the pigs? Lookit. They're going in this story and what's happening to them?*
Hannah: *They're getting fake.*
S: *They're getting fake. What were you saying, Sebastian?*
Sebastian: *They're turning into cartoons.*
S: *That's right. Look at what happened.*
Hannah: *This one turned pink, this guy turned yellow, and this one turned brown and white [points to each pig as she describes its colour].*
S: *And what happens over here? [points to recto where two pigs are exiting the nursery rhyme].*
Jeffrey: *This one looks real [points to pig].*
Sebastian: *He's going out because he wanted to be real again.*
Ms P.'s Grade 1
Ethan: *They're [the pigs] changing colours.*
S: *That's right, they're changing colours. Look at what is happening.*
Nathan: *Let's get out of here!*
S: *What do you notice about the pigs in this picture? Ethan said they're changing colour.*
Mohad: *Ah, lookit [points to pig].*
S: *This part of him looks real, but these ones, like Ethan said, have changed colour. Then what's happening over here? [pointing to pigs that are leaving the nursery rhyme].*
Jeremy: *The ones are changing.*
S: *Why are they changing colour again?*
Mohad: *I know.*
Ethan: *They are jumping out of the story, so they're real now.*

The children obviously understood how the pigs' physical appearances changed when they left their original physical space in the book and visited new spaces. The cat in *Hey Diddle Diddle* and the dragon in the medieval tale also undergo transformations when they leave their stories, and again, no words describe the physical changes. The children knew why the dragon had colour when he left his tale, and why the creature still had colour at the end of the book, even though he had returned to a 'story.' Kirstin explained, 'Because he's out of that black and white story,' and Teresa added, 'He's in a coloured story now.' Mohad answered his own question about how the dragon could still have colour. 'Because it's a *different* story. His story was just black and white ... Yeah, he was just black and white. But now in this story he has colour.'

The synergy between text and illustrations in *The Three Pigs* is fascinating – the illustrations represent, complement, extend, and contradict the text. On two pages the text reads 'and [the wolf] ate the pig up,' but the perplexed and confused wolf does not eat the two swines because the pigs have left the original tale. The children understood this semiotic contradiction. They explained that the wolf could not devour the pigs because they were out of the 'story' or 'frame' or 'storybook.' Jeffrey, in Mrs W.'s class, explained, 'Because he [the pig] got blown out of the picture.'

Nonlinear and Nonsequential Organization and Format. During the read-aloud sessions, the children in Ms P.'s class commented on the pigs leaving the various stories and looking for other stories to enter. Gurjit observed that the pigs were 'visiting a lot of stories.' When the pigs 'pulled down' *Hey Diddle Diddle*, Melissa asserted, 'They brought in another story. They brought in a nursery rhyme.' Shamah remarked on the storyboards behind the narrative of the dragon and knight stating that, 'Hey, the stories are going to go in order by stories. Like, this story first, this story second.' When the pigs discover the storyboards for their own story, the children understood that the pigs were going to reconstruct the original tale. Fernandez remarked, 'It's probably the story that they came out of. They're going to go back into the story with the dragon so that they'll be safe.' The students knew that the wrinkled storyboard near the end of the story had been the flying airplane earlier in the book. Tom stated, 'Because they made it as an airplane. They fell off the airplane, and then the plane crashed.'

During the small group read-aloud sessions with Mrs W.'s class, the children also remarked on the pigs' search for new stories to enter. The students in both classes knew that the pigs had to construct an ending to their story. Kathy stated, 'They have to put them [the storyboards] in order.'

Mrs W.'s Grade 1
S: *So, what does he mean, 'Let's go home'?*
Bishop: *Let's go home and take a rest.*
S: *OK. What's home for them? Patty?*
Patty: *Inside here [points to the storyboards].*
S: *Inside. They have to get back into the story.*
Anita: *Because they had a nice adventure, that's enough adventure for today.*
S: *Laughs. That's enough adventure for today. Let's see. So this pig says*

'Good idea, we just have to pick these up.' *So what's he saying?*
What do they have to pick up?
Patty: The frames.
S: And do what?
Bishop: And put them back together.

The children easily comprehended the nonlinear trajectory of the book. They understood that the pigs had deconstructed their original tale, flew through physical white space outside of their storybook reality, expanded their universe by visiting other stories or physical spaces, and at the end of their textual excursions, reconstructed their original story, both physically and literally.

Multiple Layers of Meaning. The children worked to make sense of the multiple layers of visual and textual information in the story. For example, when the dragon and the pig exit the dragon's story, there are several storyboards on this and the following page. The students discussed the layering of stories on this double-page spread and predicted how these visual narratives would fit with the current story:

Ms P.'s Grade 1
S: What are all of these [points to the storyboards] back here?
Fernandez: More books that they have to get people out of.
Kathy: I think they are going to start taking people, going to start taking guys out of the books.
S: From the storyboards? Taking out characters?
Robert: Guess what I know? The dragon's going to help them do that.
Kathy: Yeah, the dragon will help.
Fernandez: Look back here – there's a story with a big duck.

At the end of the book, the children recognized how the original tale was changed by the cat and the dragon joining the three pigs in their story. When the dragon answered the wolf's knock at the third pig's door, I asked the children what the wolf might be thinking. Several children in Ms P.'s class responded much like Brianna, who imagined that the wolf would be thinking, 'Hey, where'd he [the dragon] come from? He's not suppose to be in this story.' Omar suggested, 'The wolf, he's like, where'd you [the dragon] come from?' José added, 'Same with the cat.'
The entire book provides a different perspective of the traditional

story of the three little pigs. The children understood that Wiesner's rendition was an alternative version. At the beginning of every small-group read-aloud session when the children looked at the book's dust jacket, they informed me of the probable trajectory of events of the story:

Mrs W.'s Grade 1
Marnie: It might be about the three little pigs who make the houses.
S: And what do they make their houses out of?
Andrea: Bricks, straw, and sticks.
S: And what happened in that story?
Marnie: They all . . . the little brothers come to the one who make the brick house.
S: Why did they go to the brick house?
Marnie: Because they'll be eated.
S: By who?
Andrea: The wolf!
S: Well, let's see if this is the same story.

Interactive Formats. Nonlinear and nonsequential organizations and formats, multiple layers of meaning, and multiple narratives in both text and illustrations are a few of the features identified by Dresang (1999) that require a large degree of reader attentiveness and concentration (see appendix J). In addition, in *The Three Pigs*, readers and characters share the same space and time frame – readers watch as stories are deconstructed and constructed in front of them.

When the pigs pull down a bit of the green background of *Hey Diddle Diddle* from the top right-hand corner of one page, several groups in Ms P.'s class predicted that the pigs were bringing in 'oobleck.' Ms P. had recently read *Bartholomew and the Oobleck* (Seuss, 1970), a story about a king who is dissatisfied with mere snow, sun, fog, and rain. He summons the royal magicians, who create oobleck. Once the king realizes the sticky consequences of having green oobleck descend from the sky, he apologizes for his mistake. The children made an intertextual connection and predicted that the pigs were pulling oobleck into the story. Once one student realized it was *Hey Diddle Diddle*, Melissa asserted, 'They brought down another world. It's rhyme land. It's like a nursery rhyme; that's right.' When I turned to the page following the double-page spread of the nursery rhyme, the children saw the pigs and several storyboards. Nathan enthusiastically stated, 'And look, they're building a new story.' Sam agreed, 'Now they're looking for another story to go into.' Blane, in Mrs W.'s class, also noted the disruptive and intertextual nature of the nursery rhyme. 'That's not the right picture that's supposed to be in there. That's *Hey Diddle Diddle* and the pigs are not supposed to be in there. That's not the right rhyme they're suppose to be in.'

The children eagerly searched the illustrations for clues to the unfolding narratives. During one small-group discussion with children in Ms P.'s class, Robert wondered, 'Is this another story here?' when the pigs were flying on the paper airplane. Frank asserted, 'It's the same story,' and Peter stated succinctly, 'They just messed it up,' meaning that the pigs had altered the original tale. With respect to the story of the dragon and the knight, the students understood that the dragon's departure changed that particular tale. Tom stated, 'The knight can't find the dragon because he's out of the story. He can't kill him or get the golden rose.'

The children in both classes commented on the various storyboards the pigs look at as they search for a new narrative to visit. The storyboards present the pigs with multiple time and space possibilities. In the following excerpt, children from Mrs W.'s class remark on the pigs' search for a new story, make intertextual connections, and project themselves into one of the storyboards:

Anita: Oh, look at the frames, the films, I mean the picture frames. I don't want to go in there [the storyboard of the fish in the water].
S: Laughs. Why not?
Anita: Because then we'll go out of the story and we'll go down inside the water and we can't breathe.
Blane: I'm not going in that water because you would die and drown.
Katie: He's [the pig] trying to look for one [storyboard] to go in.
Bishop: Look, flying frogs [points to a storyboard]. Like the flying frogs [I had previously read Tuesday *to the children].*
S: What do you think this story is back here?
Katie: James and the Giant Peach. No, wait. Jack and the Beanstalk.
Blane: Yeah, Jack and the Beanstalk.
Anita: Hey, look the house of the three little pigs.
S: You think so?
Anita: Yeah, I see the house.
Katie: Me, too.
Blane: It's the brick house. Maybe they'll go back to their own story.

The children enjoyed the interactive nature of *The Three Pigs*. They understood how the dynamic and permeable story space of Wiesner's book created an interactive format where the pigs departed their own tale, had access to and disrupted other narratives, and connected with other storybook characters.

TYPE TWO RADICAL CHANGE – CHANGING PERSPECTIVES

Multiple Perspectives, Visual and Verbal. During our discussions the children talked about how Wiesner's tale differed from other versions of *The Three Little Pigs* that the children were familiar with. At the end of the picturebook the children noted how the presence of the cat and the dragon changed the original story. Anita explained that the story was now different 'because there's the three little pigs and there's a cat, and the fiddle, and there's a dragon, and a golden rose.' Sebastian added another detail that demonstrated his knowledge of other versions of the traditional tale: 'And it's not the same because they didn't get soup like in all the other ones.'

The Three Pigs contains multiple verbal (narrator, pigs, dragon, and cat) and visual (the storyboards and other stories) perspectives. The children liked the bird's-eye view illustration of the characters looking at the brick house. Pender remarked, 'They're looking at it upside downly.' Anita observed, 'Hey, they're stepping on the book.' Jeremy commented on the same double-page spread: 'It looks like we're looking right down at everything.' One pig discovers the storyboards from the original story on these two pages and begins to unfold the storyboard that was used for the airplane. Chris stated, 'The wolf's scared, and he was different in the other page, but he got scared,' referring to the expression on the wolf's face in the same storyboard earlier in the story. This particular storyboard appears several times throughout the story, and each time the wolf's stature and facial expressions are different.

Wiesner uses several language forms in *The Three Pigs*. For example, storybook language is used for the 'original tale' and the dragon's story. The children in each class spontaneously recited in unison the nursery rhyme language of *Hey Diddle Diddle* when I reached that part of the book. Another language form is the pigs' 'people prose' (Purves, 1994). The children did not comment about the use of conversational dialogue, but they did enjoy the dragon's discourse style. When the dragon exits his medieval story world, he too speaks in 'people prose,' but his vocabulary and grammatical structures appropriately reflect his setting. The children laughed when I read the dragon's articulations, and several repeated the phrase, 'O brave and noble swine.'

David Wiesner Fans

The Grade 1 students were enchanted, entertained, and engaged cognitively by *The Three Pigs* (Wiesner, 2001). They experienced a range of emotions as I read the book with them. Initially the children were very confident about the story's plot. However, once the first pig is blown out of the story, the students' expressions of incredulity and delight communicated their uncertainty and curiosity about the trajectory of the tale. Once they fully comprehended the significance of the pig's exit from the story, they giggled and giggled. Perry Nodelman (1996), describes the pleasure of newness of children's literature, of experiencing 'startling different kinds of stories and poems' (1996, p. 21). The children thoroughly enjoyed Wiesner's 'new' and subversive version of the tale of the three pigs.

When I asked the children to identify their favourite book or books that I read aloud with and to them during the research, their choices communicated their appreciation of David Wiesner's work. Of the twenty-three participants in Ms P.'s class, one child selected one title as his favourite, one child stated that he liked all of the books equally, ten children identified two favourite books and eleven children selected three books as their favourites. Eleven children – two girls and nine boys – selected *The Three Pigs* as one of their favourite books. Two boys liked the dragon in Wiesner's picturebook. Phillip explained *The Three Pigs* was one of his favourite books 'Because the wolf didn't blow the brick house.' Two children found the book humorous and eight children chose the picturebook because the original tale is interrupted by the pigs' departure. Some of their explanations included, 'Because it was a different version and they could come out of the story and they like accidentally broke the storyboards,' 'Because they ripped apart the story,' and 'They got out of their pages and that was funny.'

In Mrs W.'s class, ten children identified two titles as their favourite picturebooks and nine children selected three titles as their favourite books. Four girls and four boys selected *The Three Pigs* as one of their favourite books. Five of the students thought the book was humorous. Dom stated, 'I liked it because it was the funniest book.' As with the explanations provided by Ms P.'s students, five children talked about the pigs leaving their story. Kirstin explained, 'I liked it because it was funny when they jumped out of the pictures and I liked how there were word bubbles.' Three children liked the part when the pigs take flight and three students commented about the wolf's reactions to the pigs' use of the storyboard as an airplane. Patty stated, 'I liked when they made the fox into a paper airplane.' Pender noted, 'The wolf is squashed. He doesn't like that.' Two children commented about the dragon in the picturebook. Sue stated, 'I like the dragon. When the pigs got on the dragon.'

When the children in both Grade 1 classrooms talked about *The Three Pigs*, they turned to various pages in the book, often pointing to details in the illustrations to support their verbal comments. The children's fondness for and appreciation of David Wiesner's picturebook was most evident in their facial expressions, body language, and tone of voice.

Voices in the Park

Anthony Browne's *A Walk in the Park* (1977) is the 'pre-text' to *Voices in the Park* (1998). Although the books have essentially the same story elements, they differ in several respects, including the depiction of the main characters, narrative structure, and illustration style. In *A Walk in the Park*, the characters are human, a narrator tells the linear story, and the illustrative style is 'dispassionate, with a decorative quality to the design' (Doonan, 1999, p. 48). The characters in *Voices in the Park* are zoomorphic, each of the four characters tells her or his own version of the events in the park creating a 'mosaic narrative' (Douglas Yellowlees, 2001, p. 55), and in addition to 'full background treatment' (p. 48), colour and line are used to communicate information about the characters.

Voices in the Park tells the story of a mother and her son, Charles, who take their pedigreed dog, Victoria, for a walk in the park. A father and his daughter, Smudge, take their mongrel, Albert, to the same park at the same time. The canines immediately begin to interact, much to the disdain of the mother. The adults, 'divided by class, income and inclination' (Doonan, 1999, p. 47) ignore each other, but Charles and Smudge tentatively begin to play together. Charles's mother abruptly ends the blossoming friendship and each child returns home with his or her parent. The four main characters in *Voices in the Park* have human bodies and ape heads. Doonan writes that zoomorphism, 'distances the viewer, and the gap between fantasy and reality is made explicit' (1999, p. 48). Each small group of Grade 1 children remarked on the zoomorphism of the girl's father. When I turned to 'Second Voice' (the father's story) and Ali saw the father, he stated, 'Hey, he's half man and half gorilla. Look at his arms. He looks like a man but he has an ape head.' Jeffrey commented, 'Half monkey, half people,' and Andrea called the father 'a human ape.'

Voices in the Park has multiple narrators or character focalisers: each of the book's four chapters is told from the point of view of a different protagonist. Each character's version of the events in the park is depicted as occurring at a different time of year, which results in shifts in time and space relationships and indeterminacy in setting. There are additional narrative discontinuities as each character picks up the storyline at a different point in the tale. Browne reveals much about the four narrators through their distinctive type font, vocabulary, syntax (discourse style), and account of the happenings in the park.

Radical Change Characteristics

Voices in the Park, winner of the 1998 Kurt Maschler award, exhibits all of the characteristics of type one Radical Change (changing forms and formats), the multiple visual and verbal perspectives of type two Radical Change (changing perspectives), and an unresolved ending, a characteristic of type three Radical Change (changing boundaries) (Dresang, 1999). The children's understandings of and responses to the various Radical Change characteristics in *Voices in the Park* are discussed below.

TYPE ONE RADICAL CHANGE – CHANGING FORMS AND FORMATS

Graphics in New Forms and Formats. The use of a unique typeface for each character focaliser in *Voices in the Park* is one method of transmitting meaning. Doonan wrote that each character's font 'has its own effect on the psychological force of the words' (1999, p. 47) and indeed, the fonts reflect the personalities of the characters. The children were very aware of the different typographies of the characters. Some of the students remembered the different fonts from the four sentence fragments on the back of the dust jacket and book cover that we had talked about before we began reading the text. These text fragments are taken from each voice's story in the book.

Mrs W.'s Grade 1

S: [reads writing on back cover] What do you notice about the typing, about the letters that are used in each one of these?

Teresa: They're different. One of them is straight. One of them is medium kind, and one of them is really small, and one of them is really ...

Marnie: This one [points to third sentence fragment] is made out of pencil.

S: You think that one was made out of pencil?

Teresa: No, I think it was made out of marker that was very cool to use.

Sebastian: These ones [points to first, second, and fourth sentence fragments] are made out of markers and this one's [third] made by pen.

When Sebastian saw Smudge's father's font he remarked, 'Hey, it's the different writing from back here,' and he pointed to the back of the book and the four sentence fragments. Katie's comment encapsulated the comments of the students' in Mrs W.'s class about the four different fonts: 'Hey, the printing is different each time – the writing is different when someone else talks.' The students in Ms P.'s class also talked about the various typographic styles in the book. Jeremy succinctly summarized the variation in typeface: 'You know what? Any time a different character talks, there's different letters.' One group thought the father's font was bigger because the character was a 'big man.' Sam said, 'Yeah, it's bigger because he's a bigger monkey.' Phillip stated that, 'these are the same kind of printing that we use.' When another group saw the printing for Charles, Ryan observed, 'It's smaller because he's very small.' When Gurjit's group met Smudge, the fourth voice, she stated, 'Guess what, I know what the writing is. It's called gooey. It's called smudgy writing.' The children recognized the different fonts and most realized that the varying size and style of typography had significance with respect to communicating information about the characters.

Words and Pictures Reaching New Levels of Synergy. Browne's use of intense colour and line reveals information about the four narrators. Although the children did not specifically comment on this aspect, they did notice that the illustrations in Smudge's story had 'lots of colour.' On the first page of 'Fourth Voice' (Smudge's story) Marnie explained how the multi-coloured dog leash, lamp post, and tree trunk were rainbows: 'And look at all the rainbows and there's all these fruits. Red, orange, yellow, green, and purple and look, there's another rainbow, and there's another rainbow.'

The same neighbourhood street scene is depicted in the first and fourth rectos in the father's story, 'Second Voice.' In the first illustration, Smudge, her father, and Albert are travelling to the park, and in the fourth recto, they are returning home. The urban decay depicted in the first recto is transformed in the fourth recto because Smudge has cheered up her father. No text describes the symbolic transformation of the street scene – readers must look carefully to identify and understand the changes. The children were fascinated by these two pages and spent significant time flipping back and forth between the two rectos describing the illustrative transformations. Cassandra described the area in the first recto as 'all ruined with litter' and Jeffrey noted that, 'It's [the fourth recto] light and this one [first recto] is darker.' Ivan described the fourth recto as 'a good picture.'

In many instances, the synergy among the words and illustrations in the book creates indeterminancy. There are several defensible interpretations of events and characters in the text, and overall, the writerly text (Barthes, 1970) positions readers in a co-authoring role. The students noted the burning tree at the end of 'First Voice' (the mother's story) as Charles and his mother exit the park. Several children attributed the fire to Charles's mother. Sebastian explained, 'I think Charles's mom did it since she yelled so loud the leaves rubbed together and then it made a fire.' I asked the children about the illustration of Smudge and Charles sitting on the park bench, with a sunny background behind Smudge and a cloudy background behind Charles (the second verso in 'Third Voice,' Charles's story). Each group explained the illustration in a somewhat similar manner. Anita was most confident in her explanation: 'I know because he's a little bit bored and if you're bored the clouds will get on your side, and if you're happy, the clouds won't go on your side.' As evident by Anita's explanation and the following transcript excerpts, the children easily interpreted the significance of Browne's symbolic use of colour in this particular illustration.

Mrs W.'s Grade 1
S: *What is the sky like where the girl is?*
Kirstin: A happy sky.
S: *Why do you say that it's happy?*
Kirstin: Sunshine.
Sue: That means she's happy.
S: *And what about over here? [I point to the side of the bench where Charles is sitting].*

Patty: Sad.
S: How do you know that?
Sue: Because there's only clouds and rain.
Kirstin: Yeah, it's like it rained on Charles and he's sad.

<u>Ms P.'s Grade 1</u>

S: How can it be sunny on one part of the bench and cloudy on the other
*   part? The bench is the same.*
Peter: I think I know why.
S: Why?
Peter: This one [points to Smudge] is happy and this one [points to Charles]
*   is sad.*
S: Peter has a really great idea.
Chris: Well these guys [points to Charles and his mother] aren't having
*   much fun and these guys are [points to Smudge and father].*

Nonlinear and Nonsequential Organization and Format. Voices in the Park is constructed from four individual narratives, each of which is linear and sequential. The 'voices' in the story could be read in any order, but obviously changing the sequence of the narratives would affect reader interpretation. Taken as a whole, the book's framing device of stories within stories creates a nonlinear text. Doonan writes that *Voices in the Park* has 'an interlocking and interweaving of a plurality of worlds because the original story is given in four versions, each separate and complete in itself, each narrated by one of the main characters, but which taken together make another complete story, though without a linear structure' (1999, p. 47). The discursive format of chapters or voices foregrounds the narrative structure in the book. Various types of illustrative interruptions that include intertextual and intratextual connections and manifold visual and textual narratives distract reader attention and contribute to the picturebook's non-traditional time and space relationships.

The students understood the overall nonlinear structure of the book, commented on the looping nature of the four narratives, and identified intratextual connections (links to earlier episodes, phrases, actions, illustrations, and characters within the same text). When we began to read 'Second Voice,' the children identified Albert, who befriended the other dog, Victoria, from the previous chapter. Katie noted, 'Hey, that's the dog that was chasing Victoria!' Omar remarked, 'And that's the same dog as the one that was chasing the brown dog [Victoria]!' The children also identified Smudge's father.

Mrs W.'s Grade 1

*Natalie: Oh, so this guy is the girl's father. The man sitting on the bench
before.*

S: That's right.

*Dom: [Turns pages back to illustration of father on park bench]. Look, you
can tell by his clothes.*

Andrea: It looks like he is a painter.

*Dom: Yeah, and that's the same dog that was chasing and that's the same
girl that the boy was talking to.*

Blane: And I was right, that is his dog.

Ms P.'s Grade 1

Kathy: It's the same man [Smudge's father].

S: That's right. Where have you seen him before?

Robert: From those pages where she [the mother] was sitting on the bench.

S: How do you know it's the same character?

Changwei: Because I saw him on that page.

Kathy: He has the same hands – human hands and he is a monkey.

Fernandez: Oh, and the same clothes – painter's clothes.

Multiple Layers of Meaning. The co-existence of interconnecting and
looping narratives in *Voices in the Park* presents a twist on traditional
time and space relationships in picturebooks by diverting the reader's
attention and creating indeterminacies. Readers must suture the narrative disruptions, connect the stories within stories, and understand
the time switches in order to construct a cohesive 'story.'

'Intertextuality refers to all kinds of links between two or more texts'
(Nikolajeva & Scott, 2001, p. 227), but Browne's text-within-same-text
connections also create a narrative structure that is intratextual in
nature. The Grade 1 children actively worked to create unity among
the polyphonic narratives. They formed connections between the characters and their actions, and understood both the simultaneity and
interdependency of events. When I began reading 'Second Voice,' the
children identified the man from the park bench and his dog. When
asked who Charles was looking at as he sat on the bench on the second
recto of 'First Voice,' the students told me that it was the girl from the
front cover. They knew because 'she had a red shirt and jeans.' As I
started to read the 'Second Voice,' Tom stated, 'And the same thing is
going to happen to the girl because the girl is going to find the boy and
then the woman is going to yell at Charles.' They made connections to
Smudge, the other three characters, and the dogs in every individual

narrative. When we reached 'Fourth Voice,' many children recognized that we had not yet heard Smudge's story. Brianna stated, 'It's that girl's turn to talk.' The children easily understood that Browne's book contained time switches and stories within stories.

Browne refers visually and verbally to previous events, characters, or items in a way that highlights the interconnectedness of the narratives and the constructedness of the text. The children in Ms P.'s class observed connections among three of the stories as the characters left the park:

S: *Where are these pink leaves coming from?*
Ethan: *From Smudge's shoes.*
Mohad: *From the trees they were climbing.*
Jeremy: *Wait a second. All the way back here …*
Nathan: *Look, Cupid. Cupid gorilla.*
S: *Jeremy, what were you going to say?*
Jeremy: *All the way back when we first saw the leaves …*
S: *You want to go back when we first saw the leaves? OK [I turn to the illustration].*
Jeremy: *Yeah, the leaves were orange in this picture.*
S: *Right.*
Ethan: *But this time they're all nice and flowery and pink.*
Nathan: *Hey, there was just white stuff before too – like footprints in the other picture with that girl and her dad [turns to the fourth recto in 'Second Voice'].*

The students also noted how the picture on the book's cover appeared with slight modifications in two other places in the book. As Phillip remarked at its appearance near the end of 'First Voice,' 'It's the same as on the cover.' Sue stated, 'Hey look, that illustration is almost the same as the dust jacket!' The children also discussed how the second illustration near the end of 'Fourth Voice' was somewhat different from the cover:

Ms P.'s Grade 1
Gurjit: *Lookit. It's the same picture as the cover only it's different.*
Ryan: *This one [the cover] is light and that one is nighttime [second last verso illustration in the book] and that's daytime [the cover].*
S: *That's right. It's the same illustration of him giving her the flower but it is different. Good observation.*

The visual jokes (Doonan, 1999) in *Voices in the Park* create a layering effect that diverts the reader from the narratives. The children eagerly and enthusiastically searched the illustrations for 'secrets,' and I often delayed reading the text until the children had scrutinized the illustrations because their attention was focused on the pictures, not the words. Omar remarked, 'Hey a crocodile. I think he [Browne] likes to do secrets.' Some of Browne's visual jokes include an elephant's trunk and leg in the trees, a crocodile or alligator shadow, gorilla profiles in the trees and shrubs, a bicycle with two riders who are pedalling in opposite directions, two dogs that appear to be attached, fruit in the trees, a castle, dogs switching tails, a whale in the trees, and the father's toque on the statue and shrub. The following excerpts illustrate some of the children's conversations about Browne's visual jokes:

Ms P.'s Grade 1
Brianna: I see an elephant's trunk and an elephant leg.
Melissa: Oh, a trunk! Look, this here's cut off [points to the tree].
S: What's happened to the tree?
Ryan: It got sawed off.
Brianna: Hey, look that was so funny, it's ... the dogs are going so fast.
Gurjit: The dogs are going so fast that they are cutting the trees.
Melissa: The tree might fall on them!
Mrs W.'s Grade 1
Cassandra: Oh, the dogs are stuck together again.
Katie: Oh yeah! Hey, that was already in the other part [turns pages of book to first illustration where the dogs are attached] except Victoria was in front. Now this dog [Albert] is in the front and Victoria is in the back.
S: That's right. Does it make sense that Victoria is on this side of the pole and Albert is on this side?
Cassandra: Yeah, because Victoria's owner is him [points to Charles] and he's sitting on this side, and that one's [Albert] owner is her.
S: Let's see if it was like that for the other picture [turns to the illustration].
Cassandra: Lookit, she's [the mother] on this side of the bench and her dog's on this side of the tree [points to the dog and the mother during her explanation].
Katie: And he's [the father] on that side [of the bench] and that's for his side [points to the dog and the father during her explanation]. It's the exact same.

The children's comments reveal their comprehension of the symbolic significance of the visual joke as well as their recognition of the image as an intratextual connection.

Interactive Formats. Voices in the Park demands that readers be attentive because of the multiple stories, visual disruptions, and inter- and intra-textual connections in the book. The children exerted significant cognitive energy to connect the parallel and interdependent vignettes.

The students also recognized the embedded visual intratextualities in the picturebook that both connect and disrupt or interrupt the reading experience. They searched for hat shapes throughout the story because after their experiences with *Willy the Dreamer* (Browne, 1997), they knew that Anthony Browne embedded 'secrets' in his illustrations. The children identified the recurring image of the mother's hat on the fencepost, in the clouds, on the lamp posts, in the trees, on the statue, on the mother's scarf at the end of the story ('Hey, these are supposed to be flowers, but they're hats!'), and on the gateposts leading to Charles' house. Cassandra knew the identity of the figure casting a shadow on Charles in the first recto of 'Third Voice': 'It's the mom because it has the hat and there's little hats on the lamp posts and there's a hat made out of a tree and there's cloud hats.'

Mrs W.'s Grade 1
Annita: Look at the hats in the trees [first recto of 'Third Voice'].
Hannah: And the clouds.
S: Whose hat is it?
Hannah: The lady's.
Jeffrey: There are lots of hats here. Look.
Anita: And do you know what I remember that in Willy the Champ *or* Willy the Wimp *there was one banana on the picture.*
Hannah: There was one banana in Willy the Wimp *and two bananas in* Willy the Champ.
Jeffrey: When, um, in Willy the Dreamer *there was a banana with ... like the vest of Willy.*
S: Yes, that's right there was a banana with the same design as his vest.
Anita: How come everything is the mom's hat?

Ivan's comment summarized the students' opinions about the dominant image of the mother's hat that is repeated throughout the book. 'You know what? I see something funny in this [book] ... In

Willy the Dreamer, there was lots of bananas and in this one there's lots of hats.'

Lamp posts make appearances in several of the illustrations in *Voices in the Park*. In some instances, the lamp posts are 'ordinary,' but in other illustrations, Browne uses them to continue the hat motif. The students noted the mother's hat on the lamp posts, a crown on a lamp post on the first verso, and on the lamp post as Smudge and her father enter the park. Melissa observed, 'And there's a queen's or a king's crown on the lamp.' When one group looked at the illustration of Smudge and Charles on the see-saw, they noted the lamp posts in the background:

Peter: Hey, that's a Santa hat on the lamp post.
S: It looks like a Santa's hat.
Chris: And look, that's the same. I guess a lot of people are leaving their hats behind on the lamp post.
S: It seems that way.
Omar: Maybe a lot of people are forgetting their hats on the lamp post.

Several of Browne's illustrations, and some of the embedded visual jokes, are intertextual, ironic, parodic, or surreal in nature. The sophisticated and complex illustrations in Browne's book create an almost hypertextual viewing experience; there is much to choose from to 'click on' with one's eyes. The children identified many cultural artefacts in Browne's illustrations, including King Kong, the Mona Lisa, and Mary Poppins. They connected the character Charles in *Voices in the Park* to Willy, a character in several other books by Browne. The children thought that Charles 'looked like Willy.' Both Grade 1 teachers had read other Browne books (*Willy the Wimp*, 1984, and *Willy the Dreamer*, 1987) to the children.

Ms P.'s Grade 1
Frank: Oh no, who's that?
José: It's a big monkey.
Tom: I think it's a big huge monkey that's trying to get a guy.
S: Who is that big monkey?
Phillip: It's King Kong. He's a superhero.
José: And he looks like he is going to jump off the roof.
Frank: Is this in New York?
S: It could be New York.

The children's personal and cultural backgrounds affected their recognition and identification of intertexts. Although not all of the small groups identified the Mona Lisa, all the children said they were 'familiar' with the famous painting. Melissa's comment was typical of the children's responses: 'I've seen it, but I don't remember what it's called.' At least one child in each small group from Mrs W.'s class identified Mary Poppins. When asked to explain how she knew the character was Mary Poppins, Teresa stated emphatically, 'Because she has a blue dress, she has an umbrella, and she has a hat, and she has a purse.' Although only a few children from Ms P.'s Grade 1 class recognized Mary Poppins, most said they were familiar with the character once she had been named:

Sam: Oh, there's an angel flying up because it wouldn't be on the ground.
Shamah: It's a flying person.
S: It is. Do you know what story or movie that person is from?
Ivan: I know. Mary Poppins.
Shamah: I've never seen it.
Sam: She flies around with her umbrella.
Ivan: I have the movie of this.

The students were attentive to the illustrations and were able to articulate explanations for surreal events. When asked to explain the transformation that occurs to the street scene after Smudge, her father, and Albert return from the park, several small groups commented, 'It's magic.' Andrea explained the change in the heart from the first to the second street scene: 'Now the heart got fixed. Maybe it's magic and when it's morning it breaks and when it's dark, it goes back together.' In the third recto in 'Fourth Voice,' Charles, Smudge, and the two dogs are playing in a bandstand. 'As the children play upon the bandstand, Browne frees the experience from time, by depicting images of both day and night simultaneously' (Doonan, 1999, p. 52). The children struggled to explain how it could be day and night at the same time. A few students said, 'I don't know,' but many made attempts to explain the unscientific illustration. Marnie stated, 'I think it's just like, um, they're inside it [the bandstand] and there's like this border behind it and it's like it's morning.' Another group in Mrs W.'s class looked for explanations for the illogical illustration:

*Dom: Hey, this is day and this is night [points to the respective parts of the
    illustration].*
S: I wonder how that can be?
Dom: I don't know. Maybe they put up something that can look like night.
*Natalie: It's magic again. They put black ... they might have painted the
    night.*

Not only did the students try to explain the surreal illustrations in the
book, but they were quite comfortable to consider multiple interpretations of these ambiguous images.

TYPE TWO RADICAL CHANGE – CHANGING PERSPECTIVES

Multiple Perspectives, Visual and Verbal. The complex structure of *Voices
in the Park* contains textual and visual manifold narratives (Trites, 1994)
and uses stories within stories as a narrative framing device. Multistranded narratives 'are constructed of two or more interconnected narrative strands differentiated by shifts in temporal and spatial relationships, and/or shifts in narrative point of view' (McCallum, 1996, p.
406). In Browne's picturebook, each character's version of the events in
the park is depicted as occurring at a different time of year and according to Doonan, the 'settings function as a symbolic reflection of attitudes of each character' (1999, p. 48). The storyline of each vignette
begins at a different point in the story, which introduces narrative discontinuities. For example, Charles's mother starts her narration as she,
Charles, and Victoria, their dog, leave the house; Smudge's story begins
as she, her father, and Albert, the dog, enter the gates to the park.
Several of the small-group read-aloud excerpts illustrate how the children embraced a co-authoring role as they connected the multiple narratives in the book. The children understood that multiple perspectives
were conveyed in the book and that they must consider each character's point of view in order to understand the 'whole' story.
   Browne's use of shifting and multiple visual viewpoints in his illustrations intrigued the children. The illustration of Charles and Smudge
on the slide (second recto in 'Third Voice') is taken from the viewpoint
of looking up the slide, and affects readers' perception of size and distance. Teresa commented, 'Oh my gosh, that is a big slide!' The slide
appears to 'come out of the book' since the slide's bottom support
structures are outside of the illustration frame.

<u>Mrs W.'s Grade 1</u>
S: I wonder what would happen if Charles came down the slide?
Natalie: He would go right out of the picture frame.
Blane: Then he would go, whoa, right out of the book!
Andrea: He would come at me!
Blane: He'd go, 'Whee!' and I'd go [demonstrates with his hands that he
  would catch Charles and throw him back into the book].
S: You'd catch him and throw him back? [Laughs.]

The children were very interested in the visual perspectives depicted in the illustration of the mother 'blowing her top' on the first recto in 'Fourth Voice.' Jeremy called the mother 'the giant' and Cassandra stated, 'She puffed up so hard that things came flying out.' Ethan explained, 'Hey, lookit. She's so mad she blew the clouds over.'

<u>Mrs W.'s Grade 1</u>
Dom: Why is she so big and strong?
Blane: Yeah, why is she so big and strong?
S: Well, Anthony Browne has shown her really big like this. Why?
Andrea: Because she's really mad.

The children wondered how the dogs could seemingly be running through the mother's ears. They were intrigued by the proportional size of the characters and items in the illustration. Brianna stated, 'Oh I get it. They [the dogs] are like going into her ear and that one's coming out of her ear.' Hannah's comment summarized the children's feelings about having canines race through one's head: 'Eww. Yuck!'

TYPE THREE RADICAL CHANGE – CHANGING BOUNDARIES

Unresolved Endings. It could be argued that *Voices in the Park* has an unresolved ending because readers do not know if Charles and Smudge ever meet again in the park or elsewhere. The children talked about the last recto in the book, and speculated about Charles's thoughts and feelings as he is escorted out of the park by his mother and 'shielded' from Smudge:

<u>Mrs W.'s Grade 1</u>
Sebastian: Why are they [Charles and his mother] walking into the water?

S: It looks like that, doesn't it? Around their house they seem to have water. Look at the look on Charles's face. What do you think he might be thinking?

Pender: He's sad.

S: Why is he sad, Pender?

Pender: He didn't want to leave the park and go home.

Sebastian: And that's all of his crying in there.

S: You think it's from him crying?

Sebastian: Yeah, all that water around the house.

<u>Mrs W.'s Grade 1</u>

S: Look at Charles looking back.

Kirstin: He wants to go back to her … to Smudge.

S: So what do you think he might be thinking in his head?

Teresa: He wants to go back.

S: I want to go back.

Theo: Oh, please come back.

Russell: I don't want to go home.

S: Why do you think the mom doesn't want Charles to play with Smudge?

Kirstin: Oh, because she doesn't know Smudge.

Theo: She thinks Smudge is a bad girl.

Teresa: And he was playing with a stranger.

Kirstin: That's what I meant.

S: That's what you meant that she didn't know her.

Russell: And she wanted to protect him.

<u>Ms P.'s Grade 1</u>

S: How does Charles look here? [Points to the illustration].

All: Sad.

S: Why is he feeling sad?

Nathan: Because he had to leave the park.

Chris: Because he wanted to play with Smudge more.

S: What do you think Charles might be thinking?

Nathan: Um, I think he's thinking that he might see her again.

S: Wondering if he might see her again. That's a good idea. What else?

Ryan: Oh, I don't want to go home! I want to play in the park!

Mohad: I want to go back. I want to play with that girl.

The children's comments communicate their understanding of the deeper meaning of the events that transpired in the park. Overall, the children were not fond of the mother character; they believed that she treated both Charles and Smudge unfairly. For his response that accompanied his drawing, Peter wrote, 'I don't like the part when Charles's mom was keep getting him home because he can't play.' Sebastian completed the most insightful response that communicated his understanding and interpretation of the difference between Charles's relationship with his mother and his relationship with Smudge. He drew Smudge and Charles in a tree but Charles's stick legs and arms were very large and extended beyond the trunk of the tree and covered a large part of the paper. Sebastian dictated the following sentences to Mrs W.: 'Charles grows in the tree. Smudge climbs the tree with Charles but Charles is too big to climb the tree. And when Charles goes home, he shrinks.'

Student Appreciation

Voices in the Park demands a high level of sophistication and complexity in order to interpret the story and fill in the gaps. As Doonan has written, Browne assumes that his readers have great skills of interpretation (1999, p. 53). The Grade 1 students exhibited no hesitation or timidity as they participated in the small-group interactive read-aloud sessions. They exerted significant cognitive energy as they comprehended and interpreted the manifold and visual narratives. Their familiarity with Browne's illustrative device of embedding visual jokes heightened the children's interest in the book.

One girl and three boys in Ms P.'s class identified *Voices in the Park* as one of their favourite books that I had read to them during the research project. Two of the children seemed to select the book because of Browne's illustrations: Kathy liked the book 'because there are secrets in the pictures,' and Jeremy stated, 'It's good and I liked the funny things in the pictures. Like King Kong.' The other two students liked the book 'because two people get together,' and 'the girl and the boy were playing.'

In Mrs W.'s class, two girls selected *Voices in the Park* as one of their favourite picturebooks. Marnie liked the book because the characters 'became friends.' She made reference to the illustration of the different sky backgrounds for Smudge and Charles sitting on the same bench in 'Third Voice.' 'I liked when there was nothing ... when there was no dark side on them [Charles and Smudge] because they both were happy.' Teresa said, 'I liked all of it.' When I asked her if there was anything in particular that she liked about the book, Teresa turned to the first recto in 'Fourth Voice.' In this illustration, Charles's mother is very angry and it appears that the two dogs, Alberta and Victoria, are running through her head. Teresa stated, 'I like this one. It's really funny. The mother is screaming and she's like, 'Grrrr!''

Conclusion

The Radical Change characteristics exhibited in *The Three Pigs* (Wiesner, 2001) and *Voices in the Park* (Browne, 1997) increase the interactivity within the texts. These texts, along with the other selections of literature used in the research projects, demanded an active, involved style of reading from the children. They made choices as they listened, and transacted with the verbal and visual texts in various nonsequential ways. The children also explored different levels of meanings and created or expanded on portions of the story in both the visual and verbal texts (Dresang, 1999). The Radical Change characteristics in *The Three Pigs* and *Voices in the Park* give agency to readers. During the interactive read-aloud sessions, the students drew inferences, made interpretations, generated hypotheses, and created possibilities. The children also made intra- and intertextual connections during the picturebook read-aloud sessions. The picturebooks were ideal for rereading to the children as the polysemous texts afford multiple opportunities for meaning-making and interpretation. I found that the Grade 1 students eagerly anticipated the rereading of the picturebooks; their enthusiasm for and confidence in their 'knowledge' about the books were most evident during the whole-class read-aloud sessions.

Although readers should always be actively involved in the construction of meaning during the reading event (Rosenblatt, 1978), the picturebooks used in the studies require a high degree of reader participation in the creation of meaning. Picturebooks with Radical Change characteristics provide opportunities for readers to develop their abilities in comprehending text both inferentially and critically. In addition to providing pleasurable aesthetic reading experiences, these types of books can teach critical thinking skills, visual literacy skills, and interpretive strategies. Books with Radical Change characteristics can provide certain types of 'reading lessons' (Meek, 1988) for readers about the construction of narratives by authors, and about their roles as readers. The picturebooks used in the studies extended the Grade 1 students' repertoires of story schemata, and introduced the children to a variety of narrative, discursive, and illustrative devices. The children's literary understanding about the ways that stories 'work' was extended and the picturebooks provided the children with rich and enjoyable reading experiences.

3 Grade 1 Children, a Dreamer, Airborne Amphibians, and a Shortcut

In this chapter I discuss the Grade 1 children's oral responses to various metafictive devices in *Willy the Dreamer* (Browne, 1997), *Tuesday* (Wiesner, 1991), and *Shortcut* (Macaulay, 1995), three of the picturebooks used in the studies. I also discuss the students' textual engagements with some of the metafictive devices identified in appendix A. Excerpts from several small-group read-aloud sessions illustrate some of the lessons the children learned about how texts are constructed and their roles as readers. The chapter ends with a discussion about the active role of the reader in understanding and interpreting these sophisticated picturebooks, and I revisit the notion of interthinking introduced in chapter 1 to frame a discussion about the small group read-aloud sessions.

Willy the Dreamer[1]

In Anthony Browne's picturebook, a primate named Willy dreams of many things including fame, adventure, heroism, destitution, the past, and the future. The book is 'a portfolio of individual pictures': each of the twenty dreams is represented as an individual vignette in 'a full page plate in a gilt frame' (Doonan, 1999, p. 42). The dreams reveal Willy's hopes, fears, and his predilections 'in the arts, literature, cinema and sport' (p. 42). *Willy the Dreamer* is filled with intertextual pictorial connections, many of them parodic in nature, to numerous cultural products and texts. Browne includes allusions to other books and characters (including his own work), and emulates

---

1 For an outstanding discussion of *Willy the Dreamer*, see Doonan, 1999.

the work of several famous artists (Magritte, Dali, de Chirico, Bacon, and Rousseau).

The bananas on the front cover and endpapers of *Willy the Dreamer* suggest that readers will discover bananas throughout the book, and indeed, Browne does not disappoint. The children searched for bananas in every illustration and Kathy succinctly summarized the children's opinions: 'Bananas. I see bananas all over here.' When I turned to the page where Willy dreams he was a giant, Marnie enthusiastically exclaimed, 'My God! Let's look at the bananas all over the place!'

My discussion of the metafictive devices in *Willy the Dreamer* focuses on three interrelated techniques: intertextuality; 'parodic appropriations of other texts' (Stephens & Watson, 1994, p. 44); and 'availability of multiple readings and meanings for a variety of audiences' (Anstey, 2002, p. 447). An expanded discussion on intertextuality will further develop readers' understanding of the significance of the intertextual references in *Willy the Dreamer*.

Intertextuality

Although the notion of intertextuality pervades professional and academic writing on textual connections, the term is used in various ways in the literature. Some researchers describe all types of textual connections as intertextual; others describe only text-to-text connections as intertextual. Allen argued that 'intertextuality is one of the most commonly used and misused terms in contemporary critical vocabulary' (2000, p. 2).

The term intertextuality is derived from 'the Latin *intertexto*, meaning to intermingle while weaving' (Keep, McLaughlin & Parmar, 2002, ¶1) and was coined in 1966 by Julia Kristeva, a French semiotician who was influenced by the work of Bakhtin (Cuddon, 1999, p. 424). Bakhtin and Kristeva 'share an insistence that texts cannot be separated from the larger cultural or social textuality out of which they are constructed' (Allen, 2000, p. 36). According to Kristeva, 'any text is constructed of a mosaic of quotations; any text is the absorption and transformation of another' (1980, p. 66), and a literary work 'is not simply the product of a single author, but of its relationship to other texts and to the structures of language itself' (Keep et al., 2002, ¶1). She described texts as existing along two complimentary axes: 'The word's status is thus defined *horizontally* (the word in the text belongs to both writing subject and addressee) as well as *vertically* (the word in the text is oriented toward an anterior or synchronic literary corpus)' (Krisetva, 1980, p. 66). Authors 'communicate to readers at the same moment as their words or texts communicate the existence of past texts within them' (Allen, 2000, p. 39).

Like Kristeva, Still and Worton identified the two axes of intertextuality as 'texts entering via authors ... and texts entering via readers' (1990, p. 2). To Nikolajeva and Scott, 'intertextuality refers to all kinds of links between two or more texts' (2001, p. 227). They too acknowledged the reader's contribution, and wrote that in some cases, 'intertextuality may be culturally dependent' (p. 228) because a reader brings to a text all of the other texts she has read, as well as her own cultural context. An 'allusion only makes sense if the reader is familiar with the hypotext (the text alluded to)' (p. 228), such as the Grade 1 children who were not familiar with *Alice in Wonderland*, and consequently could not identify the allusions to that text in *Willy the Dreamer* (Browne, 1997).

Nodelman also discussed how intertextuality depends on a reader's background knowledge, and claimed that 'all literature and all experience of literature are tied together' (1996, p. 22). Like others, Barthes recognized that a reader is a plurality of other texts; the reader exists and works 'within an intertextual field of cultural codes and meanings' (Allen, 2000, p. 89). To Barthes, every text is 'itself the intertext of another text' (1975, p. 77), 'a multidimensional space in which a variety of writings, none of them original, blend and clash. The text is a tissue of quotations' (1977, p. 146). Finally, Fairclough wrote that texts 'are inherently intertextual, constituted by elements of other texts' (1992, p. 270). He distinguished between intertextual links to other texts and intertextual links to conventions (genres, discourses, styles, activity types) (p. 271) and described how individual and contextual factors influence a reader's interpretation of a text.

The term palimpsest, 'a parchment, tablet, etc. that has been written upon or inscribed two or three times, the previous text or texts having been imperfectly erased and remaining, therefore, still partly visible' (Guralnik, 1976, p. 1022), has been used to describe intertextuality (Keep, et al., 2002; Sipe, 2001). Sipe used the palimpsest as a metaphor to describe the 'overlapping of texts with one another' and the ways that meaning is 'gradually built upon previous meanings in a continual process of intertextual linkages,' (2001, p. 324), but the process should not be envisioned as strictly linear. Often the under-writings of palimpsests were partly visible, resulting in an intermingling of texts. When characterized this way, palimpsest seems an appropriate term to describe intertextuality. All writing takes place in the presence of other writings, and all readings are foregrounded in a 'reader's own previous readings, experiences and position' within his or her culture (Keep et al., 2002, ¶5). Making links among 'texts' (including the text of life) involves dynamic, complex, and iterative processes.

This brief discussion reveals how intertextuality is defined, interpreted, and employed in various ways in the professional literature.[2] For my purposes, the term is grounded in the belief that the text *and* the reader are synergetic constituents of intertextuality. However, it is important to remember that identifying an intertext is an act of interpretation by a reader, that hermeneutic activity gives way to intertextuality. Two types of intertextuality are described in the following discussions: intertextual (text-to-other-text connections), and intratextual (text-within-text connections).

METAFICTIVE DEVICES
'Sometimes Willy dreams that he's a movie star,' reads the text on the first verso of *Willy the Dreamer*. Willy is depicted in the accompanying illustrations as several different characters from books and movies. The Grade 1 students knew that the illustrative parodies were all Willy because, as Blane explained, 'they all have that kind of sweater on and the same face as Willy.' When I turned to this particular page Teresa exclaimed, 'Everywhere! He's everywhere!' The students also recognized King Kong, Frankenstein, Tarzan, a 'vampire' (only a couple of groups in each class called the character Dracula), the characters from the Wizard of Oz (including the 'couragey lion' and 'the metal man'), a dwarf from *Snow White and the Seven Dwarves*, Mary Poppins, and, in the words of Hannah, 'a mummy dude.' Since Ms P.'s school was producing the musical *The Wizard of Oz* during the time I was conducing my research, the children in her class easily identified the Cowardly Lion, the Tin Man, and the Scarecrow.

S: [*I turn to the page of Willy dreaming that he is a movie star and singer.*]
Nathan: Oh, way cool!
S: *Do you recognize any of these characters from movies or books?*

---

2 For further reading on the theories and practices of intertextuality, see Allen, 2000; Hartman, 1995; Lemke, 1992, 2002; Worton & Still, 1990.

Kathy: Um, the Tin Man. Frankenstein.
Nathan: George of the Jungle.
S: Anybody else?
Chris: The lion.
Fernandez: I know. He [points to the Scarecrow] was with the girl [Dorothy].
Chris: He was supposed to scare away the crows.
S: That's right. He's supposed to scare away the crows.
Kathy: He's the Scarecrow.
S: Right. What about this guy? [points to Willy as Dracula].
Fernandez: I know. It's a vampire. And there's a mummy with glasses on.
Nathan: And the big gorilla ... that's
Kathy: I know it's from a movie. It's ...
Chris: King Kong.
Fernandez: Oh, I watched King Kong in a long airport but I don't know what happened.

When he examined Browne's portrayal of Willy dreaming that he is a famous singer on the second recto, Blane exclaimed, 'He's Elvis!' and explained that 'Willy looks like Elvis with the hair and suit.' Jeremy, one of the Ms P.'s students, exclaimed, 'Hey, it's Elvis!' and observed that Willy 'has hair the same as Elvis and the same suit, too.'

Mrs W.'s Grade 1
S: Who might this singer be?
Bishop: Elvis.
S: Elvis. Why would you say Elvis?
Bishop: Because I know.
S: How do you know Bishop that it's Elvis?
Bishop: Because it looks like my toy Stitch and Stitch looks like Elvis, my toy Elvis.
S: Oh, I see.
Andrea: I think he looks like Elvis because of the hair.

Other children thought that Willy resembled Elvis, but Katie believed that Willy looked like 'the singer from *Grease*' (John Travolta). A few children in Ms P.'s classroom thought that Willy resembled the 'wedding singer.'

Every group in Mrs W.'s class believed that the illustration of Willy dreaming that he was a famous writer depicted characters from *Alice in Wonderland*. Patty stated, 'Yeah, it's like on *Alice and Wonderland*, the Rabbit says, "I'm late, I'm late for a very important date."' At least one child in every small group in Mrs W.'s class identified Alice, the Cheshire Cat, the Queen of Hearts, the Rabbit, and 'the two guys that danced around.' Shamah, a student in Ms P.'s class, believed that the illustration depicted *Alice in Wonderland* 'because in *Alice in Wonderland*, the girl is in a whole bunch of tea pots and there's a little mouse hiding in there.' Although other students in Ms P.'s Grade 1 class identified characters from *Alice in Wonderland*, many children seemed to be unfamiliar with this particular text. Each small group in both classrooms also made intertextual connections to *Jack and the Beanstalk* (Pender noted, 'It's the fee fi foe fum guy!'), Cupid (Robert stated, 'Cupid's naked and he has the face of a monkey. He has no bow and arrow and he always has a bow and arrow.'), Humpty Dumpty and Superman ('He's banana superhero!' 'His name is Banana Man!'). Thus, during every small-group read-aloud session, the children used their knowledge of one text to make sense of another.

Willy the Dreamer is an appropriate book for audiences of all ages. The Grade 1 students (and the Grade 5 children, as well as many adults with whom I have shared this book) were entertained by both the metamorphoses of Willy and the banana motif. For those children who recognized the hypotexts in Browne's book, there was an additional level of delight and meaning. The Grade 1 children were not familiar with Browne's reference to the artwork and style of Magritte, Dali, Rousseau, and de Chirico, but those who recognize these intertextual references will appreciate Browne's illustrative appropriations. The book warrants additional readings because of the indeterminacy of many illustrations and the possibility of multiple interpretations.

Overall, the children thoroughly enjoyed and appreciated Anthony Browne's *Willy the Dreamer*. Most of the six students in Ms P.'s class, five boys and one girl, who selected *Willy the Dreamer* as one of their favourite books that I read aloud with them provided more than one reason to explain their choice. Four children said they liked the bananas ('There's so many bananas!' observed Ivan), four children thought the book was funny, two children commented on Browne's illustrative style ('Because he puts in secrets and stuff,' explained Nathan), two children remarked on Willy's dreams ('I liked it because he can imagine what he was and that stuff,' remarked José), and Ali commented about a specific metamorphic dream ('Because I liked the how Willy the Dreamer was flying').

Ten students in Mrs W.'s class, six girls and four boys, selected *Willy the Dreamer* as one of their favourite picturebooks and again, most children provided more than one reason when asked to explain their choice. Seven students enjoyed the transformations of Willy or other characters in the book, four students commented on Browne's use of bananas ('I liked all the tricks with the bananas,' said Katie), three children thought the book was funny, three students identified specific characters that they liked ('Well, because I liked King Kong and I also liked the sumo wrestler and I like the rock star and Humpty Dumpty and "Fee fi fo fum. I smell the blood of an Englishman,"' explained Theo), two children liked Willy's dreams ('Because he had all those cool dreams'), two children articulated general appreciative comments about the illustrations ('I liked the pictures,' Anita said), and Katie's remarks about the book's visual images reflected her appreciation of Browne's illustrative techniques ('And these tricks [points to the title page] because that's ... because they aren't the right words').

Willy the Dreamer was the first picturebook that I read aloud to and with the children in both Grade 1 classrooms. I knew the children would find the book entertaining and enjoyable. I also knew that it would teach the children about intertextuality and about the importance of looking carefully and thoroughly at illustrations. I have the greatest regard for Anthony Browne and his work because he, like other authors and illustrators such as David Wiesner, David Macaulay, Chris Van Allsburg, Peter Sis, John Burningham, Shaun Tan, and John and Janet Ahlberg, shows great respect for children and for their abilities as readers.

Tuesday

In the United States, the Randolph Caldecott Medal is awarded annually to the author or illustrator of the most distinguished children's picturebook. David Wiesner received the prize in 2002 for *The Three Pigs*, but he was awarded his first Caldecott Medal for *Tuesday* (1991), a wordless picturebook about airborne amphibians (Pantaleo 2003b).

Where did Wiesner get the ideas for *Tuesday*? In his Caldecott acceptance speech, Wiesner stated that 'the imagination needs no outside stimulus' (1992, p. 416), and explained that he neither had a pet toad, lived near a swamp, nor had a 'thing' for frogs. Wiesner recounted his personal history as an artist, and how he was inspired 'to explore the possibilities of wordless storytelling' (p. 418). Once Wiesner graduated from Rhode Island School of Design and began to work as an illustrator, one of his goals was to publish a wordless picturebook. *Free Fall* (1988) was the culmination of his many ideas. However, Wiesner wanted to investigate other possibilities and longed 'to do a book that was wildly humorous, almost slapstick' (p. 419).

Cricket magazine approached Wiesner to do a cover illustration for an issue that would contain stories about St Patrick's Day and about frogs. Wiesner used old *National Geographic* magazines for reference and began to draw. He discovered that the creatures 'were great fun to draw – soft, round, lumpy, and really goofy-looking' (1992, p. 419). Coincidentally, Wiesner himself was 'in flight' when he began sketching images of the flying frogs that eventually became the characters in *Tuesday*. Within an hour he had worked out a complete layout, 'which remained essentially unchanged through to the finished book. Everything was there: the story, the use of the panels, the times of day, and the title' (1992, p. 420). According to Wiesner, he chose the title of the book because of the 'ooze quality' of the pronunciation of 'Tuesday' (p. 420).

On the front dust jacket flap of *Tuesday* readers are warned that if they disbelieve the events in the book, there is always another Tuesday. On the frontispiece, three air-framed illustrations, banded horizontally to depict the passing of time, foreshadow events as three sleeping frogs on lily pads become three airborne amphibians. The title page includes a lily pad, further foreshadowing of the water plant's salience to the story.

The book begins 'Tuesday evening at 8:00 p.m.' (unpaginated). Frogs at a pond become airborne when the lily pads on which they are sitting mysteriously become miniature flying carpets. The facial expressions of the frogs convey their individual personalities and emotions as they soar toward a nearby town on their lily pads. The airborne creatures chase some unsuspecting crows, cruise by a window as a man enjoys a late-night snack (11:21 p.m.), become entangled in laundry on a clothesline, visit an elderly lady who has fallen asleep while watching television, and pursue a dog. As dawn approaches, the lily pads lose their ability to fly and the frogs tumble to earth. The grounded amphibians hop back to the pond, and sit wistfully on new lily pads, musing over their night's adventures. In the morning, perplexed police officers and detectives examine the evidence of the frogs' flight, the discarded lily pads. Frog-shaped cloud formations in the background of one double page spread provide further clues to the previous night's events. The following Tuesday at 8:00 p.m. the sky is once again inhabited, but on this Tuesday, a different creature is airborne.

In his Caldecott acceptance speech, Wiesner discussed the reader interactivity required by wordless picturebooks. He noted that 'the reader is an integral part of the storytelling process' (1992, p. 421) and that his version of *Tuesday* was 'no more valid than anyone else's who reads it' (Caroff & Moje, 1992/1993, p. 287). My discussion of visual parodies in *Tuesday* is just one interpretation of Wiesner's wordless picturebook, and my list of parodies is neither exhaustive nor definitive. I concur with Wiesner's statement that 'each viewer reads the book in his or her own way' (1992, p. 421). Readers access their unique literary and linguistic reservoirs when they construct meaning (Rosenblatt, 1978); others may disagree with my interpretation of Wiesner's work, identify other parodies, or interpret differently the parodies I have identified.

Parody: A Historical and Conceptual Review

The root of the term parody is the Greek noun *parodia*, which means 'counter-song' (Hutcheon, 1985, p. 32) or 'mock song' (Cuddon, 1976, p. 640). *Para* can also mean 'beside' or 'subsidiary' in Greek. Hutcheon wrote that parody is 'repetition with difference' (p. 32), 'a bitextual synthesis' that 'incorporates the old into the new' (p. 33). Others who have written about the intertextual nature of parody include Dentith, 2000; Lewis, 2001; McGillis, 1996; Rose, 1993; Stephens, 1992; and Waugh, 1984. Lukens wrote that 'a parody reminds us of something known, then gives fresh pleasure by duplicating form that contrasts to new and humorous meaning' (1999, p. 224), and many of the children I worked with found Anthony Browne's parodic intertextual references in *Willy the Dreamer* very amusing. McCallum (1996), Stephens and Watson (1994), and Waugh (1984) included parodic appropriations in their lists of metafictive devices.

Dentith defined parody as 'any cultural practice which makes a relatively polemical allusive imitation of another cultural production or practice' (2000, p. 37). He believes that Genette's (1982) terms hypotext (original text) and hypertext (parodic transformed text) are useful when the intertextual nature of parody is discussed. Although all parodies are intertextual in nature, not all intertextual connections are parodies. Dentith noted the paradoxical effect of parody as it preserves the very text that it imitates (p. 36), and distinguished between specific parodies that are 'aimed at a specific precursor text' and general parodies that are aimed at 'a whole body of texts or kind of discourse' (p. 7). Parody 'is to be thought of as a mode, or as a range in the spectrum of possible intertextual relations,' and can be 'irreverent, inconsequential, and even silly' (p. 37).

Rose has observed that over the ages, parody has been 'a form rich in complexity as well as contradiction' (1993, p. 284). Dentith, writing of the place of parody in the history of literature, noted that 'the discussion of parody is bedevilled by disputes over a definition' (2000, p. 6). Dentith and Rose believe that various definitions of parody must be considered with respect to their historical specificity. Rose traced the historical evolution of definitions of parody and found that by the fourth century BC, parody was understood and used to describe works that were 'both comic and meta-fictional, and ambivalent towards their targets' (1993, p. 272). In contrast to the modern reduction of parody to '*either* meta-fiction *or* comedy' (p. 273), Rose described the postmodernist understanding of parody as 'both comic and meta-fictional' (p. 272).

How the postmodernist understanding of parody differs from previous definitions has been explored by a number of writers. According to Stephens and Watson, one feature of postmodern style is 'the elevation of parody as a mode.' They have argued that postmodern parody is not necessarily satirical and 'may offer some kind of tribute to the original' (1994, p. 53). Rose observed that 'Bradbury's, Lodge's, Eco's and Jencks' reaffirmations of the laughter of parody have been "postmodern" in returning some recognition of the comic or humorous aspects of parody to it' (1993, p. 271). Dentith (2000) also maintained that it is important to reconnect parody to the comic aspect found in ancient uses of the term.

Although my study is focused on visual parodies, both specific and general, similar issues surround parody in various semiotic systems. For example, like linguistic parodies, the 'social and cultural meanings of [visual] parody ... can only be understood in the density of the interpersonal and intertextual relations in which it intervenes' (Dentith, 2000, p. 37). Further, although writers, illustrators, and artists may create parodic texts of some kind, it is the reader or the viewer who interprets the text; interpretation of text as parody is dependent on recognition or knowledge of the original or hypotext.

In *Humor in Art: A Celebration of Visual Wit* (1997), Roukes discussed parody as a triggering mechanism of humour in visual art. Like Dentith, Roukes identified a range or spectrum of parodic forms that include 'mimicking, burlesquing, spoofing, comic representation, 'roasting,' or lampooning' (p. 14). Roukes defined parody in visual art as 'a humorous spoof or "take-off," mimicry or comic imitation of a selected subject' (p. 149) that 'seeks only to amuse by the comic inter-pretation of human nature and customs, behaviours, silly fads, prod-ucts, icons and art. Parody is entertainment, pure and simple' (p. 135). The humour of the visual parodies in the book is the aspect of *Tuesday* that I emphasize in the following discussion. Wiesner writes that his intent the book, as a whole, was 'to make people laugh' (1992, p. 421), and indeed the visual parodies in the book are very humorous.

I am not suggesting that the Grade 1 students were able to recognize the visual parodies in *Tuesday* as 'parodies.' Rather, the excerpts below exemplify how the children responded to, interpreted, and appreci-ated some of the visual parodies that I identified in *Tuesday*.

VISUAL PARODIES IN *TUESDAY*

Wiesner commented on *Tuesday* that the 'whole point of the book is that it is a flight of imagination' (Caroff & Moje, 1992/1993, p. 287). Wiesner was actually on board a plane when he 'got around to think-ing seriously' about his frog book (1992, p. 419): 'If I were a frog, and I had discovered I could fly, where would I go? What would I do?' (p. 420).

The flying lily pads parody other tales with flying carpets such as *Aladdin* and *The Arabian Knights*, or flying characters such as Peter Pan, literary or visual precursors that some of the students recognized. When Blane saw the framed illustration on the back of a book of an air-borne frog on a lily pad among some cattails he commented, 'The frog's flying. It's kind of like a magic carpet, but it's a magic lily pad.' When Anita viewed the first double-page spread in the book in which the frogs are sailing over the turtle on the log, she remarked, 'It's like Aladdin, because the lily pads are flying and Aladdin got a carpet.' Another student in Mrs W.'s class thought the frogs in the frontispiece illustration were imitating a behaviour he had observed at a magic show:

S: *Now look, what's happening in this picture [the frontispiece]? What are the frogs doing?*

Sebastian: They're doing this [makes humming sound – hmmmmm].
S: What are they doing, Sebastian? What is that [hmmmmm]? What do you mean by that?
Sebastian: They're making themselves float by doing that [hmmmmm].
S: Do you know what that's called?
Sebastian: On a magic show when I went there, a girl, she had two poles beside her, she had her legs crossed, she closed her eyes, and then she did this [hmmmmm], and she was starting to float up.
S: And she was starting to float?
Cassandra: I saw that one too.
S: You saw that one too?
Sebastian: I saw you [Cassandra] at the magic show.
S: Do you know what that's called when people do that and they go hmmmmm? Have you ever heard of meditating?
Sebastian: No.
Cassandra: I have.

Interestingly, a few groups of students in Ms P.'s Grade 1 class generated similar explanations for the flying lily pads:

Tom: He's waving.
S: Hello! [Imagining what the frog might be saying if it could talk.]
Evan: And look! Wait, wait, wait. Look, he's meditating.
Fernandez: He's meditating.
Tom: No, he's doing yoga.
Fernandez: He's doing yoga.
Evan: And then he's doing yoga and then he's going up, up, up.
S: Okay, so you think that's how they're able to fly because they're doing yoga, meditating.
All: Yeah.
Fernandez: Yoga.
S: How else might they be able to fly?
Evan: I think they're doing tai chi.
S: Tai chi?
Fernandez: What's tai chi?
Evan: Want me to show you some moves? I'll show you at recess.

As the awed spectators (fish) watch incredulously, the squadron of flying amphibians leave the pond. The frogs begin to fly in formation, like planes in an air show. Soon the frogs break out of formation and some engage in aerobatic manoeuvres including flying upside down. A few rather reckless amphibians pursue some surprised crows:

Ms P.'s Grade 1
Brianna: How can they control their lily pads?
S: That's a good question.
Gurjit: They should have a steering wheel.
S: Laughs. They should have a steering wheel.
Melissa: It looks like he's controlling it [the lily pad] back here.

Several students wondered how the frogs were able to fly upside down on their lily pads. Some children thought the lily pads were sticky, others thought the frogs were 'holding on very tightly,' and several thought it was magic.

Mrs W.'s Grade 1
Katie: They're not falling off.
Sue: They're sticky.
S: It could be. Look at this frog ... he's not even using his hands [third recto, framed illustration].
Marnie: Maybe he's holding on with his feet and holding them together and it's sticky and he put glue on them and sticked on them.
S: Maybe.
Sue: Maybe it's magic.
S: Maybe.
Ms P.'s Grade 1
Robert: They're flying! They're flying!
S: I wonder how they are able to fly like that.
Mohad: Their lily pads.
S: So, what is it about their lily pads that's letting them fly?
Frank: Maybe it's just a magic trick from a witch.
Shamah: Maybe it's a spell.
Mohad: Yeah, a witch did a spell.

The frogs look very self-assured as their flight continues. Wiesner has noted that in the air, the frogs 'clearly felt dignified, noble, and a bit smug' (1992, p. 419). Judging by the reactions of the Grade 1 students, the amphibians' night flight was also very noisy. As well as much laughter, the read-aloud sessions were filled with the children's accompanying sound effects for the driving/flying amphibians: Zooom! Errrrr! Wheee! Whoopee! Whaaa! Ahhhh! Yipeee! Vooom!

Some of the 'lily pad drivers' crash into laundry on a clothesline, and the collision is reminiscent of many cartoon crashes. On the verso that follows the double-page spread of the laundry collison, Wiesner frames four frogs that are wearing sheets or tablecloths from the clothesline – a parody of Superman or other flying superheroes. There was much giggling when the frogs collided with the laundry, and when the children saw the frogs with their capes on the following page:

Mrs W.'s Grade 1
All: Lots of laughing.
Sebastian: The super toads! Super toads and super frogs!
S: All right, so back here if you remember the clothesline with the sheets on it.
Kirstin: Look at this picture – look at him [points to frog in framed illustration closest to reader].
Sebastian: Him super frog!
Cassandra: He's leading the group of frogs.
S: He looks like he's really proud like, 'Look at me!'
Sebastian: He's super toad!
Kirstin: Or he could be like the king, he's pretending like he's so proud and he's got that look like he knows everything [she sticks her nose in the air and displays a haughty facial expression].
Ms P.'s Grade 1
All: Laughing, engaging in overlapping speech and making flying noises.
Chris: He tied a cape.
José: He's got a baby cape.
Ivan: I know he's pretending he's Superfrog!
S: Superfrog. It's like … Superfroooog.
Ivan: Yeah, he's a superhero.
Chris: There's two.
José: It's like he's on his battleship. Vooom!

Another parody is foreshadowed by the illustration on the cover of *Tuesday*: an aerial invasion. Rusty the dog looks to the sky in wonderment as green lily pads descend upon the town. When the students were discussing the cover and predicting narrative events, Katie hypothesized that 'The frogs are going to come and they are going to destroy the world!' There certainly is a sense of impending invasion as the frogs approach the town. Cassandra remarked, 'The frogs – they're all over the whole planet! It's a froggie attack!' But the attack is not ominous – it is a humorous invasion by creatures for which flying is indeed an 'alien' activity.

The lily pads represent an unmistakable parody of flying saucers. In his Caldecott acceptance speech, Wiesner explains that when he was working on the *Cricket* magazine cover, he drew a frog on a lily pad: 'That shape ... the round blob with the saucerlike bottom. Suddenly, old movies were running through my head: *Forbidden Planet* and *The Day the Earth Stood Still*. Together the frogs and lily pad looked like a fifties B-movie flying saucer!' (1992, p. 419). Interestingly, one group of children called the flying amphibians 'saucer frogs.' Ivan commented, 'Yeah, it's like the frogs are Martians and space invaders and they land with their flying saucers.'

The invading amphibians fill the night sky and soar over the town in large numbers. But the aliens are friendly – even when they pursue Rusty, there seems to be no intent of malice. The dog just seems to be getting his comeuppance for having chased one of the frogs. As they fly past the window of a house, one frog smiles and waves to a startled man who is having a late night snack. Patty suggested the man would think, 'This is wrong! There's no flying frogs in this house! I'm up late. I'm tired!' and Dom hypothesized, 'I can't believe my mind! There's no such thing as flying frogs!' Wiesner engages in a sly self-parody here, as the man at the table is a self-portrait of the author. Wiesner's sense of the ridiculous is well developed. He observed that 'If, after reading *Tuesday* one evening before bed, they [children] look out the window and see frogs flying by – well, we should all be so lucky' (1992, pp. 421–2). By drawing himself into the story, Wiesner was able to mediate his own luck and see those flying frogs. I asked the children what they would think if they were the man in the illustration. Several students said they wouldn't believe their eyes, and some said they would think they were seeing creatures from another planet. Mohad stated, 'I would think they're weird, weird aliens!'

The invaders enter a 'human's house' through an open window and chimney, but inquisitiveness seems to be the reason for their exploration. How does the human species live? An elderly woman's cat witnesses the frogs' visit but like Rusty, the feline is unable to assist the humans when they investigate the lily pad phenomenon on Wednesday morning. The end of the picturebook features a parody of an UFO investigation complete with reporters, detectives, police officers, tracker dogs, witnesses (human and animal), and the mysterious evidence of the lily pads:

Mrs W.'s Grade 1
Sebastian: Lookit. An investigator.
Cassandra: They're looking at the lily pads
Sebastian: And then the dog is like this [makes sniffing sounds].
S: What does that dog [Rusty] know?
Kirstin: He knows that there were frogs flying last night.
Cassandra: Yeah, the froggies were chasing the doggie.
All: Laughing.
Kirstin: And the cat knew.
Sebastian: Those are the same ... this is the dog that was chasing the frogs and the frogs were chasing that dog and that was the cat out in the old lady's house ...
Kirstin: And the man who was eating a sandwich.
Cassandra: Who was eating a sandwich when the frogs went by.
S: That's right, Cassandra. So why do you think this man is going like this? [I imitate the man's gesture in the illustration of putting up my arm and looking skyward.]
All: I saw frogs up in the sky! [imagining what man would be saying to reporter.]
Sebastian: He's on television.
S: Yes, there's a camera and the woman, the reporter, may be asking him to tell her what he saw. Now why is the investigator picking up the lily pad with a pencil?
Cassandra: Because he doesn't want to be poisoned.
S: OK. Why else might he pick it up with a pencil?
Kirstin: Because he doesn't know where it came from and it could be poisonous.

Ms P.'s Grade 1
Ali: It's their lily pads.
Fernandez: Why is the police have it there?
Ali: Because, because they're frogs.
Tom: They're trying to look at the flying saucers.
S: They're doing an investigation.
Ethan: Because the frogs.
Fernandez: Why are they doing an investigation?

S: *Because they're wondering … OK, you tell me. Why are they doing an investigation? What are they investigating?*
Tom: *Oh, I know. Maybe they think the lily pads are flying saucers that let all the aliens out.*

On the double-page spread depicting the investigation, Wiesner has cleverly included two clouds shaped like frogs on lily pads – hovering spaceships perhaps? The cloud frogs may parody the beliefs of some people that we are not alone or that 'Big Brother is watching.'

The strange events, magic, and mystery in *Tuesday* parallel and echo the use of those devices in fantasy and fairy tales. Wiesner acknowledges that he highlighted the mystery in *Tuesday* by using 'clocks, such as the clock tower on the cover, clocks scattered throughout the pictures, and the times of day in the text' (Caroff & Moje, 1992/1993, p. 285). Mystery surrounds the frogs' ability to fly as well. Is magic used on the lily pads, and if so, what is the source of the magic? Based on the cover illustration, some students predicted that there would be flying lily pads and frogs in the book:

Mrs W.'s Grade 1
S: *So now the author gives you another hint about what the book is about.*
Dom: *Frogs.*
Jeffrey: *A floating frog.*
Teresa: *It's on a lily pad and about the night.*
S: *And about the night, that's right. The frog is floating. How do you think it's able to float?*
Teresa: *Because it's on a lily pad.*
Dom: *It could be a balloon.*
S: *It could be a balloon. Teresa, you said because it's on the lily pad. What do you think has happened to the lily pad to make it float?*
Teresa: *Magic, fairy dust.*
S: *Fairy dust. Any other ideas?*
Dom: *I know. It could be since like it's so, uh … it doesn't have very much weight so it can float.*
S: *Because it's so light you think?*
Dom: *Yeah. Just like feathers.*

Time plays a very important role in *Tuesday*. Why did the flight occur at night? As dawn approaches, the lily pads loose their power of flight and the frogs' airborne adventure ends. Ryan hypothesized, 'I think at night the frogs can float but then when the daylight comes they can't fly anymore.' Dom suggested that 'They can't fly in the sun.' Anita explained that 'they flew too long and the magic is running out.' Like Cinderella at the ball, the frogs' magic ran out at a certain time. The children had several ideas to explain the termination of the frogs' flight:

Mrs W.'s Grade 1
S: Well, let's see – there's lily pads lying around. What do you think has happened here?
Kirstin: All their lily pad magic has come off.
S: OK, why do you think they've lost their magic?
Kirstin: Um, because they stayed out too long.
S: They stayed out too long?
Sebastian: No, I think because they didn't do that long enough.
S: They didn't do what long enough?
Sebastian: Like – hmmmmm.
S: Oh, I see. They didn't go 'hmmmmm' for long enough.
Sebastian: Yeah.

At the end of the book it's the pigs that become airborne, but again time determines this event because it takes place 'Next Tuesday, 7:58 p.m.' (unpaginated). I asked each small group of students to explain how the pigs were able to fly. Katie thought it was because 'the stars they are magic. They're made out of diamonds and magic.' Note Sebastian's consistency of reasoning to explain the pigs' flight:

Mrs W.'s Grade 1
All: Pigs are flying!!!
Sebastian: Look at that piggy [points to pig in upper left-hand corner of last illustration], he's like ahhhhhhhhh!
S: Do you think this one likes flying? [I point to the same pig.]
Sebastian: No he hates it.
Cassandra: That one sure does, he's like an angel [referring to pig with eyes closed by E and N on weather vane].
S: That's a really good way to describe him, Cassandra.
Kristin: He's like this [she closes her eyes and makes a face of contentment similar to the pig's].
Sebastian: The pink ones [pigs] don't, but the green ones [pigs] do.

S: *Now these pigs, they don't have lily pads, so how are they able to fly?*
Sebastian: *Oink, oink, oink, oink.*
S: *Pardon? How are they able to fly?*
Cassandra: *Um, maybe the curse of the five p.m. thing.*
S: *What do you mean? Like the curse of the eight p.m.? What happens at eight p.m.?*
Cassandra: *Yeah, like it's like a curse at that time.*
Kirstin: *Or a wizard came and made them fly whenever they want.*
S: *OK, so maybe there's a wizard. Sebastian, what did you say?*
Sebastian: *Like, you know what I think, I think they did this ... I think how they flew is like the frogs ... but these ones didn't do it that way [hmmmmm], they said, 'Oiiiiiiiiiiiiiiiiiiiiiiiink!'*
S: *So that's how they were able to fly?*
Sebastian: *Yeah, by doing, 'Oiiiiiiiiiiiiiiiiiiiiiiiiiiink.'*
All: *Laughing.*

<u>Ms P.'s Grade 1</u>
S: *I wonder how the pigs are able to fly. They don't have lily pads.*
Melissa: *They have special food to make them fly.*
S: *They eat special food and that makes them fly. Sam?*
Sam: *They have this power and they have special little flying saucers as small as an ant, but you can't see them and they're flying.*
S: *What a great idea, Sam.*
Changwei: *Maybe they have magical ears.*
S: *Magical ears. Good idea. A couple more ideas?*
Peter: *I think they have invisible rocket boosters on their feet.*
All: *Laughing.*

Wiesner parodies some people's hypnotic absorption with television when he depicts the frogs mesmerized by the television in the elderly woman's home. She has fallen asleep while watching television, and all but one frog seems to be engrossed in viewing the television. One particularly talented amphibian is channel hopping (another parody of typical human behaviour) by using his tongue on the remote control. When he saw this illustration, Bishop commented, 'Look at this guy [frog with the remote control]. He's saying I'm going to change the channel to a channel I like!'

<u>Mrs W.'s Grade 1</u>
S: *OK, whose house is this? Whose house do you think it might be?*
Cassandra: *It's the man's house – the guy who was eating a sandwich.*

S: The man's house?
Sebastian: No, it's that ... it's that dog's [Rusty on the cover].
Kirstin: Oh, it's an old lady's house.
Sebastian: Yeah, and it's that ...
Kirstin: Laughing. Look! That frog's turning the remote on with his tongue.
Cassandra: Thank God the lady's asleep!
All: Lots of laughing!
S: Laughing. Why do you say thank goodness the lady is asleep?
Cassandra: If she wasn't asleep she would scream, 'Ahhhh! Ahhhh!' And
    call 911. [she is very animated; lots more laughing.] 'There's frogs in my
    living room!'
Kirstin: 'It's a frog attack!' [imagining what the lady would say.]

One lone frog's attention is focused on a landscape painting in the lady's living room – a picture that depicts an environment where the frogs might live. Is the lone frog's removal from the parodied event a reminder to readers of the dangers of the technological world disregarding the natural world? Or does the scene parody Dorothy's refrain from *The Wizard of Oz* that 'There's no place like home,' and foreshadow the amphibians' ultimate return to the pond? Sebastian commented, 'Look at that frog, he's looking at the view.'

Ms P.'s Grade 1
José: He's looking at the picture over there.
Ivan: Yes, he's going to walk through it.
Chris: Yeah, there's a pond. Like his home.
Ivan: Maybe it's like in The Three Pigs. *They got out of the story.*

Wiesner (2002) admits to watching a lot of Bugs Bunny and talks about his affection for comic books when growing up (Caroff & Moje, 1992/1993). The frogs' collision with the laundry, the chase scene between the crows and the frogs, and especially the dog–frog then frog–dog chase frames are reminiscent of scenes from cartoons and comic books. In comic-book-like panels we see one frog apply the 'brakes' to his lily pad when he encounters Rusty, the dog depicted on the cover. The students readily provided sound effects for the screeching brakes. The frog quickly turns around his lily pad to escape the dog, but on the next page the situation becomes reversed as a group of frogs chase the incredulous dog:

Mrs W.'s Grade 1

S: [I turn the page and read 4:38 a.m. The children look at the illustration on the recto and make barking sounds].

S: So what's happening? It's becoming almost morning time. So what's happening to the sky?

Teresa: It's getting sunny!

S: It's getting lighter, that's right. So here's this frog. What's he doing?

Teresa: He's almost on the ground. He's flying along and then he stopped!

S: If you could make sound effects what would they be?

All: Make braking sounds – screeching.

Anita: There's a dog.

S: Look at the frog. What do you think he's thinking here?

Jeffrey: Yikes!

All: Yikes!

S: Now watch this [I turn the page].

All: Laughing.

Jeffrey: All the frogs are chasing the dog.

Dom: Now look at the dog.

Jeffrey: The dog is scared of the frogs.

Teresa: What's his name?

S: Rusty, that says Rusty on this collar [spells name]. So, here the dog he's chasing the frog and then all of a sudden …

Anita: All the frogs are chasing him.

Dom: That's funny!

Tuesday could also be interpreted as a parody of the tourist adventure in the vein of the country mouse/town mouse story. The frogs travel to a new 'world,' explore and experience human culture without getting into too much trouble, and leave artefacts to inform the humans of their visit. The following excerpts are taken from two groups' discussion of the double-page spread that depicts the frogs' return to their pond.

Mrs W.'s Grade 1

S: Well, look at these guys. What are they doing?

Anita: They're walking.

Teresa: Hopping, they're hopping to their … they're hopping to the pond.

Dom: Look at this frog – it's a big one that can eat a mouse, and the female is bigger than the male. That's what I saw on a television show.

Anita: Dom, look at this one [points to a frog in far right-hand panel on recto].

S: Right. Look at this one. Anita is saying Dom look at this one. Look at this guy. How do you think he's looking?

All: Mad.

Dom: Mad.

S: He looks grumpy. Why do you think he might be angry and grumpy?

Teresa: Because he's back at the pond.

Dom: Because he fell down.

Anita: And maybe that all the adventure that they had ...

Jeffrey: He wants more exploring.

S: Just a minute Jeffrey, please. Anita, say that again – what you said.

Anita: It looks like the adventure that they had is all finished and he's mad.

S: So you think he wants more adventures, and Jeffrey, you think that he wants to do more exploring?

Anita and Jeffrey: Yeah.

<u>Ms P.'s Grade 1</u>

S: Look at this guy. Look at the way he's sitting [points to the frog in the far right-hand panel on the recto].

Chris: He's saying, I know what he's saying. He's saying, 'What a terrible trip!'

José: I don't think he likes to ride.

Chris: He's thinking, 'What a tough trip!'

S: He said, 'What a tough trip!' because look at all that happened to them. They flew and then they fell. What are you saying, José?

José: He doesn't like the trip.

S: He didn't like the trip. What else might he be saying?

Ivan: He's saying, 'That was dangerous falling on the roof!'

Chris: I know. He's saying, 'Boring pond.'

Overall, *Tuesday* was a very popular book with the Grade 1 children. Of the nine boys and two girls in Ms. P.'s class who selected *Tuesday* as one of their favourite picturebooks, eight said they liked the flying frogs. Nathan said, 'It's so crazy with those flying frogs.' Two children thought the book was funny, two students commented on the flying pigs, and one student, Omar, liked *Tuesday* 'because the frogs are flying and the pigs are flying.' Peter commented on the humour of the book and enjoyed the mystery surrounding the flying amphibians: 'It's kind of funny. The pigs fly at the end and we don't know why the frogs are flying and ... it's funny.' Jeremy chose *Tuesday* 'because I like frogs and they're making jokes about frogs.' Finally, Changwei selected *Tuesday* as a favourite book because she liked the illustration of the frogs flying by the window as the man was eating his late-night snack.

In Mrs W.'s class, four girls and five boys chose *Tuesday* as one of their favourite books that I read aloud with them. Four students liked the flying frogs. Natalie explained, 'I liked it because the flying frogs were so funny.' Two students liked the flying pigs, and one student explained that *Tuesday* was one of his favourite books 'because the frogs and pigs could fly.' Three children thought the book was humorous. Patty said she liked 'the funny part when the frogs fall down in the morning.' Three students selected *Tuesday* because they enjoyed the illustrations in the book.

The Grade 1 children in my studies were able to recognize and appreciate the parodic elements of *Tuesday* with a degree of sophistication beyond their limited experience of literature. McGillis has written that 'writers and illustrators who employ parody show a respect for young readers' and that 'children receive one of their first lessons in criticism and critical detachment' by reading parody (1996, p. 124). Developing an understanding of parody as a form of intertextuality, and recognizing how it can be used as a metafictive device (McCallum, 1996; Stephens & Watson, 1994; Waugh, 1984) will contribute to an individual's growth as a reader. Meek writes that children 'quickly learn the rules for "how things work around here." Having done so ... they know that the rules can be broken, by parody for example' (1988, p. 18). Awareness and understanding of parody will assist children as they become older and encounter parody in other picturebooks, novels, movies, television programs, advertisements, and computer and video games. The children's responses to and interpretations of several visual parodies in *Tuesday* emphasizes that parody can also provide readers and viewers with aesthetic pleasure. Enjoyment of literature is the essential constituent to becoming a lifelong reader.

Shortcut

The frontispiece of *Shortcut* (Macaulay, 1995) provides readers with an introduction to the book's cast of characters: June, Albert, Patty, Pearl, Professor Tweet, Sybil, Clarinda, Clarinda's cockatoo, and Bob. Macaulay's picturebook is organized into nine chapters and an epilogue. In chapter 1, readers are introduced to Albert and his horse,

June. Each week on market day, they travel to town to sell their ripest melons. Albert and June regularly stop at a bridge along the way; Albert tosses a coin in the water and makes a wish. On this particular day, he decides to take the shortcut up a steep hill. Albert removes his coat and hangs it on a signpost so that he can more easily help June haul the wagon up the hill. The signpost points travellers in the direction of the 'shortcut' and the 'long long way.' When they reach the top of the hill, Albert retrieves his coat from the signpost, and he and June continue their journey, stopping only at the Railway Café for something to eat. At the market, their melons are popular and the wagon is soon empty. Albert and June arrive home before dark.

Chapter 2 introduces readers to Patty and her pig, Pearl. How is this chapter connected to the first chapter? On their way to the market, Albert and June set in motion a dramatic chain of events (a hot air balloon sailing out of control, a missing pig, a train on an abandoned railway line, a speeding driver, a sinking boat) that ultimately involves the other characters on the frontispiece. However, none of the characters in *Shortcut* is aware of the actions of the other characters in the book.

Some of the metafictive devices that are evident in *Shortcut* include both textual and illustrative manifold or multiple narratives, the narrative framing device of stories within stories, disruptions of traditional time and space relationships in the narrative(s), and nonlinear and nonsequential plots including narrative discontinuities. The interdependence of the metafictive devices in *Shortcut* enhances their overall effectiveness.

Metafictive Devices in Shortcut

Russian Formalist literary theory of narrative distinguishes between story and plot, between form and content. In Formalism, the term 'fabula' (the story) refers to the way in which an event unfolds, the 'brute chronology' (Holquist, 1990, p. 113) of the narrative; the term 'syuzhet' refers to the plot, 'the order and manner in which events are actually presented in the narrative' (Cuddon, 1999, p. 328). The mediated telling of events by an author is a construction, while the chronology of events might be varied in some way for a particular effect (Holquist, 1990, p. 113). In Macaulay's *Shortcut*, the whole point of the book is how the telling differs from the chronology of actual events. The syuzhet of *Shortcut* is nonlinear and nonsequential, and the narrative is multistranded as multiple stories and perspectives are presented in the text and illustrations. Many diversions in the picturebook disrupt time and space relationships in the story, and sidetrack reader attention. The multiple narratives of *Shortcut* create indeterminacy – readers must fill in the many gaps of this writerly text (Barthes, 1970). The syuzhet of *Shortcut* establishes its metafictional status as text and fiction.

Readers first meet Albert and June in chapter 1. The story of their trip to market is both sequential and linear. However, subsequent chapters present readers with new narratives about Patty and Pearl, Professor Tweet, the Darlington Cannonball, Sybil, and Bob. Readers must suture these narrative disruptions in order to unify the visual and verbal manifolds. Although the characters in *Shortcut* are unaware of each other, they are connected through a bizarre chain of events. Some links among the multiple narratives and characters are revealed through words and others are disclosed solely through illustrations. Visual clues provide details that enable readers to make associations and connections between the various stories and characters, to foreshadow upcoming events, to fill in the gaps, and to unravel the interdependent, yet synergistic subplots, and hence the overall plot.

Multistranded narratives 'are constructed of two or more interconnected narrative strands differentiated by shifts in temporal and spatial relationships, and/or shifts in narrative point of view' (McCallum, 1996, p. 406). The co-existence of several interconnected and looping narratives creates a discursive structure that differs from traditional time and space relationships in picturebooks, and that may be disruptive for some readers. The use of chapters as an organizational format also foregrounds the narrative structuring in *Shortcut*. The text is multilayered, and readers must be attentive and 'see not merely look' (Macaulay, 1991, p. 419) in order to weave a story (or two) within the framework provided by Macaulay. Indeed, there is no 'shortcut' to constructing a cohesive fabula from the individual narratives in the picturebook.

The intratextual connections among the multiple and multistranded narratives are plentiful in the book as Macaulay refers visually and verbally to previous events, characters, or items that highlight the construction of the text. The students were able to make connections between the actions of Albert and June and the fates of subsequent characters. They understood both the simultaneity of events and the ensuing chaos in some narratives. For example, June is tied to the railway switch outside the café, stretches to reach some tasty clover, and moves the switch, changing the course of the train, the Darlington Cannonball:

Ms P.'s Grade 1
S: *How could a train be coming down the track? I thought it was an abandoned railway line?*
Ethan: *Well remember how the horse pulled on it [the railway switch] when it walked away from the switch? Well instead of going on the track that it [the train] wanted to go on, it got onto the abandoned one when the horse made it switch.*
Mohad: *And now the train is going to hit the pig!*
Mrs W.'s Grade 1
Marnie: *Hey, look at Pearl's back end!*
Sue: *There's a train coming.*
S: *How do you know a train is coming?*
Sue: *Because there's a shadow right here [points to shadow].*
S: *That's right. See the shadow on her behind? Is there suppose to be a train on this track?*
All: *No!*
Cassandra: *It's abandoned.*
S: *So how do you think the train got on the tracks?*
Marnie: *Maybe someone switched it.*
Cassandra: *No, because June switched it.*
S: *Good for you, Cassandra. Do you want to go back and find that picture?*
All: *Yes. [I turn back to illustration of June stretching for clover and moving the switch.]*
Cassandra: *There. She switched it and that's why.*

June's actions affected not only Pearl. The train's new trajectory resulted in the train colliding with a camper on a truck:

Ms P.'s Grade 1
S: *What happened here?*
Kathy: *The sign says 'Closed' [points to sign].*
Robert: *The train went through there and then it cut the house!*
S: *Exactly, the train went right through these people's trailer. Would the people be expecting a train to be on these tracks?*
All: *No.*
S: *Why not?*

*Fernandez: Because trains don't go through there anymore, but it did
because it went on the wrong track because of the horse.*

As Albert and June continue on their journey to town to sell their
melons, they unknowingly untie Professor Tweet's hot air balloon
when it impedes their way:

<u>Ms P.'s Grade 1</u>
S: Why is the balloon breaking free?
Gurjit: I know, cause they [Albert and June] untied it.
*Ryan: Because accidentally they untied it and nobody knowed they were up
there. That's why they untied it and then the balloon went away and then
the glasses and his hat went down.*
Brianna: And that paper [points to paper in illustration].

As Professor Tweet's balloon sails toward the church spire in
Fauxville, skimming the rooftops, the children made further connections. They noted the bird lying in the eaves trough of one house and
made intratextual links to information provided visually on the book's
frontispiece and half title page:

<u>Ms P.'s Grade 1</u>
Ivan: There's that bird!
S: Do you remember that bird from before?
Sam: That escaped from that cage in the front of the book.
S: Does that look familiar? [points to feathers sticking up on head]
Shamah: His hair is sticking up.
Sam: It's the same bird.
<u>Ms W.'s Grade 1</u>
Kirstin: Lookit. There's a bird on top of his [Professor Tweet's] head.
*S: That's right. Have you seen this white bird before? [points to bird in
eaves trough]*
Kirstin: Yeah. It's her bird [turns to frontispiece].
Pender: At the beginning.
Patty: Right there [points to Clarinda and photograph of bird].
Kirstin: That's why she's crying!
S: Why, Kirstin?
*Kirstin: Because she lost her bird, and that's her bird [points to photograph
of bird].*
Patty: We seen him, and him, and her [points to three characters].

Dom: Not that one [points to Sybil].
S: Not her and not?
Dom: Him [Bob].
S: That's right, so we still have to meet those people yet.

Chapter 5 begins with 'Sybil is off to the market,' but a time disruption returns readers to events that were depicted in chapter 1. The fourth page in chapter 5 shows Sybil driving by the signpost shortly after Albert puts his jacket on it, obscuring the direction to the short-cut. Albert's legs are visible in the top part of the illustration, pushing the wagon up the hill. The children understood the simultaneity of events in the multistranded narratives:

Mrs W.'s Grade 1
Hannah: She thought that that way is the shortcut.
S: But is it really?
Hannah: Because it says shortcut and then the arrow.
S: That's right. But is it really the shortcut?
Anita: No.
Hannah: No. It's the long way.
S: The long, long way. Right. So back here when Albert does this … [turns back to the pages in chapter 1 showing the signpost on the verso, and Albert pushing the wagon up the hill and his coat hanging on the signpost on the recto].
Hannah: There it is!
S: That's right. Look you can see Albert walking up the hill. And here he is in this illustration [turns to back to chapter 5] walking up the hill again just as Sybil drives by.
Hannah: And lookit. She is right there taking the long way and Albert took the short way up.
Theo: She didn't see him.
S: It doesn't seem so, does it? So when Sybil gets over here [points to her in the recto], what happens?
Theo: He went back down the hill and got his coat.

The children were able to understand the temporal, spatial, and narrative shifts in *Shortcut* and make associations between the new and previous characters and events. Further, many of the narratives are linked only visually. When the children saw the illustration of Bob floating in his boat at the beginning of chapter 7, they recognized the bridge from chapter 1 and most commented on the crest on the bridge:

Ms P.'s Grade 1
Tom: It's the same bridge that they [Albert and June] crossed over.
S: How do you know that?
Frank: Because you can see those signs [points to the crest on the bridge].
José: Yeah, those. There's the hill, there's the bell, there's the money, there's … I can't remember what that one is.
Mrs W.'s Grade 1
Katie: Here! There it is again.
S: There's what?
Katie: That same bridge with that crest thing.
Russell: Yeah. There's the coins for that man with the watermelons.
S: Right. Who does the hat belong to?
Katie: I know. I know. The Professor. And the bell …
Bishop: Is the pig's.
Katie: We haven't seen the hill yet.
S: Are you sure? Who does the hill belong to?
Russell: Him [flips back in book to an illustration of Albert].

As Bob's exploits unfolded in chapter 7, the students made further connections to other narratives in the book. They understood that one character's story was indeed part of another character's narrative. The children knew the sandbags were from Professor Tweet's hot air balloon and the money at the bottom of the river was Albert's:

Ms P.'s Grade 1
S: 'Chapter seven. Bob sleeps all day. He loves the peace and quiet of the river. In his favorite dream …'
Changwei: These are the Professor's [points to the sandbags] – they are going to go bonk!
Robert: It's going to land on his head.
Peter: I think it's going to land on his face.
S: Good connecting! 'In his favorite dream, he is admiral of the fleet.' And look, as Changwei said, here comes the Professor's things [I turn the page; the next double-page spread shows Bob falling in the water and sinking to the bottom of the river].
All: SPLASH!

Changwei: I knew it!
Kathy: He's going to get the coins.
<u>Mrs W.'s Grade 1</u>
S: 'Chapter Seven. Bob sleeps all day. He loves the peace and quiet of the river.'
Dom: Oh, Bob's the one that is in the water upside down [referring to the illustration on the frontispiece].
S: *You think so?*
Dom: Yep.
S: 'In his favorite dream he is admiral of the fleet.'
Patty: Oh, those are the bags that Professor Tweet throwed, the sandbags.
Dom: See this is Bob.
Kirstin: You know what? Lookit right there [points to crest on bridge].
Dom: Oh yeah. The penny and the bell and the hill with the trees.
S: *That's right. The shield that Kirstin called it. So here's Bob ...*
Patty: And look at that duck.
Pender: The rabbits are laughing and now there's only three.
S: *I wonder why they're laughing.*
Patty: Because those sand bags are coming down and then ... plop [uses her hands to show the descent of the sand bags landing on Bob].
S: *Let's see [I turn the page].*
Kirstin: Oh, the sandbags hit him so hard! Ohh! Lookit! He might have wished for money and then he saw all that money!
S: 'Suddenly he is thrown from his boat. Fortunately he sinks to the bottom, which is how he makes his dream come true.' *So where did all the money come from?*
Patty: Um, from people up there.
Pender: The people that made wishes.
S: *That's right. Who was making wishes?*
Kirstin: Albert.

The Grade 1 children clearly worked actively to create unity among the nonlinear and nonsequential plots, the multistranded narratives, and the stories within stories, demonstrating 'that it isn't necessary to think in a straight line to make sense' (Macaulay, 1991, p. 419). Readers must go the 'long long way' to construct a coherent, consistent, and unified fabula in *Shortcut*. The children understood that even though Macaulay's mediated telling of the syuzhet included narrative discontinuities and disruptions in time and space, the multiple stories and characters interacted and were ultimately connected. The excerpts illustrate the children's participatory behaviours as they co-created the text.

Four boys and one girl in Ms P.'s class chose *Shortcut* as one of their favourite books that I read aloud with them during the research project. When asked to explain why they liked *Shortcut*, four children talked about Sybil and her driving abilities. Sam stated, 'because she could drive so fast ... she drives so crazy that she almost drove over people and she ran over the guy on the bike.' Two children believed that Sybil was sent to jail for her driving violations. Melissa said, 'the girl was in jail and it was the man's fault.' Peter explained that he liked the book 'because it was funny and a lot of clues were left behind.'

In Mrs W.'s class, three girls and three boys selected *Shortcut* as one of their favourite picturebooks from the read-aloud sessions. Five students thought that the book was humorous including Hannah, who explained 'it was funny when he put his coat over the sign because she (Sybil) thought it was the shortcut.' Four children identified particular events in the story that they enjoyed. Natalie 'liked the part when the pig almost go runned over by the train.' Patty enjoyed 'the part when um, Albert left his jacket on the sign and helped June up the hill.' Theo said that Macaulay 'makes the funniest pictures,' and he showed me several illustrations in the book that he liked.

Metafiction and the Child Reader

The transcript excerpts reveal how the Grade 1 children competently handled the visual and narrative metafictive devices in *Willy the Dreamer*, *Tuesday*, and *Shortcut*. Books such as these with metafictional devices provide certain types of 'reading lessons' (Meek, 1988) about the construction of narratives by authors, and about the role of readers. An extensive understanding of '*the nature and variety of written discourse*' (Meek, 1988, p. 21) can enrich students' literary understanding about the structures of stories, increase their knowledge about the ways that stories work, and help develop literary competences (Culler, 1980). Through their textual engagements with the picturebooks, the Grade 1 children experienced 'reading lessons' about intertextualities, multistranded narratives, narrative framing devices (stories within stories), disruptions of traditional time and space relationships in narratives, nonlinear and nonsequential plots, parodic appropriations, and indeterminacy.

The picturebooks used in my study extended the students' repertoires of story schemata and introduced them to a variety of narrative, discursive, and illustrative devices. The abilities to tolerate ambiguity (Meek, 1988) and to understand irregularities and complexities (Spiro, Coulson, Feltovich, & Anderson, 2004) are fundamental to children's growth as readers and to their future successful transactions with more sophisticated texts. In her review of the literature on the developmental nature of reading fiction, Mackey wrote that an awareness of 'some sort of distance between reader and story' was seen as 'essential to full adult reading' (1990, p. 180). Through their experiences with picturebooks with metafictive devices, children will grow in their abilities as readers; their metafictive awareness will assist them as they encounter similar devices in other print and digital texts. In Anstey's opinion (2002), postmodern texts with metafictive devices provide a site for developing new literacies. She identified eight metafictive devices commonly found in postmodern picturebooks and discussed how these features can provide readers with the necessary understandings to be multiliterate in the twenty-first century (p. 448).

McCallum wrote that 'underlying much metafiction for children is a heightened sense of the status of fiction as an elaborate form of play, that is a game with linguistic and narrative codes and conventions' (1996, p. 398). In many ways, the Grade 1 students' reading work resembled play-like behaviours as they constructed meaning. The metafictive devices in the picturebooks used in the research gave agency to the young readers and required them to adopt a coauthoring role to become even more involved in the creation of meaning. During the read-aloud sessions, the students drew inferences, made interpretations, generated hypotheses, created possibilities, and made intratextual and intertextual connections. In assuming a collaborative role when reading, the students manifested involvement, alertness, responsibility, flexible thinking, a questioning stance, and 'an openness to alternative formulations of experience' (p. 399). Books with metafictive devices can provide pleasurable aesthetic reading experiences as well as teach critical thinking skills, visual literacy skills, and interpretive strategies.

According to Goldstone, research shows that 'children can handle quite sophisticated and visual and narrative devices' (1998, p. 51). My picturebook read-aloud experiences with the Grade 1 children fully corroborate Goldstone's statement. Peter Hunt wrote that 'it may be correct to assume that child-readers will not bring to the text a complete or sophisticated systems of codes, but is this any reason to deny them access to texts with a potential of rich codes?' (1991, p. 101). The answer is a definite no.

Using Talk as a Tool to Think Collectively

I have used Mercer's term 'interthinking' (2000) to describe how talk allows us to think collectively, to engage with others' ideas through oral language. Mercer coined the term as a means to link the cognitive and social functions of group talk. The transcript excerpts in chapters 2 and 3 show the nature of the interthinking that occurred during the small-group interactive read-aloud sessions with the Grade 1 children.

Exploratory talk is a fundamental aspect of interthinking. Barnes (1976, 1992) described exploratory talk as 'thinking aloud' that enables individuals to monitor and reshape their own thoughts, talk as 'a means for controlling thinking' (1992, p. 28). Barnes explained that exploratory talk 'is very important whenever we want the learner to take an active part in learning, and … is one means by which the assimilation and accommodation of new knowledge to the old is carried out' (p. 28). Mercer examined exploratory talk in his book *The Guided Construction of Knowledge: Talk Amongst Teachers and Learners* (1995). He described three ways of talking and thinking: disputational, cumulative, and exploratory. To Mercer, exploratory talk involves individuals engaging 'critically but constructively with each other's ideas … Challenges are justified and alternative hypotheses are offered' (p. 104). Exploratory talk was also part of the taxonomy Klein (1977) generated for designing a talk environment in classrooms. In Klein's words, exploratory talk creates 'new perceptions of or feelings about an idea or thing' (p. 10). He further subdivided exploratory talk into *moving-in exploring talk* that 'takes as its beginning point a task or problem, however narrow or general in nature, and creatively "solves" it' and *moving-out exploring talk* that its more open-ended, 'its purpose mystery-generating rather than problem-solving' with suggestive rather than resolved and closed results (p. 10). Klein also suggested that students should have experiences with formal talk, dialogue, small group discussion, and dramatic talk in classrooms. Barnes, Mercer, and Klein each use the term 'exploratory talk,' but my use and meaning of the phrase resembles both Barnes's description, in which students talk their way through and into ideas, and Klein's moving-out exploring talk.

The transcript excerpts in chapters 2 and 3 reveal how the students and I thought through ideas together and built on one another's thoughts, suggestions, and comments, that is, how we engaged in exploratory talk. The children used oral language to think collectively; their exchanges served a multitude of functions including scaffolding interpretations, extending understandings, exploring significances, and constructing storylines. As the students participated in each small-group read-aloud session, they 'learned' about how to participate in this particular context. Indeed, the children's identities were influenced by the interaction patterns of the small-group discussions. As Ryan and Anstey have written, 'All readers have an identity which is derived from their life experiences and which provides them with resources as a reader' (2003, p. 11). The types of interactions that took place among the students influenced their repertoires of literary and life experiences (Rosenblatt, 1981), and the social and discursive practices established during the sessions affected their language and literacy development. The students' intertextual histories – their knowledge about literature and about how to talk about literature with other people – were constantly changing as they listened to and talked about each picturebook. Their language and behaviours affected each other and the group as a whole, and the group affected the individual: individual and collective identities were constantly changing, adapting, and emerging. Berk and Winsler wrote that 'social engagement can be a powerful force in transforming children's thinking' (1995, p. 14) and 'ways of thinking are socially situated' (p. 15). However, children's thinking is also influenced by their engagement with media and pop culture outside of the school context.

During the small-group read-aloud sessions, the children had opportunities to try out, think through, and reflect on their ideas. Barnes (1992) wrote of the importance of giving children opportunities to 'talk it over,' so they can learn by talking and through talking. Vygotsky believed that collaboration with others was a source of cognitive development. He wrote that 'All higher mental functions ... are initially created through collaborative activity; only later do they become internal mental processes' (Berk & Winsler, 1995, p. 20). Children are able to rehearse and try out their ideas when they orally share their thoughts with others. By listening to their own talk and to the talk of others, children can develop their understanding of themselves and their world. As Mercer wrote, 'individually and collectively, we use language to transform experience into knowledge and understanding' (1995, p. 67).

The nature of the literature I read to the Grade 1 children facilitated interthinking during the read-aloud sessions and required a high degree of reader participation in the creation of meaning. Although picturebooks have always challenged readers to fill in gaps and generate predictions on multiple levels, picturebooks with metafictive devices and Radical Change characteristics demand a more active, involved reading. 'Talking it over' was an essential component of the interactivity and connectivity, the developing sense of community that occurred during the read-aloud sessions.

Dewey (1966) maintained that social interactions, like small group discussions and peer dialogue, encourage learning. Klein wrote that small group discussion 'represents the highest order of human relations and language interaction ... [and] represents an opportunity to develop languaging, thinking, and human relations skills, at the same time' (1977, p. 44). The small-group discussions demonstrate how the Grade 1 children's comments and questions offered 'insight into their literary and literacy interpretations' (Torr, 2004, p. 182).

Although teachers do not generally have the luxury to engage in small-group read-aloud sessions like those described in this book, they can employ both shared reading and group interactive read-alouds in their classrooms. Research on effective reading instruction has found that effective teachers engaged in an interactive style that encouraged active student involvement (Taylor, Peterson, Pearson, & Rodriguez, 2002) and 'posed more "open" questions, to which multiple responses' were appropriate (Allington, 2002, p. 744). Texts with Radical Change characteristics and metafictive devices are ideal for rereading to children; the polysemous texts afford multiple opportunities for meaning-making and interpretation. As Meek wrote, 'Don't explain everything; leave some of the artist-author's secrets for another time' (1988, p. 19). Morrow (1988) found that repeated readings of stories with young children fostered 'a wider variety of response and more, interpretive comments than did single readings of stories' (Martinez & Roser, 2003, p. 804). The students in my research enthusiastically anticipated the rereading of the picturebooks and enjoyed sharing their knowledge about the books during the whole-class read-aloud sessions. Time should be allocated for students to look closely at texts, and to engage in talk about them with both their peers and teacher. Given the time, children are often able to discover 'secrets' in the illustrations that may be missed by adults (Meek, 1988).

Teachers should be familiar enough with the literature they read aloud to understand and appreciate the possibilities for discussion. In addition to understanding the importance of the peritextual features of picturebooks such as the dust jacket, cover, endpapers, title, half-title, and dedication pages, and the frontispiece, teachers need to be aware of how these features contribute to the overall text and to students' reading transactions. Conversations about peritextual features should be considered an integral part of storybook read-aloud or literature discussions, so that concepts and vocabulary can be introduced in meaningful contexts.

Teachers can enrich read-aloud sessions by adopting particular pedagogical practices in their teaching and learning. To cultivate 'an environment rich in high-quality talk about text' (Duke & Pearson, 2002, p. 208), teachers can encourage students to create connections between texts and their lives, and to build links within and between texts. Research on exemplary teachers has found that 'In these classrooms, teachers and students were more likely to make connections across texts and across conversations' (Allington, 2001, p. 96). Students should be allowed time to follow up on their intertextual initiations (Oyler & Barry, 1996) and to acquire the metalanguage for talking about literary devices and conventions such as intertextual, intratextual, or text-to-life connections. Teachers must model these behaviours and discuss how they use textual connections to construct meaning and to enrich and deepen their own reading, writing, and viewing experiences. Further, teachers and students need to discuss how the social and cultural specificity of some intertextualities affects their inclusion, identification, and interpretation by the class.

As the most influential member of the students' interpretive community, a teacher must be critically aware of how she or he uses language in the classroom and of how children are encouraged (or discouraged) to use language. Teachers can periodically audio-record discussions during guided reading, in learning centres, inquiry groups, cooperative learning groups, or literature discussion groups. Teachers can also video or audio-record their read-aloud sessions to provide information about the language behaviours of both themselves and their students.

As a teacher and a researcher, I learned a great deal from the Grade 1 students about how six-year-old children talk and think in general, and specifically about how they interpret and respond to a collection of sophisticated picturebooks. Like many other researchers and teachers, I continue to be challenged by the multifaceted role of the teacher in student discussion groups. By reading the transcripts, I learned that I talked too much, even though I was cognizant of the quantity of my oral contributions, that I missed some 'tender shoots' of response (Britton, 1968, p. 4) that could have been fostered and explored collectively, and that I asked too many questions. The transcripts also revealed that I used various techniques to guide the children in their construction of knowledge. I also believe my behaviours and articulations communicated to the children that their contributions were valued, that they were most capable of constructing meaning from the sophisticated texts, that multiple interpretations of literature should be recognized, considered, and celebrated, that reading is an enjoyable and pleasurable experience, that readers should be actively involved in the construction of meaning when they read, and that adults can learn (a lot) from children.

After working with Grade 1 students for two years, I was interested in exploring the responses of older elementary students to picturebooks with Radical Change characteristics and metafictive devices. Chapters 4 and 5 describe some of the findings from the two studies I conducted with three classes of Grade 5 students.

4 Grade 5 Children Reading Literature with Radical Change Characteristics

Subsequent to my research with the Grade 1 students, I conducted two studies with three classes of Grade 5 students during the fall of 2003 and 2004. I was interested in exploring the responses of older elementary students to a similar collection of contemporary picturebooks with metafictive devices and Radical Change characteristics.

This chapter describes the research contexts and data analysis processes, and focuses on some of the Grade 5 students' responses to the picturebooks they read during the studies. I describe the findings about their favourite picturebooks and the books they found most challenging to read, and I share the children's oral and written responses to *Zoom* (Banyai, 1995) and *Re-zoom* (Banyai, 1995), the first books the students read during the research. I also detail my findings of the analyses of the students' written responses to *The Three Pigs* (Wiesner, 2001), *The Stinky Cheese Man and Other Fairly Stupid Tales* (Scieszka, 1992), and *Who's Afraid of the Big Bad Book?* (Child, 2002), three of the students' favourite books, as well as *Black and White* (Macaulay, 1990), one of the books the children found most challenging to read. The chapter ends with a discussion of the students' opinions about what they learned about reading picturebooks from their participation in the studies.

Research Site and Participants

Year Three

Ms H.'s Grade 5 classroom was in a kindergarten to Grade 5 independent elementary school located in an affluent residential area of a city in western British Columbia, Canada. Of the approximately 160 students enrolled in the school, the majority were from upper socio-economic class families. All eleven girls and nine boys in Ms H.'s class participated in the study. For one boy and two girls in the class, English was not the only language spoken at home. One child was Asian and spoke Mandarin and English, another student was South Asian and spoke Gujrati, Kuchi, and English, and another child spoke German and English.

According to Ms H., who was in her thirteenth year of teaching, all of the students in her class were meeting provincial grade level standards in reading and writing, and three students exceeded expectations in these areas. One student was in an individualized educational program (IEP) and received regular assistance in language arts from the learning resource specialist. The students were on a six-day cycle timetable and received language arts instruction for between seventy and eighty minutes each day. Hereafter this class is referred to as 5A.

Year Four

I worked with Ms H. and her Grade 5 students the following year as well. During my second year in the school I was on study leave and was able to work with both classes of Grade 5 students with whom Ms H. taught language arts. Hereafter, the 2004 Grade 5 classes are referred to as 5B and 5C.

All eight girls and eleven boys in 5B participated in the study. Fifteen children were of Euro-Canadian ethnicity, two children were Chinese-Canadians, one child was of Filipino heritage, and one child was biracial (Chinese and Euro-Canadian parents). For two of the children, two languages were spoken at home all of the time (English and Manadrin, and English and Chinese). Three other children indicated that although English was spoken most frequently at home, they also spoke another language (French and Croatian).

According to Ms H., one student was exceeding provincial grade level standards in reading and writing, and two students were fully meeting expectations in these areas. Although the other sixteen children met Grade 5 level provincial standards in reading and writing, their work represented a continuum of proficiency. Ms H. indicated that four students were competently meeting expectations and two other students were minimally meeting expectations.

In 5C, all seven girls and twelve boys participated in the study. Fourteen children were of Euro-Canadian ethnicity, one child was South Asian, one child was South American, one child was Chinese Canadian, and two children were biracial (Japanese and Euro-Canadian parents, and Chinese and Euro-Canadian parents). One student in the class was designated as legally blind. Two children indicated that they spoke a language other than English at home (Japanese and Punjabi).

According to Ms H., one student was exceeding provincial grade level standards in reading and writing, and six students were fully meeting expectations in these areas. Of the other twelve children who were meeting Grade 5 provincial standards in reading and writing, five were minimally meeting expectations. One child was designated as gifted and three students received regular assistance in language arts from the learning resource specialist.

The six-day timetable schedule had been revised from the previous year. Language arts was scheduled on five days for a total of 385 minutes of instruction. The students also had a scheduled library period of 35 minutes in each six-day cycle.

Research Methods

Year 3

I began visiting the Grade 5 classroom in mid-September of 2003. Ms H. and I planned our lessons together and we began our eleven-week research journey with the students by talking about the notion of 'response.' Through a variety of activities, we reinforced how humans are constantly responding to various stimuli in their lives, and that there are various kinds of responses and ways to respond. We also facilitated a class discussion about what the students do in their heads as they read and connected their reading to the idea of response. Finally, we spent time talking about small-group discussions with the goal of developing a communal understanding of the expectations, behaviours, and protocol of 'successful' discussions. A few role-playing activities were implemented to demonstrate some of the students' ideas about appropriate interactions in discussion groups (how to change topics, how to piggyback on someone else's ideas, how to disagree politely). Two short stories from Cynthia Rylant's *Every Living Thing* (1985) were used for lessons on generating 'good' discussion questions.

I used the picturebook *Willy the Dreamer* (Browne, 1997) to introduce or explicitly identify the semiotic notion of intertextuality. I initially showed the children in 5A several coloured overhead transparencies of artwork by Magritte, Dali, and Bacon. The students shared their thoughts about the artwork, talked about the feelings that were evoked by viewing the paintings, and generated possible titles for the pieces of art. Once I shared the name and artist of each painting, we talked further about each selection. Ms H. and I then each took ten students and read *Willy the Dreamer* to them. The children were amazed and intrigued by how Browne had transformed the original artwork and were fascinated by Browne's intratextual connection of bananas. The Grade 5 students' experiences with *Willy the Dreamer* underscored the importance of 'reading' the illustrations in picturebooks.

The first picturebooks we used to introduce the 5A students to literature with Radical Change characteristics were *Zoom* (Banyai, 1995) and *Re-zoom* (Banyai, 1995). The girls read *Zoom* and the boys read *Re-zoom* (I had ten copies of each book). The boys and girls exchanged books after they had written predictions about their book based on only the front cover, completed two journal entries (one midway and one after finishing the book), and discussed the book in small groups. Finally, each student created her or his own 'Zoom' book by emulating Banyai's illustrative technique.

The other picturebooks used in the study were, in order, *Why the Chicken Crossed the Road* (Macaulay, 1987); *Shortcut* (Macaulay, 1995); *Voices in the Park* (Browne, 1998); *The Three Pigs* (Wiesner, 2001); *Starry Messenger* (Sis, 1996); *The Stinky Cheese Man and Other Fairly Stupid Tales* (Scieszka, 1992); and *Black and White* (Macaulay, 1990). With the exception of Banyai's two wordless picturebooks, each student had her or his own copy of each book. The students were asked to make predictions in their response journals for all of the books except *Starry Messenger*. In that case, I accessed their schemata about Galileo, provided background information about Ptolemy's and Galileo's views of the universe, and explained the reasons for the church's involvement in the debate and in Galileo's ultimate imprisonment. The students did not generate predictions for *The Stinky Cheese Man and Other Fairly Stupid Tales* because most class members had previously read the book. Subsequent to reading each picturebook independently, the children completed at least one entry in their response journals, then engaged in small-group discussions of three or four members, assigned by Ms H. Each group had a tape recorder and the students were responsible for recording their conversations. During the peer-led discussions, Ms

H. and I circulated among the groups and eavesdropped on the students' conversations, but we did not participate. Following each group discussion, I led a whole-class discussion that introduced and reinforced the metalanguage of the Radical Change characteristics evident in each book. The students' participation during the whole-class discussions was also audio-recorded.

As a follow-up activity to reading and discussing *Black and White*, the students viewed a two-minute clip of the movie *Timecode* (Columbia/Tri Star Studios, 2000), in which the action takes place simultaneously in four frames. The students wrote a response about their viewing experience and again, they shared their ideas in a whole-class format. Following the work with the picturebooks, Ms H. and I engaged the children in a discussion about their observations of the existence of Radical Change characteristics in their lives outside of school, including other books, movies, television programs, video games, and Internet sites.

Throughout the project, the school's librarian, Ms H., and I brought other picturebooks with Radical Change characteristics into the class for the children to peruse. The students had approximately twenty minutes of daily silent reading time at the beginning of language arts, and often used this time to look at these picturebooks.

The next part of the research involved the Grade 5 students reading novels with Radical Change characteristics. All of the students read *Seedfolks* (Fleischman, 1997) and engaged in peer-led small-group and whole-class discussions about the novel. After they listened to book talks that described the novels, the students selected one of the following to read: *The View From Saturday* (Konigsburg, 1996); *Holes* (Sachar, 1998); *Walk Two Moons* (Creech, 1994); and *Flipped* (Van Draanen, 2001). Each student wrote two responses and created a poster about the novel he or she read. The posters included four layers: a central visual that was significant to the novel; quotes from the novel that were powerful or important; a visual border using symbols that represented important events, characters, items, or ideas; and phrases or singular words that described important ideas or themes in the novel.

Once the posters were completed, Ms H. and I once again facilitated a class brainstorming session about the Radical Change characteristics that the students had learned about through their experiences with the picturebooks, the novels, and the class discussions about video games, movies, television shows, and Internet sites. Near the beginning of the study we had informed the students that they would be writing their own stories with Radical Change characteristics as the culminating activity of the project. The children were told that they were to include a minimum of three Radical Change characteristics in their work. The students in 5A had approximately eleven school days to complete their stories. Eighteen of the twenty students wrote the text of their stories on computers. All of the children worked at home on either writing the text and/or creating the accompanying visuals. Ms H. and I circulated and monitored as the students created their stories and assisted with editing and securing materials for the construction and publication of their books, which had laminated covers and were spiral bound.

The students in 5A were interviewed individually three times during the study about the picturebooks they read, the multilayered poster they created for the novel they read, and the story they wrote. All of the interviews occurred during class time and were audio-taped and subsequently transcribed. During the interviews about the students' stories, I inquired about the origin of the ideas in their books and asked the children to describe how they went about writing their stories. I also asked them if any of the picturebooks influenced their work, to identify the Radical Change characteristics they included in their stories, to explain the most challenging aspect of creating their work, and to describe what, if any, changes they would make if they had the opportunity to rewrite their story. Finally, the students completed an end-of-study questionnaire in which they were asked to describe themselves as a reader and a writer. They were also asked to explain what they learned by participating in the research project, what they learned specifically about reading picturebooks, and what they enjoyed most about the research project.

Year Four

Most of the methodological procedures I used in year three were repeated in year four. However, certain procedures were revised due to the previous year's experiences and time constraints.

I began visiting the Grade 5 classrooms in mid-September, 2004. Once again, we embarked our ten-week study with the students by talking about the notion of 'response.' The children also engaged in activities that featured intertextuality, the active role of the reader in comprehension and interpretation, and small-group discussion behaviour, etiquette, and protocol. We devoted additional time to teaching the students about response writing and small-group discussions.

Once again, the first picturebooks we used to introduce the students to literature with Radical Change characteristics were *Zoom* (Banyai, 1995) and *Re-zoom* (Banyai, 1995). The same procedures and activities were used with these books as in year three. The other picturebooks used in the study were, in order, *Why the Chicken Crossed the Road* (Macaulay, 1987); *Shortcut* (Macaulay, 1995); *Voices in the Park* (Browne, 1998); *The Three Pigs* (Wiesner, 2001); *Beware of the Storybook Wolves* (Child, 2000); *Who's Afraid of the Big Bad Book?* (Child, 2002); *The Stinky Cheese Man and Other Fairly Stupid Tales* (Scieszka, 1992); and *Black and White* (Macaulay, 1990).

The students wrote predictions about and responses to the picturebooks and participated in single- and mixed-gender peer-led small-group discussions and in whole-class discussions of each picturebook. All the discussions were audio-recorded. After the students read *Zoom* and *Re-zoom*, we distributed a chart that listed a number of Radical Change characteristics and features, similar to appendixes J and K. The rows of the chart consisted of all of the characteristics of type one, one characteristic of type two, and one characteristic of type three Radical Change. The columns of the chart contained the titles of the picturebooks. As we completed the chart for each book during the whole-class discussions, the language of Radical Change characteristics and features were taught and reinforced.

Once again, other picturebooks with Radical Change characteristics were brought into the classroom for the children to peruse throughout the project. Following the work with the picturebooks, Ms H. and I engaged the children in a discussion about their observations of the existence of the Radical Change characteristics in their lives outside of school.

Timetable disruptions and cancelled language arts classes during year four resulted in the children neither viewing the clip of the movie *Timecode* (Columbia/Tri Star Studios, 2000), nor reading *Seedfolks* (Fleischman, 1997). However, they did have time to read and write two responses to one novel with Radical Change characteristics. After they listened to the book talks, the students each selected one of the following: *The View From Saturday* (Konigsburg, 1996); *Holes* (Sachar, 1998); *Walk Two Moons* (Creech, 1994); *The Tale of Despereaux* (DiCamillo, 2003); and *Flipped* (Van Draanen, 2001). The students read their novels during the same time period in which they were working on their stories. Time constraints meant that the students in 5B and 5C could not complete the poster project.

The students knew from the beginning of the research that they would be writing their own stories with Radical Change characteristics as the culminating activity of the project. The children were to include a minimum of five Radical Change characteristics in their work. All of the 5B and 5C students wrote the text of their stories on computers, and all of the children worked on their stories at home. The students had nine or ten school days to complete to their stories and the finished products were spiral bound with laminated covers. One boy in 5C did not write a story at the end of the study.

The students were interviewed individually on two occasions during the study, about the picturebooks they read and the story they wrote. All of the interviews took place during class time and were audiotaped and subsequently transcribed. The interview questions were the same as those used in year three.

Data Analysis

The data I collected during years three and four comprised researcher and teacher field notes, photocopies of students' journal entries, transcriptions of small-group and whole-class discussions, photographs of students' posters, coloured photocopies of students' books, transcriptions of the interviews with each student, and transcriptions of discussions between Ms H. and myself. I also wrote daily entries in my researcher's diary throughout the studies. The same data analysis procedures were used for both the year three and four students' small-group discussion transcripts, written responses, stories, and interview and questionnaire data.

Small Group Discussions, Written Responses, and Student Interviews

Techniques similar to those applied to the Grade 1 students' transcripts were used to analyse the Grade 5 students' oral and written responses. Although the students in 5A were given discussion questions or prompts for most of the picturebooks, they had the freedom of and responsibility for generating their own discussion topics or issues for each book. Data analysis of the transcripts was thus both deductive and inductive. I used the discussion questions or prompts as guides when analysing the data. The transcripts were read, reread, compared, and contrasted (Glaser & Straus, 1967). Overall initial categories and subcategories were generated that reflected emerging patterns.

Further readings of the transcripts resulted in progressive modifica-
tion of categories and themes.

A similar iterative process was used to analyse the students' written
responses, and interview and questionnaire data. I generated categories that reflected patterns and themes in these data. With respect to
the student interview data, I also tallied the number of selections of
each picturebook.

To analyse the Radical Change characteristics evident in the stories
that the children wrote, I created a chart that included all of the characteristics of type one, one characteristic of type two, and one characteristic of type three Radical Change (see appendix J). I use the term
characteristic to refer to the categories of each type of Radical Change
and the term *features* to refer to the multiple ways that each characteristic can be evidenced in literature (and the in Grade 5 students'
stories). (Dresang does not make the latter distinction in her work.)
Most of the features were taken from Dresang's book *Radical Change*
(1999), but I added two, 'synergy among multiple stories' and 'new
perspective(s) on existing literature,' that were evident in the children's writing but not explicit in Dresang's descriptions. I did not use
Dresang's feature of 'pictures, maps, or graphs play a predominant
part in a book that might be expected to have mostly words' (p. 82) for
the characteristic 'graphics in new forms and formats' of type one
Radical Change. This feature was not relevant to the stories crafted by
the Grade 5 students.

Each time I reread the students' books I completed a new chart that
identified the Radical Change characteristics and features in their
work. By comparing my charts and rereading the books I was able to
resolve the few inconsistencies in my charts. Finally, I read the interview transcripts several times and searched for instances where the
students identified intertextual connections in their books. I recorded
the students' connections to literature, movies, and other cultural artefacts, as well as their incorporation of Radical Change characteristics.
I also examined the metafictive devices evident in the stories created
by the students.

Student Interviews about the Picturebooks

During the individual interviews, the students were asked to identify
their favourite picturebook or books from the selections they read
during the studies. The Grade 5 students' choices and their reasons for

selecting particular books are shown in appendixes D, E, and F. I also asked the children to identify the book or books that they found the most challenging to read. I explained to the students that I was using the term 'challenging' to describe a book that was more difficult to make sense out of or 'to put together.' Appendixes G, H, and I show the students' choices and the reasons for their selections.

The data for the three Grade 5 classes were not combined because they did not read the same collection of books. The tables show that the three books that were not read by all three classes – *Starry Messenger*, *Beware of the Storybook Wolves*, and *Who's Afraid of the Big Bad Book?* – played a dominant role in the children's selections.

Year Three, Class 5A

When the students in 5A were asked to select their favourite picture-book from the titles read during the study, five children (four girls and one boy) identified one title, eight students (three girls and five boys) selected two titles, six children (three girls and three boys) identified three titles, and one girl selected four titles. Every book used during the study was selected as a favourite book by at least one student in 5A. Most students provided more than one reason to explain their reasons for selecting specific books.

The Stinky Cheese Man and *The Three Pigs* were 5A's favourite books, and accounted for approximately one-half (53.5 per cent) of the class's selections. With respect to gender, *The Three Pigs* accounted for 30 per cent of the boys' total selections and *The Stinky Cheese Man* accounted for 25 per cent. However, *The Stinky Cheese Man* accounted for over one-third (39.1 per cent) of the girls' total selections of favourite titles. *The Three Pigs* and *Starry Messenger* were each selected three times as favourite picture books by the girls; each book accounted for 13 per cent of the girls' total of favourites.

The two main reasons the students expressed for selecting *The Stinky Cheese Man* as one of their favourite books were the book's humour and the fractured nature of the stories. The students also commented favourably on the interaction of characters with the reader and the book's peritextual features:

Amy: Well, I thought it was really funny that some parts ... like the chicken interrupted in the story, it wasn't like a regular kind of story. They changed all the stories and made them into, like, a more funny kind of story, and some of the stories, they made it up out of, like, when you were reading it. That's what I really liked about it.

Tyler: *Well, I think it would probably be* The Stinky Cheese Man and Other Fairly Stupid Tales *because I like that they remade fairy tales ... Well, I liked that they talk to you. Like at the beginning when it said right here where you can see that Chicken Little never got her own page and she was always trying to get Jack. She said, I found a kernel of wheat, says little red hen, and she tries to continue her story. And then I always liked the fonts too, like when they put things in abbreviations and the surgeon general's warning, and then the dedication page . . . and when the table of contents ... they made it out of a story, like that's how they did a story, they just made that fall on them, and 'The Boy Who Cried Cow Patty' was lost, and it was actually right on the dust jacket.*

The students who selected *The Three Pigs* as a favourite book gave as their most frequent reasons Wiesner's illustration style, the unique version of the traditional tale, and the interaction of characters with each other in front of the reader – the way the characters entered and exited the stories. Several students also enjoyed the contradictions between the illustrations and the text, and the humorous nature of the book:

Eddie: *Because it's, like ... I don't really like the normal* Three Little Pigs, *but this one I like. Everything is like wrong because the words say something, but the pictures say another thing. And they have different looks in different stories, like look here [points to illustration]. He seems just a little fuzzy and when he's out of the story he looks like real almost.*

Amber: *It's just I like it how they made them go into different stories. When they're out that was funny when the wolf blew him out of the story and then it says he ate the pig up and he's just like, 'Hmm. Where did the pig go?' And the people say he ate it and then he's like, 'I'm hungry. I must go eat another pig.' And then the pig ... and then that guy says, 'Come out of the story.' And then the text goes, and he ate the other pig up, and he's [the wolf] like, 'I did?' I just like those types of stories, and then he jumps out before the wolf can climb through the chimney.*

Each of the four boys who selected *Re-Zoom* as one of their favourite books explained how they enjoyed the book's overall structure and format. The three girls who chose *Starry Messenger* as a favourite picturebook noted how they gained new knowledge or information by reading the book.

When asked to identify the picturebook or books that they found the most challenging to make sense out of, thirteen students (six girls and seven boys) chose one book and seven students (five girls and two boys) selected two books. *Black and White* was selected by over 40 per cent of the students, and *Starry Messenger* was selected by approximately 30 per cent. Each double-page spread in the *Black and White* is divided into four sections so that the four narratives about trains, cows, parents, children, a dog and a thief unfold simultaneously. The students noted that it was challenging to make connections between the four parallel, yet synergistic stories:

Shazia: Black and White. *When I first read it . . . like, in each of the pages there was like four different sections, so I thought you were supposed to read 'Seeing Things,' 'Problem Parents,' 'Waiting Games,' 'Udder Chaos.' I thought, 'What's going on?' because it looked like there was all these things and it doesn't make any sense, and I kept on reading. This is the boy's first trip alone [points to various stories as she talks] and then there's just this picture, and then I would read this picture and this picture, and I would keep . . . I went on like that until like the middle of the book and I didn't understand any of it. So then I thought, maybe I'll just read one story at a time, so I read this one, and this one, and this one, and this one. Because it sort of all connects in a way, because it was a bit confusing to find out how to do that. Like, I had to read it a couple of times to sort of get what the story was sort of about.*

Starry Messenger details the life of Galileo. The text is augmented by handwritten messages taken from Galileo's own works and other primary documents. According to the children, the book was challenging because of the historical content and the handwritten text:

Bert: I think Starry Messenger, *because it's sort of, well, just facts and stuff sort of, and instead of just like a picturebook, it's more of a ... an old book, older book, but it's not older, but it's sort of tells about the old background. Yeah, except these books they just very barely have any text ... and tons of pictures, but this book, it has all different sorts of patterns of writing and stuff, and then they have a little paragraph in the corners, and then on every page there's always some . . . something, a fact that you never knew about, maybe.*

Year Four, Class 5B

When asked to identify their favourite picturebook, fifteen children (five girls and ten boys) identified two titles, three children (two girls and one boy) identified three titles, and one girl identified four titles. *The Three Pigs* and *Who's Afraid of the Big Bad Book?* were the most popular books with the students in 5B, accounting for approximately one-half (51.2 per cent) of the total number of selections. About one-quarter (27.9 per cent) of the children selected *The Three Pigs* as one of their favourite books. The children articulated many reasons for choosing this particular picturebook, including the interaction of characters in front of the reader, the reworking of a familiar tale, Wiesner's illustration style, the humorous nature of the book, and the synergy between the text and illustrations:

Morrie: Because it's really funny because they go out of their own story and interrupt other stories, and it just ... it's really funny how they put it that way, and then the text is still going on, like the wolf ate the pig and there's no pig because he jumped out of the story.

Devon: Well, I like the illustrations in this book and how, like, when they get out of the book they have to save all the other characters from bad things happening to them. And when they get blown out of the story they have like a cartoon sort of like a texture, and then when they get blown out they turn into more real.

Nine of the ten students who identified *Who's Afraid of the Big Bad Book?* as one of their favourite books commented on Child's illustration style. The children thoroughly enjoyed and appreciated Child's illustrative mixed media collages of ink drawings, fabric samples, wood grain, and photographs:

Jase: Who's Afraid of the Big Bad Book? *had a lot of synergy and so to me it was a real good book. There are a lot more characters in there, he goes to a lot more different places, a lot more characters interact with him, and there's synergy between the words and the pictures.*

Katherine: Well, I liked how it would ... like he'd go into stories that you knew and it'd be different, and also I liked how she used like real ... like she'd get something that looked like wood, and then she'd cut it out and put it so it was like real, and then she'd have some that was illustrations, yeah, like the tree trunks and stuff.

The other main titles selected as favourites by 5B were *The Stinky Cheese Man and Other Fairly Stupid Tales* (two girls and four boys), *Black and White* (three girls and two boys), and *Voices in the Park* (three girls and two boys). Like 5A, students in 5B liked the humour and the fractured nature of the stories in *The Stinky Cheese Man*. The children who chose *Black and White* appreciated the picturebook's overall format and structure, as well as its intratextual nature. With respect to *Voices in the Park*, the students liked Browne's illustrations and the structure of the book, in which each character told his or her story about the events in a park.

When asked to identify the most challenging book to make sense out of, all of the students in 5B selected one title. Overall, two titles accounted for over three-quarters of the students' selections: *Why the Chicken Crossed the Road* was chosen by eight children (five girls and three boys or 42.1 per cent) and *Black and White* was selected by seven students (two girls and five boys or 36.8 per cent). The students found the story structure of *Why the Chicken Crossed the Road* challenging because of the continuous introduction of new plot events and characters:

Sashami: Why the Chicken Crossed the Road, *it's sort of confusing because ... I guess there are lots of time switches and, like, people going back and forth and stuff, and sometimes they added things that didn't really make sense . . . Like first they're ... something happens at Zembo Ice Cream Company, and then you just go over to the others . . . and like there's this person, and then this person, and then this person, it never stayed on one person for that long.*

The students in 5B also found the structure and format of *Black and White* challenging. They experienced difficulties making intratextual connections among the stories in the four quadrants:

Nathaniel: Because it has four stories, but all the four stories happen at the same time, and because ... see the parents come home dressed in newspapers, right? They come home dressed in newspapers because they were at the train stop, the train stop is the toy one there, so it's all happening at the same time.

Year Four, Class 5C

In 5C, two boys identified one favourite picturebook, thirteen children (seven girls and six boys) identified two favourite books, three boys identified three favourite titles and one boy identified five favourite books. Three books, *Who's Afraid of the Big Bad Book?*, *The Three Pigs*, and *The Stinky Cheese Man and Other Fairly Stupid Tales*, accounted for over two-thirds of the total number of selections in the class (23.8, 23.8, and 21.4 per cent respectively). However, significant gender differences existed in the selections of these three titles. *The Stinky Cheese Man* was selected as a favourite book by nine boys and zero girls, *The Three Pigs* was chosen by eight boys and two girls, and *Who's Afraid of the Big Bad Book?* was selected by six girls and four boys.

With respect to *Who's Afraid of the Big Bad Book?*, the children in 5C appreciated Child's pastiche illustrative style. The students also enjoyed the book's humour, intertextual nature, and unique engineering features such as upside down pages, and holes and gatefolds in the pages:

Riley: I think the ones by Lauren Child were my favourite because they were funny and she had really good characters. Like, there were lots of intertextual connections I found, and I liked how she did the illustrations like cut holes in the pages, and made flaps for the doors.

Jerry: My favourites were probably the ones by Lauren Child. Who's Afraid of the Big Bad Book? *that's probably my first favourite because of all the interactivity with the reader, and other parts like the text, and how it was placed with the illustrations. The gatefold was interesting. And how there was that whole cut out and the upside down page. I like that stuff that was interesting.*

The ten children who identified *The Three Pigs* as a favourite book provided several reasons to support their choice including the reworking of a familiar tale, the interaction of characters in front of the reader, and Wiesner's illustration style:

Nidhiki: Well, I liked it how they popped out of the panels and they made their own story, if you know what I mean. Because they kept on coming into different stories and getting them [the characters] to come out, and then at the end they actually returned to their first story.

Mary: I liked the way they come out of the story and the way it changed from cartoony to like realistic. And just the different language forms that they used in it, that made it different, and different perspectives as well.

Like their peers in 5A and 5B, the nine boys who chose *The Stinky*

Cheese Man as a favourite book explained that they liked the humour and the fractured nature of the stories:

Andrew: I liked it because there are a bunch of different stories and there are really funny ones, there are like unrealistic things happening in the them that's different than the original stories ... they didn't just take fairy tales and change them like a little bit, they made some new ones and totally changed some ... and they did it in a different format than a lot of books.

Beware of the Storybook Wolves accounted for over one-quarter or 28.6 per cent of the girls' total selection of favourite titles. The four girls who selected *Beware of the Storybook Wolves* commented on Child's mixed media collages. Overall, Child's two books accounted for 71.4 per cent of the girls' favourite selections. The three boys who chose *Black and White* liked the book's format, structure, and intratextual nature. The two boys who selected *Voices in the Park* as a favourite commented on the book's unique structure of four voices.

When asked to identify the most challenging picturebook they read during the study, of the nineteen students in 5C, fifteen children (eleven boys and four girls) selected one book and four students (one boy and three girls) chose two books Twelve students identified *Black and White* as the most challenging, which accounted for 52.2 per cent of the total number of selections. Over two-thirds of the boys chose this particular title and all twelve students found the picturebook's structure and format challenging. Interestingly, only the boys expressed difficulties with connecting the stories in the four quadrants:

Fred: I didn't know which one to read first, so I was ... no, at first I thought it was all four. I just thought these were just a bunch of different things, so I went here, here, here, and here [points to different quadrants explaining the order in which he read them], and these two made sense, but it made no sense it sounded like these people lived on the train. Because like why is he coming back? And it's like I hear the train. The train is going to stop soon. And then up here it's like when is it going to stop, and that kid looks just the same as that kid [points to boy in 'Seeing Things' and 'Problem Parents'].

Two girls and three boys identified *Shortcut* as the most challenging book to make sense out of. The children seemed to experience difficulties with the nonlinear sequenced plot, as well as with the numerous illustrative intratextual connections. According to three girls and one boy, *Why the Chicken Crossed the Road* was the most challenging picturebook to put together because of its story structure:

Andrew: Well, in Shortcut *there were so many different stories and in some stories there were words where you had to pay lots ... more attention to them. You have to be paying attention to so many different stories at once, and at the end you had to put it all together and it was hard to remember what went where and what order they were in.*

Riley: Why the Chicken Crossed the Road *was really ... like it kept going off topic sort of. It just kept changing the topic, and sometimes it didn't finish the stories.*

Some general trends emerged from the data analysis of the students' favourite and most challenging picturebooks. *The Three Pigs* was identified as a favourite book by all three classes, with the boys selecting the title more often than the girls. Although the children provided a number of reasons for choosing the tale, the main reasons included the characters interacting with each other, the unique version of the traditional tale, and Wiesner's illustration style. Several children also commented on the synergy between text and illustrations, the contradictions between the illustrations and the text, and the humorous nature of the book.

Many children in 5A and 5C selected *The Stinky Cheese Man* as a favourite picturebook. In 5A, Scieszka's metafictive book accounted for nearly 40 per cent of the girls' and 25 per cent of the boys' total favourite selections. However, in 5C only boys chose *The Stinky Cheese Man* and it accounted for nearly one-third (32.1 per cent) of their total favourite selections. The students indicated that they enjoyed the humour and the fractured nature of the stories in *The Stinky Cheese Man*.

Although several students in 5B and 5C identified *Who's Afraid of the Big Bad Book?* as one of their favourites, the book was chosen more often by the girls. The girls in 5C were especially fond of Child's book and it accounted for 42.9 per cent of their overall favourite selections. The children thoroughly enjoyed and appreciated Child's illustrative style.

Students in all three classes identified *Black and White* as a challenging book to read or to put together. In 5A, both genders equally identified Macaulay's Caldecott award-winning picturebook as challenging to read, but in 5B and especially in 5C, the boys selected *Black and White* with greater frequency than the girls. The children explained that they experienced difficulties with the book's structure of four discontinuous narratives on each double-page spread. When compared to the girls, the boys expressed greater difficulties in making connections between the four parallel stories in the book.

Starry Messenger accounted for 25 per cent of the girls' and 36.4 per cent of the boys' total selections of challenging picturebooks in 5A. In 5B, *Why the Chicken Crossed the Road* accounted for 62.5 per cent of the girls' and 27.3 per cent of the boys' total selections of books they found challenging to read or put together. *Why the Chicken Crossed the Road* was also identified as a challenging book by 17.4 per cent of the students in 5C, and 21.7 per cent of the students in this class also described *Shortcut* as book that was difficult to put together.

In the next section of this chapter I discuss the students' oral and written responses to some of the picturebooks. I examine *Zoom* and *Re-zoom* in detail as they were the first books read by the students and the books' wordless nature made them unique from the other literature used in the research. Following the discussion of Banyai's books, I share the data analysis of the students' written responses to *The Three Pigs*, *The Stinky Cheese Man and Other Fairly Stupid Tales*, *Who's Afraid of the Big Bad Book?*, and *Black and White*.

Zoom and *Re-zoom*

The illustrations and words in picturebooks work together to convey a message and both sign systems are necessary for constructing meaning. However, in wordless picturebooks, the reader/viewer is presented with only one sign system, the visual text. The reader provides the verbal or written texts. Like all forms of literature, wordless picturebooks vary in their level of sophistication and complexity. Some, like *Zoom* (Banyai, 1995) and *Re-zoom* (Banyai, 1995), are visually demanding, and readers experience substantial visual gaps. The written and oral responses of the Grade 5 children to Banyai's books provide a window into their reading transactions with the works (Pantaleo, 2007a).

Banyai uses the same concept and design in both *Zoom* and *Re-zoom*. He takes readers/viewers on a visual journey as an imaginary camera pans out backwards to show an increasingly distant perspective of the previous scene. His technique resembles mise-en-abyme, as each scene is indeed a small part of a larger one, and on several occasions, one that is totally unanticipated. The books could be likened to matryoshkas, Russian stacking or nesting dolls, in reverse, as each page turn reveals the former illustration as part of a larger artwork. Although the reader's view of the original scene is continually broadened, narrative connectedness is retained. Both books have black glossy verso (left-hand) pages that serve 'almost as stage curtains in their dramatic severance of one act from another' (Stevenson, 1995, p. 189). The detailed, flat-coloured illustrations outlined with black pen line on the recto (right-hand) pages present multiple visual perspectives, and playfully suggest that 'things are not what they seem' (p. 190).

Zoom begins with a close-up view of a rooster's comb. More zooms reveal that the rooster is part of toy farm set that is part of an advertisement on a magazine being held by a boy on a cruise ship. And the ocean liner is really a poster on a city bus that is on a television show being viewed by a man in the Arizona desert. At one point near the end of the book, Banyai zooms back and also alters the details in the scene. The outward expansions continue until readers see the world as a white dot.

Kudo, one of the Grade 5A boys, described his reading of the first few rectos in *Re-zoom* in his response journal:

First I thought it was a bird. Then I thought it was a person, and then I thought it was a bird person! I turned the book all sorts of ways, upside down and sideways and then right side up. On the third page I saw a man with a bow shooting a woolly mammoth in a watch. Then I saw it was placed on a HAIRY pincushion! On the third page there was a man who was very hairy that was painting with the watch on! On the next page it had the hairy man and he was in a building. Then I turned some pages and the building was in a strange triangle and I turned it all around again just like page one.

The 'strange triangle' Kudo refers to is the Paris Obelisk, the first obelisk in modern time to be removed from Egypt. The book shifts in locale from Paris to a movie set supposedly set in a jungle, but the movie set is actually a decoration on a steamer trunk that turns out to be part of a painting. More complex perspective shifts and numerous intertextual connections that include the Paris Obelisk, Place de la

Concorde, the Goodyear blimp, Napoleon, the Eiffel Tower, Alfred Hitchcock, and numerous well-known individuals on a subway car, complete the book. Various mediums of communication and modes of transportation are represented in the scenes. The metafictive ending reveals that every scene in the book is in the magazine being read by an adolescent male on a subway train. The book ends with two red dots – the tail lights of the subway train.

Data Collection and Analysis

Of the fifty-eight Grade 5 students, half read *Zoom* and half read *Re-Zoom*. In 5A and 5B the girls read *Zoom* and the boys read *Re-zoom* (I had ten copies of each book); the two books were read by both genders in 5C. The children were asked to begin their reading experiences with a very focused lens and generate predictions about the books by looking solely at the front covers. Their reading experiences reflected the zooming technique in the books as their reading lens kept broadening. Once the students wrote their predictions, they read to the midway point of the books. The students were then asked to write a journal entry about what they were feeling, thinking, wondering, questioning, or imagining as they read. The children read the rest of their books and completed another personal response. When they finished their second journal entry, the students were instructed to read their books backwards and to write another response about that particular reading experience.

The overall question that guided my analysis of the students' written responses was, 'How did the children read the books?' I discovered that they wrote about the books' structure and format, their responses to reading the books back-to-front, and their sense- or meaning-making processes. The use of 'Z' and 'RZ' after students' names indicates whether the written response was about *Zoom* or *Re-zoom*.

Students' Written Responses

Most of the students who wrote about how the books work, their format and design, focused on more than one aspect. Some students expressed surprise at the wordless nature of the books, and recognized the need to read the pictures. In Shazia's midway response to *Zoom* she wrote, 'You can't read it. You look at the pictures. It's about a picture turning into a picture. I wonder what will happen next?' Devon wrote about *Re-zoom*, 'I was shocked that there were no words and just pictures in pictures,' and Jordan wrote, 'I liked how the pictures tell the story, not the words so you make it whatever you like – it's like all in your imagination, not the illustrator's.'

Most students wrote about Banyai's zooming technique in either their midway or final response. As part of her midway response to *Zoom*, Riley wrote, 'In my mind I think of how a camera works because it has a zoom lens.' The students recognized the intratextual nature of the books created by Banyai's framing device of nesting illustrations:

Katherine (Z): I liked how the book would zoom into something and then it would turn out to be a postage stamp or something. I also found why it's called Zoom. *It's because they are zooming into everything. I thought it was neat because you look at everything from a different perspective.*

Mark (RZ): There were no words, because you had to read the pictures. It was weird because in the end the boy was reading a book and every page we flipped, he flipped too. It all just comes out of literally two books. I thought that book was really cool because it was like reading two books except it feels like I'm in only one book and then coming out of two. It was like reading two books at the same time. And also kind of being two people. It's the guy on the subway reading a book and I'm in it but I'm also reading a book in real life, too. Man, this is hard to explain. That's not part of the response.

Many students expressed confusion and curiosity about the shifting images on each subsequent recto. Alyssa's question, 'How could that be?' encapsulated most students' initial responses to the first few pages of the books:

Alyssa (Z): At the beginning, I thought to myself, 'How could that be?' I turned back a page and realized the letters in the corner. After that, I started to look for hints in the pictures. In the Arizona scene, the third one, I knew it was a stamp because of the edge for example. But I was a little confused at the ending – I thought it was going to go back to the rooster!

Trent (Z): It had a lot of pictures and then kept on zooming out and showed the background over and over again. I thought it was sort of confusing and interesting because you didn't know what was going to happen. I think it was very random and it was nothing that I was thinking. It was hard at the first 4-5 pages because it had no letters.

A few students wrote about the author's choices, talents and mistakes. As part of Sandra's midway response to *Zoom* she wrote, 'I think it is really cool that when you flip to the next page you also see more, but not just that everything is still in the exact same position but farther away. I think that being able to do that is a real talent.' Only a few students wrote something about Banyai's use of black pages. However, the children contributed many insightful and perceptive comments about the significance of the black verso pages during their small-group and whole-class discussions.

The format and design of the books allows them to be read/viewed from back-to-front. I was amused by the students' facial expressions when I instructed them to read the book backwards. Several looked puzzled at receiving permission to violate this cultural reading convention. Other children smiled, somewhat mischievously, and a few whispered conspiratorially, 'I already did.'

The students' reactions to reading *Zoom* and *Re-zoom* from back-to-front varied. Three students did not write a response, three children thought there was no difference, and seven students found it less exciting and preferred reading the picturebooks front-to-back. Five students still found the books interesting because of the different perspective offered by reading the books backwards, even though they knew the content of the books. Eight children preferred reading the book backwards because they found it more interesting and according to them, the book made more sense. The remainder of the students explained their thoughts or feelings when they read the book back-to-front. They described the zooming sensation they experienced as they read the book one way and then the other. Many students used similes to describe the physical sensations of reading the book backwards:

Shecara (Z): I liked reading it backwards because it was like a magnifying glass on a big picture. Rereading it backwards was really fun because you knew what was coming but it was from a different point of view.
Nidhiki (Z): When I read it backwards, it seemed like it was zooming in on the rooster in the magazine on the cruise ship sign on the bus on the TV, on the stamp, on the airplane view on the Earth. I liked reading it backwards because it looked like I was falling through the pictures.

*Jordan (RZ): Flipping back into the book was like taking a ride into a book
the way it took you on a rollercoaster through the book. It was extraordi-
nary how the illustrator organized the pictures and emphasized the
photos. The way he took you and put you in the pictures going backwards
it was like a vortex sucking you in with all its might, power and grasp. It
shot you right through the book and you would be going so fast but still
see the story at hand.*

The students' written responses also revealed how they tried to
make sense of the picturebooks. They described their reading strategies and explained what they were thinking, feeling, wondering, and
understanding. Several of the students reflected on their interest in the
real and unreal aspect of the books; others wrote about the books'
never-ending potential:

*Michelle (Z): The pictures were getting bigger and bigger. I wondered why
they were getting bigger and bigger. First I thought the first picture was
real and on and on and on. Then I was almost positive that the girl in the
magazine was real. Then the same with the cruise ship.*
*Mark (RZ): It was like everything looked live but it was only getting
painted or it was on a picture. It was also like backing up and seeing what
it really was. I was wondering if it would ever come to an end. Now I
know why they called it Zoom I think. Because it's like zooming out of
the picture.*

Some students thought there were multiple stories in the picturebooks, some thought the stories were interconnected, and some
thought there was no story at all:

*Andrew (RZ): The book was mainly about random pictures of things. I
would have liked the book better if it wasn't just random things and if
there was a story to it.*
*Jerry (RZ): I liked that it kept zooming out and all the pictures were linked
together but each had a different story. My favourite part was the Asian
elephant and from then on because it was very interesting how the author
came up with all these ideas and how they linked to each other.*
*Cochim (RZ): I was thinking how the next scene was going to relate to the
page I was reading. I was also thinking about what the book is about and
how to write it down. I was thinking about what time period that picture
book took place in and why the illustrator placed that picture there.*

Many children's responses reflected their anticipation of and fascination with the evolving visuals in the books. The students explained their thoughts about the pictures and guesses about successive illustrations. The written responses of several students shared their excitement, enjoyment, and surprise:

Lily (Z): I thought the book was very interesting. I liked how the little farm became a toy magazine and then the magazine ended up in the boy's hand and then so on ... I would try to predict about what the next picture would be like. I thought the cruise ship would end up as a postcard but it was an advertisement on a bus. I also thought when the world was going to get smaller and show the other planets.

Sandra (Z): The second half does the same thing by getting farther away. At the end, the world almost turned into nothing. It gets you really excited once you know what is happening because it makes you really want to see the next page. I wish the ending didn't finish so fast because I wanted it to go on.

Jenny (RZ): In the first picture it looks like a lot of lines and colour. I assumed it was the man's painting. On page 8, I thought the man was in a pyramid but on the next page, I thought otherwise. I didn't get how the tall oblong-gated pyramid got into the middle of the city but again on the next page I saw why. It's cool how it turns into a movie set in Egypt. I thought the movie set was in France but it was in the middle of the forest.

Small-Group Discussions

The Grade 5 students' discussions about their reading experiences of Banyai's two wordless picturebooks suggest one of the sentences on the back cover of *Re-zoom*: 'Open this wordless book and take off on a mindbending visual journey full of twists, turns, and surprises.'

The students were provided with a few discussion prompts and questions for *Zoom* and *Re-zoom*. The discussion questions for 5A differed somewhat from those given to the children in 5B and 5C: 1) How many stories were in the book and what were the stories? 2) How and why do you think the author/illustrator created the book? and 3) The black pages – why do you think the author/illustrator used black pages – could he have used red or green or? This group of students addressed the prompts/questions after they had shared their personal observations, feelings, questions, opinions, and sensemaking processes.

Most groups in 5B and 5C also generated their own discussion topics or questions but they talked about the assigned questions before moving on to other subjects. Unfortunately, one of the girls' groups in 5B did not record their discussion of *Zoom*. The students in 5B and 5C were given the following discussion questions: 1) What were you thinking when you read the first few pages? 2) How many stories do you think there are in the book? Explain your opinion. What are the stories about? 3) Why do you think the author/illustrator created the book? His purposes? and 4) How do you think the author created the book?

Although all of the students talked about the mysteriousness of reading the first few pages of the books, the children in 5A devoted much less time to discussing their initial thoughts about what was going on in the books. During their open 'wondering' conversations when the students verbalized their interpretations of some of the images in the two books, they devoted significant time to discussing reality and illusion. In the excerpt below, a group of girls share their opinions about what they thought was real and unreal:

Zoe: *Whenever … when I first looked at the poster, I was like that should be real, like, you see how … I thought the two little kids were real, but they're just dolls right so I thought … and then when I turned to the girl playing with the farm I was, like, she should be real, and then when I turned to, like, the …*

Jessy: *The next one.*

Zoe: *Yeah, the next one, I thought it should be real, and it's still not real.*

Judy: *Yeah, I know. It's just going on forever and the only real one is the one in the jungle where they're reading the maps.*

Jessy: *No, and the traffic one actually.*

Zoe: *And the traffic, yeah.*

Judy: *Yeah, and the traffic.*

Jessy: *No, the traffic's on the TV.*

Zoe: *Yeah, but it's still real.*

Jessy: *I know it's still real, but it's like not there, it's not kind of the real scene, it's … well anyway. OK, so it goes from the toy magazine to on a cruise ship, a boy is holding a toy's magazine in his hand.*

When students in 5B and 5C were answering the discussion question, 'What were you thinking when you read the first few pages of the book?' most of the students talked about how perplexed they were by the initial pages. Although they were uncertain about the nature of the book, they were simultaneously intrigued by the unknown and were curious to discover what would happen next. The students seemed to experience a kind of cognitive disequilibrium that fostered a wondering stance toward the book. They discussed their speculations and verbalized their sense-making processes. Two recurring phrases during their discussions to the first question were 'I thought' and 'I was thinking.' Excerpts from two different discussion groups follow.

Ethan (Z): There was a picture where I really didn't know what was going on. It was where they have a scene of a farmhouse and of all the stuff going on at the farm, and these arms on the table. And by that time I had realized that it was a model, but I just didn't really know what was going on, whether she was building it or what. And then I saw that it was probably a magazine because there was ... on the next page there was a sign – 'oys' or at least that's what it looks like, and then a girl with closed eyes. So I realized that it was probably something from the literature. Then even on the next page there were some hands as though it was a magazine. That was until I saw the third page that I was just talking about. It was really hard to sort of get the idea of what was going on.

Peter (RZ): Well, when you looked at the watch you're like, 'What? What's this happening?' I mean the first part when it looked like a painting to me, but then when you zoomed out then you saw ... like, the watch and then it made sense. But then it was on the guy in the painting, then it like, went back more, and it just kept making no sense and then making sense and just like that.

The students recognized the zooming technique after a few pages and in their discussions they used examples from the books to describe Banyai's method. When they described the zooming technique, they generally placed themselves in the book using the pronouns 'I' or 'you.' Recognition of the pattern facilitated a type of enlightenment where the unknown became known. In the excerpt from a small group discussion about *Re-zoom*, the boys share their moments of recognition of Banyai's technique:

Cochim: I thought it was really odd at the beginning because it takes a long time to get out of this tomb. See there's like ten pages before you actually got to see what it was, but other than that ... What page did you start to realize what the idea of this book was? I realized it at the ...

Zachery: I'd say right at the pool thing, right over here at the pool thing ...
   wait a second, like ...
Cochim: The pool?
Zachery: Yeah, yeah, this nice pool thingee with uh ...
Cochim: Oh really? I noticed it right there in the Goodyear [blimp] one,
   where the ... but yeah, Zachery is talking about the one with the soldiers
   [eleventh recto]. Which page did you ...
Jase: I noticed it when just before the big tower was ...
Cochim: This one?
Jase: Yeah, but not ... yeah, the one that's just a little high up with the
   Egyptian signs [ninth recto] and the [overlapping speech].
Cochim: Oh, yeah, so the one right before the Goodyear one.

Another discussion prompt asked the students to consider how
many stories were in the books and to describe what they thought the
stories might be about. Most of the groups were of the opinion that the
picturebooks contained multiple stories. Some students believed that
each recto was a separate story and other students divided the book
into story sections. A very small number of children thought that there
was one continuous story or no story at all. Excerpts from three different discussion groups follow.

Nicky (RZ): I think there were four stories in the whole book because there's
   one with this person doing the Egyptian exhibit thing in the city, then
   there's the movie set, then there's that painter painting that thing, the
   picture, then there's the person who ended up to be in a magazine.
Jase (RZ): I think that it was like ... it's one story, but it was explaining ...
   a picture means a thousand words, like the old saying, and now I actually
   know what the old saying means, a picture means a thousand words.
Amy (Z): And I think each page has a story because each page ... well not
   each page, but each page that shows at least, like, kind of the same pictures, because it's kind of hard to tell, but maybe there's only one story in
   the book, because each thing has to do about things, so I think this whole
   book is about one story and maybe a lot of stories.
Lisa: So each page has something to do with another story so and that makes
   ... it's kind of like a chapter book, kind of. So I think it's just like one
   whole story and it's a very interesting book.
Amy: And each page tells ... well to me, like, every time you look at it, it
   tells a different story.
Lisa: Yeah, I know, I know. It's just like chapters in a chapter book.

Amber: Yeah, like sort of like a never-ending story.

Shazia: Yeah, like a never-ending story. Like you could read it back and forth, back and forth, lots of times without ... [All the girls talk at once].

Shazia: Anyways, you could read it backwards and forwards several times. Like, read it forwards, then backwards, and then read it forwards. And each time it'll like keep going forever and ever.

Amy: Yeah, I think it's different stories.

The students also talked about enfolded stories, how the stories grew into other stories, and how the stories 'opened out' or 'turned out to be' something else than they had started to be. The children explained the unfolding and shifting images by the zooming effect. In general, the students thought that the stories were about everyday life events; a few children believed that Banyai was depicting a kind of trajectory, like Cochim, who explained, 'I think it [*Re-zoom*] was also telling you how the world has changed from the very beginnings of technology, so this drawing on the wall, or that's what it seems like the first time you see it, until a subway light in the distance at the very end.' Two discussion excerpts follow.

Tyler (RZ): I think that there's really just one story here that keeps on going backwards. I mean it starts out with this, what you think is particles on a blue background, then as you look it looks like a caveman with a bow, then if you look again you see a caveman with a bow on a watch shooting a mammoth. And if you keep on going back it shows what you think is a pyramid, but then it's actually a tower that's either in France or Rome, somewhere in Europe I think. And then it just proves that it's actually just on a little magazine thing for a movie. And then if you keep on going back you see a guy who's riding an elephant with two other people. And then if you keep on going back they're only on a chest. And then if you go back again you think that it's just a little boy's toy. And then it's actually an artist painting that, and actually that artist painting is only on a Japanese fan, and the Japanese fan is on the thing for 1-800 Re-zoom. And then that turns out to be on a book, which a little kid is reading in a subway train, and then the subway keeps on going back until you can only see two lights.

Jessy (Z): You're zooming into the rooster.

Jenatine: Yeah, like it's almost like the rooster is in the centre of the earth because you know that the rooster is supposed to be cock-a-doodle-doo when it's morning. It's like this is the beginning of time when he cock-a-doodle-doos or whatever he does.

Maddie: Cock-a-doodle-doo, ha, ha.

Jeantine: I don't know, then ... then ...

Maddie: You end up in the end of time. And once you get to the world showing, like, not seeing anymore islands anymore and it turns black and then once you get to the little tiny dot, all the ... it's just all black besides the little tiny dot.

Jenatine: Yeah, but you can ... it's almost like a tiny ... there's so much inside just that tiny little dot because it has like everything, cruise ships, everything comes to be compact inside that tiny little dot.

During their small group discussions, most of the children talked about the wordless nature of the books. Overall, the students liked that *Zoom* and *Re-zoom* were wordless because they were able to 'write' the text themselves. Amy made an interesting comment about the wordless nature of the book: 'I think the author created the book because, like, it helps you sort of think clearer. Like, usually you depend on words to see stuff, but, like, instead you rely on pictures.'

Cody (Z): I think the book shouldn't have words because then you can make up your own story as you go along, and when you get to the very end you think wow, that was a great story and we're going to read it ... like look at it again or something.

Lily: I like the idea how it didn't have words like Cody said, because every time you can make up a different story instead of the same one every time.

A few students expressed a desire for some written text to accompany the illustrations:

Edward (RZ): It should have some words.

Evan: Yeah, I think it should actually have some words.

Kyle: Yeah, I mean, like, something at the beginning. To make the no sense things make sense.

Jase: You know, it's cool without the words, but you know, it could have used a few words.

Evan: Yeah, well, it doesn't really need words because we could make them up ourselves.

Kyle: Yeah, that's actually a good idea. I think that this book is for all ages from kindergarten to adults ... not quite adults, for, like, maybe from kindergarten to Grade five, since Grade five they can think make up the words and they can do, like, work with it, and also in Grade kinder-

*gartens and ones they can, you know, like, try to make up their own
stories with it and they kind of like that type of stuff, and they like pictures, you know.*
Edward: Yeah, they can if they wanted to.
Kyle: Yeah, and you know, they would like all that type of stuff.
*Edward: Like this: Once upon a time there was a man who was made of
sand, he had a bow and arrows, but he was practising targets, but once he
flipped another page you actually see it's actually a caveman with a
mammoth.*

When the Grade 5 children 'read the story' in their groups, they
either read the images descriptively, providing a commentary about
the content of the images on the pages or they created a narrative as
they read the images, as Lily's does:

*Lily (Z): Well, there's this rooster that sits on the fence all day long and
people watch him, and they watched him for a long time. And they live on
this farm out in the wilderness, and it has all the animals like horses,
chickens, pigs, cats, dog. And one time this giant came and took away
their whole city, and it was all over the news and giants bigger than those
giants ... or no, then all the other giants were reading this magazine
about the giant that took away the small human village, and it ended up
... it ended up all over the news on cruise ships and stuff. People were
talking about it, and in the city, and guys in Texas found out too, and it
became famous and ended up on a postage stamp in Hawaii, and the guy
in the airplane took the postage stamp all the way out, farther and farther
and farther into the clouds until he was, like, practically out of the world,
and the world got smaller and smaller.*

When I asked the children to speculate on Banyai's reasons or purposes for creating the books, their ideas fell into two main categories:
to stimulate cognitive engagement and to create a book with a unique
format. Many students believed that Banyai wanted his readers to
'think.' Some children compared the book to a puzzle in which the
reader had to search for clues to guess subsequent images:

*Sandra (Z): Why do you think the author/illustrator created the book, his
purposes? Well, I think he made it because there's not many books around
that you can start from the beginning and it looks like you're going back-
ward and getting farther and farther away, and I think that's pretty cool,*

*because you don't just go around in the library and find books like these.
So I think he made it so there'd be a different type that you could look
through.*

*Nicky (RZ): Why do you think the author/illustrator created the book? His
purpose?*

*Sharon: I don't know, I think the purpose maybe was to, like, get kids going
to think, 'Holy, this is a weird book because it has no words, but it's
getting interesting.'*

*Nicky: I think he wanted to show that not all books have to be with words,
just like you can tell a story with the pictures.*

Mary: I think his purpose was just like Sharon said, to get kids thinking.

*Jenny: I think he drew the book because instead of he ... like in some books
there are story lines and you don't think they really go with the pictures,
and this you get to imagine the story to go with the pictures.*

During their discussions about why Banyai created the picturebooks
the students expressed their appreciation of his abilities as an artist
and their enjoyment of the books. Matt's comment is representative of
the students' opinions: 'You'd have to be smart to do this. Like, you're
looking out at the world through a watch to a train.' Overall, the children were fascinated by the zooming technique used in both books:

*Ethan (Z): Yeah, like one day you zoom out so that you see the picture of the
boat on the side of the car, and then the next page after that I was looking
for mistakes on the page even after that when you zoom out, as they see
the person's foot, I was looking for mistakes and there really aren't any ...
any mistakes at all. It's all perfect. It's just amazing how he was able to do
it. I mean the people are in the same place, the lights are even the same
colour, the building edgings is the same, it's ...*

*Donald: Yeah, it's like spectacular how ... and it's amazing how good he can
draw ... there's so much detail. Yeah, to look at the original stamp it looks
like somebody tore it off.*

*Ethan: Yeah, it's not just a piece of paper. There's detail on the cactus,
there's thorns, there's stuff like that and if you look at the letter it says via
airmail, and he put a lot of stuff in there like Arizona and stuff like that.*

Donald: The hand looks, like, realistic because it's like ...

*Ethan: Yeah, he's cramming so much stuff into one thing, which is what
makes it great, and it's ... there's just so much life like you can connect to
the book. It's just, like, all the same except it's different in a good way, and
so it's a great book.*

The students in 5A were asked to discuss Banyai's use of black verso pages. Most of the children thought he wanted readers to focus on the recto pages. Sammy stated, 'I think each page is black because if there's like a bunch of colour on one side of the page, and then on the left side there's black, the only thing you can look at is, like, the colourful page, because black is black.' Amber thought that the black pages made the rectos 'look more real.' Excerpts from three discussion groups follow.

Fritz (RZ): It's more ... it's more surprising this way [with black pages].
Matt: Yeah, it's more ...
Fritz: I actually kind of like the black pages. If it was blue or white ... if it was white like ...
Matt: If it were blue it would distract me from the book.
Fritz: Black makes a comment.
Matt: Yeah.
Nick (RZ): If you look at the book you would notice that all the left-hand pages are black. I think they're black to make you not look at the black page, but make you focus on the right ...
Tyler: To attract attention to the right-hand page is what the black pages are for.
Eddie: So Nick, do you think they could have made it a different colour, the black pages on the left-hand sided of the book always?
Nick: Maybe, yeah. Although it probably wouldn't have worked as well to make you focus on the right-hand pages.
Eddie: I guess, because if it was white or something that might make you think that was the picture maybe.
Tyler: Yeah.
Jenatine (Z): I think why the writer or illustrator person used black pages to really focus you on the coloured ones because you can't really like get distracted by the other page. You have to really concentrate.
Maddie: Like if it was white, if it was white then ...
Jenatine: You'd think like somebody erased it or something.
Maddie: Yeah.
Jenatine: Like what happened there? Isn't there supposed to be something there? But then if every one is black, right, it looks like it's always supposed to be black.
Maddie: Or maybe, I thought maybe when I was reading it that you're wearing a pair of binoculars and you can't see through one of the binoculars.
Jessy: That's a great idea.

Discussion of Students' Written and Oral Responses

The students' written and oral responses reflected their intellectual and affective engagement with the picturebooks. As co-authors, the students had to fill in the visual gaps between each recto, as well as create 'text' as *Zoom* and *Re-zoom* for the visual narratives. The children worked to interpret the visual signs, fill the signifiers with meaning, and make new signs (Kress, 2003b).

Iser wrote that one means authors use to intensify a reader's imaginative activity is to cut to new characters or even to different plotlines, so that the reader is forced to try to find connections between one story in the present and new, unforeseeable situations. He or she is faced with a whole network of possibilities, and thus begins to formulate missing links (1978, p. 192). In Banyai's books every recto is a 'cut' and the children worked to connect the scenes. As the students constructed associations, they engaged in other reading strategies such as accessing their background knowledge, imagining possibilities, anticipating events, and revising predictions. The students' reading experiences reflect Iser's ideas about a reader's wandering viewpoint, how readers are 'continually forming and modifying both expectations of what is to come and interpretations of what has previously been read' (Thomson, 1984, p. 21). The Grade 5 students made sense of the wordless picture books 'by using sense-making processes similar to those used in the reading of print-based texts' (Crawford & Hade, 2000, p. 66).

Several students wrote about the novel format and design of *Zoom* and *Re-zoom*. The children's schema for wordless picturebooks was expanded by their experiences with Banyai's books. The illustrative framing device of zooms challenged or disrupted their reading/viewing expectations. Banyai's books require readers to tolerate ambiguity (Meek, 1998) and uncertainty, and this skill, along with an understanding of irregularities and complexities, is fundamental to children's growth as readers and to their future successful transactions with more sophisticated texts. The multiple concepts represented in Banyai's works contribute to students' development of 'cognitive flexibility ... of having a diversified repertoire of ways of thinking about a conceptual topic' (Spiro, Coulson, Feltovich, & Anderson, 2004, p. 645).

The children's interactions with *Zoom* and *Re-zoom* also provided them with lessons about metafiction (Lodge, 1992; Waugh, 1984). The students were simultaneously engaged with the books and aware of how the texts were working. Reading *Zoom* and *Re-zoom* gave the students opportunities to read images, an aspect of visual literacy. Although not writing specifically about wordless picture books, Kiefer believes that 'experts in the field of visual literacy have often neglected the potential of picturebooks to develop visual literacy' (1995, p. 10). Yenawine defines visual literacy as 'the ability to find meaning in imagery' and states that 'many aspects of cognition are called upon ... but subjective and affective aspects of knowing are equally important' (2005, p. 845). The students' oral and written responses reveal their construction of meaning in imagery, and their cognitive and affective engagement. The children's responses support the findings of Walsh (2003) and Arizpe and Styles (2003) that reading pictures is a complex act.

The students were inspired and amused by *Zoom* and *Re-zoom*. The picturebooks stimulated the children's powers of imagination, inquisitiveness, and interpretation and they communicated their curiosity, enthusiasm, wonderment, surprise, and enjoyment in their written work and in their small-group discussions. As they read the books, they also expressed their aesthetic responses physically through their facial expressions, gestures, and body language.

In the remainder of this chapter, I share some of the Grade 5 students' written responses to four other picturebooks read during the research projects: *The Three Pigs*, *The Stinky Cheese Man and Other Fairly Stupid Tales*, *Who's Afraid of the Big Bad Book?*, and *Black and White*.

A Trio of Swine

The Three Pigs was a top favourite of the students in all three Grade 5 classes for a number of reasons. The children liked the characters interacting with each other, the unique version of the traditional tale, and Wiesner's illustration style. Several children talked about the synergy between the text and illustrations, the contradictions between the visual and the verbal texts, and the humorous nature of the book. Similar themes emerged when I analysed the students' written journal responses to *The Three Pigs*:

Lily: I loved how the author really changed the story. Instead of just the plain old 3 pigs story he changed it. He had the pigs fold up a page and fly off to other stories. The author is right that no one asked the pigs how the story goes. I really thought the illustrations told the story. If there weren't words, I bet I would know how the story goes. I liked at the end how the pigs were collecting letters to make soup! I think that when the pigs went into different stories it was an intertextual connection because it connected with other stories like the Hey Diddle Diddle story. It was like they were part of the stories because they kept going into them.

Jenny: At the beginning you think it's just the old story of the three pigs but then you end up outside the story and they kind of write their own story by deleting the wolf from the book. On the first page the book starts off by showing the pigs gathering straw, sticks and bricks so it makes you look at the title page and the author and the illustrator. The wolf gets confused because the story says he ate the pigs but the pigs escape so he doesn't know where they are. It's like there's a second story being told but not in writing of what could happen if the book was forming before your eyes – it didn't seemed rehearsed like most stories. They make their own story by flying on the paper airplane and crashing it – sooooo funny! On two pages the pigs turn cartoony and enter a different story by pulling down the top of another page. The story doesn't make sense but it's funny. The cat follows them through his panel and turns real (he's cute) and the dragon comes too and turns colourful.

Jerry: I was surprised that the pigs actually came out of the story and depending on what story they were in, the illustrations changed and when the characters came out of the stories, there was more detail. It was also different because the characters interact with the text like where the dragon and the cat from 'Hey Diddle Diddle' all were in the third little pig's home and knocked over the text. The text wouldn't change but the illustrations would because the pigs escaped the story. I think this is my favourite story so far because it's very funny and different because there's a lot of interaction: the characters interact with the text, other stories, and between the illustrations. The illustrations change because characters leave their stories. Overall, I enjoyed the story.

All of the Grade 5 students wrote about more than one topic or idea in their response journals. About two-thirds of the children's responses included comments about the aesthetic pleasure they experienced from reading *The Three Pigs*, and evaluative statements about the book. The above written responses convey the children's enjoyment and appreciation of Wiesner's picturebook. At least one-third of the students included each of the following ideas in their writing: the book's illustrations, the pigs' departure from the original story, the interaction of characters, the uniqueness of the fractured fairy tale, the intertextualities in the book, and the humorous nature of the book. Approximately 20 per cent of the students' written responses included comments about the contradictions between the illustrations and the text, the pigs' flight on the storyboard airplane, the pigs' construction of the story in front of the readers, and Wiesner's use of various typographic elements.

A Collection of Fractured Fairy Tales

The Stinky Cheese Man and Other Fairly Stupid Tales accounted for one-quarter of the boys' and over one-third of the girls' total selections of favourite titles in 5A. In 5B, two girls and four boys selected Scieszka's collection of fractured fairy tales as a favourite book. In 5C, nine boys selected *The Stinky Cheese Man* as a favourite picturebook, accounting for over 20 per cent of the total selections in the class. The boys who chose *The Stinky Cheese Man* as a favourite picturebook explained that they liked the humour and the fractured nature of the stories.

The students' written responses to *The Stinky Cheese Man* revealed that over half of the children commented on the humour in the book and wrote about the fractured nature of the tales (see Pantaleo, 2007g, for an in-depth discussion of Grade 5 student responses to the parodic reversions in *The Stinky Cheese Man*). Nearly half of the children made evaluative comments that identified aspects of the picturebook that they liked, admired, or believed could be improved. Over one-third of the students wrote about the intertextualities in the book by making connections to the original tales or to other books they had read during the research project, and over one-third of the children wrote about their favourite stories in *The Stinky Cheese Man*.

Jordan: That's a classic book – the tales are stupid but that makes them funny. Seriously the stupider the book, the funnier it is. I especially liked the chicken because she has her own thing going on and nobody would help her, which makes it interesting. I liked how he created the book in front of you (RC characteristic) and he doesn't stick to the rules – he goes outside the lines or the box. He used different materials for the illustrations, not just one. If he used just one then would be boring and not exciting. I like on one of the pages the font size goes from big to tiny which makes if fun to read as opposed to the same font. I liked the pictures because of the different colours and styles used. I really like the pictures of the big giant and of the chicken. What I noticed was that in the Cinderella story it says she is beautiful when she's ... how do I say this ... ugly!

Zachery: Well, first of all, I don't get why it is called The Stinky Cheese
Man *because it isn't about the Stinky Cheese Man but the title does
make you wonder. Right? Well, this book has a lot of stories and the
stories in my opinion are funny because the author changed a lot of the
story. Say for example, Chicken Licken's story was changed a lot
because the table of contents squashed on them. If you look at the illustrations, there is a lot going on. For example on 'Cinderumpelstiltskin,'
if you look out the window, you see the Giant and Jack and the
beanstalk. If you look at the pictures in detail, you probably see what
you didn't see last time.*

*Jenny [writes her response as she reads the book]: I don't get why they wrote
a story on the dust jacket. Why not inside the book. I wouldn't have
looked there if you teachers hadn't told me! This doesn't make sense – it
just doesn't. I don't know how to explain it. The font is different for each
story but it kind of goes with the story – like the Ugly Duckling his
writing is big and bold and the story is also big and bold. That poor poor
duck!*

*I take back what I said – these stories are funny! EWWWW that would
be disgusting kissing a frog – the poor princess!*

*That's better – the chicken's inside the book and not on a really non-
noticeable place. The Giant's funny – he cut parts of other stories to make
his own and it doesn't even make sense! Lazy Giant. AUGHH! That is
one annoying chicken!*

*Nicky: I thought this book was very creative and one of the most funny
books I have read. The author would have to use a lot of his imagination
and have a hilarious sense of humour. When Jack forgot to put the 'Table
of Contents' and it crashed on the chickens and fox, I loved how the 'Table
of Contents' was shown all scrambled and disordered. It was sort of like*
Who's Afraid of the Big Bad Book? *when Herb climbs the words to
escape from Goldilocks. I thought the way the author put a twist on all of
the stories was very interesting. The way the illustrator used the collage
type picture was different. It was as though he wasn't afraid to be different and it had a sinister look to it. I loved this book and I might recom-
mend it to my brother!*

Approximately one-quarter of the students commented on the illustrations in the book, and all but three liked Lane Smith's style. One
quarter of the students wrote about the interactive nature of the picturebook and commented on how the characters interact with each
other in front of readers, how the narrator, Jack, interacts with readers,

how several stories are created in front of the readers, and how readers must be attentive due to the number of interruptions and disruptions in the book.

Another 20 per cent of the students noted generally that *The Stinky Cheese Man* exhibited many Radical Change characteristics and some wrote about specific characteristics in the picturebook. Approximately 20 per cent of the children commented on the interactivity of the book, and wrote about Scieszka's use of varying size and style of fonts, the multiple stories in the book, and the interruptions by the Little Red Hen (see Pantaleo 2007c for a detailed discussion of how the Little Red Hen's character and behaviours draw reader attention to the defiance of convention in *The Stinky Cheese Man*).

In at least 10 per cent of the responses, students wrote about their favourite characters in the stories, questioned the appropriateness of the book's title, commented on the book's unique dust jacket, wrote about the table of contents falling on the characters in 'Chicken Licken,' described some of the processes they engaged in as they read the book, and commented on the illustrations in the Giant's story.

Falling into a Book of Fairy Tales

Who's Afraid of the Big Bad Book? was a popular choice with the students in 5B and 5C but was not read by the students in 5A. *Who's Afraid of the Big Bad Book?* is Lauren Child's second book about Herb and his inter-actions with storybook characters. Herb falls asleep one night with a book of fairy tales on his chest and awakens to discover that he has fallen into the book. He encounters many storybook characters who are disgruntled because he has tampered with the book by defacing characters and removing or altering various artefacts from their stories. Herb needs the Fairy Godmother's assistance to escape from the angry storybook characters (see Pantaleo, 2006b, for a detailed dis-cussion of the metafictive devices in *Who's Afraid of the Big Bad Book?*).

In both 5B and 5C six girls and four boys selected *Who's Afraid of the Big Bad Book?* as one of their favourites. The book accounted for approximately one-quarter of 5B's and 5C's total favourite selections. During my individual interviews with the students, they talked about their appreciation of Child's pastiche illustrative style, and their enjoyment of the book's humour, intertextual nature, and unique engi-neering features. Content analysis of the students' journal entries revealed similar comments.

Katherine: This is definitely my favourite book so far! I think it's great how she uses real things in the book, like the wigs are hair cut out from magazines. I love how she cut a hole in the book and had the two pages upside down. She uses mise-en-abyme three times in the book. On the front cover, on the page with the monsters (basically), and the page with the Three Bears' house (the book he's reading in bed). And I think that's really cool! I think it's neat how the stories changed because of things that Herb has done. Also I noticed an intertextual connection on the page when he's running though the forest, there is a small green caterpillar like the Big Bad Wolf from the other story. I really enjoyed the book!

Cochim: This book is much better than Beware of the Storybook Wolves *because there are so many jokes and puns. For example Goldilocks is extremely rude and says, 'This is my page. Get off!' It's probably more realistic because Lauren Child stuck photographs on the paper and the background is cartoony. Also we know that this was all a dream because it said that he drifted asleep and that makes it more realistic. This book is extremely like the movie 'Shrek' because one character explores lots of fairy tales. P.S. I think it would be good to use the idea of text being topsy-turvy and using text in the story (when Herb climbs up the text to escape the world of the book). I also think it's a great idea to use stickers in a book because it is sometimes funny and it's original. I think it would be neat to use the fabric sort of style in a different story and the things that the fairy godmother loses when she falls out of the book.*

Nolan: I really liked how in the pictures she made some of it realistic and the rest cartoony. It was also neat when Herb was in the Evil Stepmother's house and his words were one side up and the Evil Stepmother's were the other side up. When he was in the ballroom, the stuff he drew on the people looked like pen but it in the end it says they rubbed it off with eraser. When Herb is running through the forest did you notice the Big Bad Wolf as a caterpillar? It said on the back that there was a special guest appearance from the Little Bad Wolf but he wasn't really in the story at all. On the dedication page there is a sticker that says, 'Bananas about bananas.' It is the same sticker that is stuck on Baby Bear. I liked the story more than Beware of the Storybook Wolves *because there were more characters from other fairy tales and how they kind of made fun of them and they had lots of more intertextual connections.*

The children's written responses communicate their aesthetic appreciation of Child's picturebook. Nearly two-thirds of the thirty-seven students wrote evaluative comments about the book, commented on

Child's illustrative style, and wrote about the intertextual nature of the book. Approximately one-half of the students wrote about the fractured nature of the stories, the level of character interactivity, the unusual engineering features, the typographic elements, and the similarities and differences to Child's other book, *Beware of the Storybook Wolves*. About one-third of the children wrote about the humorous nature of the book. I introduced the students to the term 'mise-en-abyme' when we looked at the dust jacket of the book and over 20 per cent of them wrote about this illustrative feature in their responses.

'Seeing Things,' 'Udder Chaos,' 'Problem Parents,' and 'A Waiting Game'

During the individual interviews, several students identified *Black and White* (Macaulay, 1990) as a challenging book to read. In Macaulay's book, four discontinuous but parallel stories are told in a unique manner, unfolding simultaneously on each double-page spread. In 5A, both genders equally identified Macaulay's picturebook as challenging to read but in 5B and especially in 5C, the boys selected *Black and White* with greater frequency than the girls. The children explained that they experienced difficulties with the book's narrative structure. The boys expressed greater difficulties than the girls in making connections between the four parallel stories.

When I analysed the students' written responses to *Black and White*, several common themes emerged. Of the more than three-quarters of the students who wrote about the number of stories in the book, some thought there was one overall story and others suggested that the book contained multiple stories (two, four, five, or 'lots of' simultaneous narratives):

Bert: On the first page the boy is wearing a white and black shirt! That's the colour of Desperate Dan's shirt and the dog looks like he has a bandit mask on him and that's what Desperate Dan wears. The book was really confusing. There were four stories going on at once but if you wanted, you could just make it all one story by connecting them. The kid's train is the train that the boy is in who is heading to the train station that his parents are waiting for him. When the road is blocked by 'boulders' it's actually the dog and Macaulay makes the fur look like cows. When I was reading it I connected them together just like I said – on each page I read it top to bottom.

Nicky: I loved how this book had two stories going on at once. You really had to use your imagination on how to read this book. It really got you thinking. You would have to have a lot of imagination to come up with such a book. I thought David Macaulay had to put a lot of thinking into the illustrations because he connected the two stories only in pictures. He also had to be very talented to use both watercolours and I think very thick oils.

Close to half of the Grade 5 students discussed each of the following aspects of *Black and White* in their writing: the order in which they read the stories; the connections among the individual stories (intratextual connections); the inclusion of Desperate Dan; and their evaluation of the picturebook. Their responses reveal how the students read the book in varying ways: one story at a time; left to right and top to bottom; verso to recto; and from the bottom right-hand corner of the recto ('Udder Chaos') and then on to the other stories.

Judy: This was actually the best book! But it was very confusing because of the cow story. And Desperate Dan was kind of a different character. And also because all of the different stories all in different places so you would read one story all through the book and then go back and read another story until all of the stories are done. That's how I read it. I read 'Problem Parents' first because that was that one that came to my head. And I did not want to read it in order either. Because this is a book that you can ready anyway you want. Anyway then I read all of the other stories. I also kept turning the book upside down to see if there was another picture or a different story.

Amber: Black and White *is a really good book. I think it's a book for all ages. It's really cool because it has four stories in it. In* Black and White *the story called 'Udder Chaos' – I like how he put Desperate Dan in that story – like how they put him in jail in* Why the Chicken Crossed the Road, *but in this book, he gets out of jail and steals some cows. I was thinking, 'Why did Desperate Dan steal cows?' And did you know that Desperate Dan is in all the stories? Well, he is. 'A Waiting Game' relates to 'Problem Parents' because you know how the parents come home wearing newspaper? Well in 'A Waiting Game' when they are all reading the newspapers, they start making stuff like clothes and decorations. I think the parents were waiting for the train and in 'Seeing Things' and Desperate Dan is the old lady. I read 'Udder Chaos,' then 'Problem Parents,' then 'A Waiting Game' and then 'Seeing Things.'*

Nidhiki: Well, Desperate Dan was in the story. But the only NORMAL humans were the problem parents. The blizzard was the falling newspapers and the cows stampeding over the tracks were caused by Desperate Dan. I also noticed that every story looks different. 'Seeing Things' was blurred watercolours, 'Problem Parents' was old cartoon strip, 'A Waiting Game' was today's cartoon strip and 'Udder Chaos' is like Shortcut.

Over one-third of the students wrote about the intertextual connections they made between *Black and White* and other picturebooks they read. Approximately one-quarter wrote about each of the following aspects of their reading experience: the aesthetic pleasure they experienced; the discomfort or confusion they experienced; and the different fonts, colours, and illustrative styles in the book. Finally, approximately 15 per cent of the students explained events that were occurring in the individual stories, commented on the difficulty of making sense of the book, expressed enjoyment in looking for hidden pictures in the illustrations (searching for the squirrel and Desperate Dan, for example), and identified which of the four stories they most enjoyed:

Jase: This book was very interesting. I liked how there were all the different ways that you could look at it. For example the train could have been the toy one at the kid's house and the roadblock was the dog laying on the tracks or the cows could have been the road block. The parents are not just crazy, but getting the idea from the people at the train station, etc., etc. I also like how there were different kinds of illustrations for the different stories.

Lily: There were four stories going on at once. It was a bit confusing at first but when I got into it, I understood. I liked how in every picture of the train station there was a squirrel doing something. When the train stopped the so-called boulders were the cows that escaped. In the newspaper that the parents had in their hands, if you turn it upside down it said, 'Cows Escape.' And on the T.V. that the kids were watching, it showed that wanted guy – Desperate Dan (at least it looked like him).
I read the book from the first one to the first one on the second page. Then the second one on the other page and then the second one on the other page.

Although several children commented that *Black and White* was challenging to read, most students were willing players in Macaulay's games (see Pantaleo, 2007d for a discussion of Grade 5 students' responses to and interpretations of various kinds of narrative and illustrative play in *Black and White*). Macaulay plays with any number of literary devices, including indeterminacy, contingencies, synergistic stories, colour, art styles, typography, types of discourse, jokes, puns, picturebook form and format, intra- and intertextual connections, and narrative conventions and codes. His playfulness engages readers by arousing their curiosity, making them think, and inciting them to 'see things' in his story. By participating in the various kinds of play at work in *Black and White*, the children were actively involved in the process of co-authoring the text.

Private Lessons

One of the questions I asked the Grade 5 students on the survey that I distributed at the end of each research project was, 'What have you learned about reading picturebooks by reading the picturebooks in the study?' Some students answered the open-ended question by contrasting their former reading behaviours with newly learned skills, and all of the children identified more than one lesson that they had learned during the studies. Two interrelated ideas came up most frequently that reflected the nature of the sophisticated literature used in the research. Over three-quarters of the students explained that they had learned to 'read the illustrations' – to look carefully at and to study the pictures – and over two-thirds of the children mentioned the importance of careful reading, of readers taking their time when reading picturebooks:

Zoe: I learned that you couldn't just flip through the pages. You have to really look at the pictures. You have to read the pictures! Sometimes I had to read the text over and over again to understand the pictures.
Katherine: Before I flipped through the books quickly. Now I read slowly and go over the pages once or twice. Before I read the text and then went on to the next page. Now I look at the illustrations carefully and then read the text. Before I would go right to the first page of the book. Now I look at the cover and the title page before starting the book.
Cochim: I learned that there are just as many stories (or more) in the pictures. Before I thought nothing about the saying 'a picture tells a thousand words' and I read picturebooks as fast as I could. Now, however, I read picturebooks quite slowly and pay more attention to the illustrations.

Fred: I learned that when I used to read the picturebooks so fast, I never did see the pictures. Now I spend more time on a page. I did not look for eyes in bushes or squirrels in a tree but now I do, I really do.

The lessons the children learned about the value and importance of reading the illustrations in picturebooks contributed to their development of visual literacy skills. Arizpe and Styles wrote that 'analyzing visual text, and the relationship between word and image, makes demands on what are often called "higher order reading skills" (inference, viewpoint, style and so on) and involves deep thinking' (2003, p. 238). The illustrations in many contemporary picturebooks have become increasingly sophisticated over the years, and changes in printing technology have affected the range of artwork possible in picturebooks. Although the illustrations in picturebooks are a 'source of aesthetic delight,' *everything* about the illustrations conveys 'information about how viewers are being invited to [read and] respond' (Nodelman & Reimer, 2003, p. 278). The Grade 5 students clearly understood and appreciated how artists contribute to a picturebook, and were well aware of the multifaceted viewing and interpreting skills required of them as readers.

The students less frequently described other reading behaviours that they had learned about, such as the importance of rereading text and pictures, of looking for hidden items or details in illustrations, and of recognizing the relationships between text and illustrations. Several students described how the knowledge they gained about Radical Change characteristics affected their reading of picturebooks:

Max: When I read the picturebooks I used to look at the pictures and whiz through the books. Now I look for more detail, like Radical Change, and hidden stuff in the pictures and if it's nonlinear or if there's synergy.

Sandra: I've learned to look for small details and RC characteristics. I read books more slowly and carefully now. I think ahead and keep an open mind. If something doesn't make sense I read it over and over again trying to make sense out of it instead of just keep reading. I enjoy picturebooks more now because I now how to read them slowly and carefully.

Angie: Before, I started to just look at pages in the beginning and just look at the pictures, read and then flip the page. Now, I learned to look for things hiding in the back or try to find interruptions. Each page in a book to me is now like flipping channels on a T.V. screen.

Jerry: I look for RC characteristics. I've learned that picturebooks aren't just

*for kids. I've learned to read them slower to find hidden things. I've
learned that some books contain more than one meaning. I've learned to
view different styles or art and format (i.e. four squares for each double-
page spread telling 4 stories). I've also learned many new words (i.e.
synergy, Radical Change, etc.).*

The students' answers to the survey question reflected a new respect
for and understanding of picturebooks. The children seemed to have
developed an increased appreciation for the abilities required to comprehend and interpret various sign systems (Gardner, 1993, 1995). In
addition to providing the students with pleasurable aesthetic reading
experiences, the picturebooks taught them about literary and artistic
codes and conventions. In the next chapter I discuss how the children
used what they learned from the picturebooks in creating their own
writing.

5 Grade 5 Children Writing Texts with Radical Change Characteristics

The Reader in the Writer

Margaret Meek wrote that 'If we want to see what lessons have been learned from the texts children read, we have to look for them in what they write' (1988, p. 38). She acknowledged that when they write, children will 'draw on the whole of their culture if we let them' and maintained that, 'we have to be alert to what comes from books as well as from life' (p. 38).

The discussion of Grade 5 students' writing in this chapter reveals how they drew upon their symbolic tools, specifically those developed as a result of their experiences with particular kinds of texts, both inside and outside of the classroom. Barton embraced the use of an ecological metaphor to explain how literacy is 'a set of practices associated with particular social systems and their related technologies' and to understand how literacy is embedded in 'social life and in thought, and its position in history, language and learning' (2007, p. 32). The crafting of the students' work was influenced by their literary and experiential reservoirs as well as the nature of the literary practices of the classroom community.

Near the beginning of my studies, the Grade 5 students were informed that they would be writing their own stories with Radical Change characteristics as the culminating research activity. I provide a detailed discussion of the stories written by three of the Grade 5 students: Eddie, Jenatine, and Bert, because these students created some of the most complex stories with respect to narrative and visual structure, narrative composition, and incorporation of Radical Change characteristics.[1] I used Dresang's Radical Change framework to construct a chart to analyse the students' stories (see appendix J). A description of the parameters of the chart can be found in the discussion of appendix J on page 114. Following a description of these three stories, I discuss some of the general findings about all of the Grade 5 students' stories.

Eddie: Profile

According to Ms H., Eddie was successfully meeting Grade 5 level provincial expectations in reading and writing. Eddie confidently expressed his opinions to peers and adults, and his ideas contributed to the depth of classroom discussions. His quick wit and sense of humour were appreciated by all. Here are Eddie's comments when asked to describe himself as a reader and a writer on the end-of-project questionnaire:

Reader – I like to read comics. I am a very good reader. I also like to read adventure books.
Writer – I mainly write rhyming poems. To find the right rhyming word, I just find absolutely any word that rhymes at the end of the word.

Eddie participated enthusiastically in all activities during the study and was very eager to read each picturebook. He responded to the queston, 'What did you learn by being in the research project?' by writing: 'Everything about Radical Change! Every single characteristic.' He explained that he enjoyed reading books where the characters interacted with one another such as *The Stinky Cheese Man and Other Fairly Stupid Tales*. When asked what he had learned about reading picturebooks by reading the literature in the study, Eddie wrote, 'There are more formats than one. Sometimes I had to go to another page to understand a page. It's kind of like one page is a door and another one is like a key. The pictures were often like puzzle pieces because you had to look at them all to understand them. They also can be a key to text phrases.'

---

1 See Pantaleo, 2007b for an analysis of another sophisticated work completed by one of the Grade 5 students. See Pantaleo 2007b, 2007c, and 2007e and Pantaleo & Luce-Kapler, 2006 for further analysis and discussion of the Grade 5 student's written work.

The Three Weird Pigs and Other Awkward Stories

Eddie's nine-page book was created on 8½-by-11-inch paper. It contains four stories, 'The Three Weird Pigs,' 'Bill and the Burglar,' 'Mary Had a Little Lamb Chop,' and 'F.A.T. (Formally Annoying Turtle).' A small wolf dressed in a black suit and bow tie appears in the right-hand bottom corner of the cover with a large thought/image bubble that shows the wolf imagining himself with the three pigs inside his stomach. The title of the book is written inside the wide mouth of the wolf in the thought bubble.

Eddie explained how he came up with the ideas for the first story, a version of *The Three Little Pigs*:

> E: *Well, I was just in my bed one night, I was just like, 'Hmm, what should I do for my story? Some sort of fairy tale.' And I was hungry so I started thinking of food, and I was thinking of the Three Little Pigs at the same time. So I'm like, 'Hey, whoa! House, food, good story.'*

The three pigs in his story speak in a type of pop-culture prose: the word 'dude' is used in almost every utterance. Unlike the original tale, Eddie's pigs construct their houses out of cheese, seafood, and gelatin. The wolf is very polite in his interactions with the first two pigs; instead of devouring them, he eats their houses. When the wolf reaches the house of the third weird pig, he becomes very angry – and the font used for his talk changes from pink italics to large red capitals. By the time the wolf consumes the third pig's house, he is too full to even attempt to eat the pig. The story ends with the 'boss' congratulating the actors on their excellent performances: the story is actually a movie being 'filmed' in front of the reader.

Eddie explained that his second story, 'Bill and the Burglar,' was based on one of his dreams. In this tale, Bill is holidaying with his family in Germany at an elephant ranch when a burglar threatens everyone with a gun. When Bill seizes the burglar's gun, he realizes that the weapon is in fact a flame thrower. As the burglar escapes, Bill burns off the back of the thief's pants and reveals the burglar's pink heart boxer shorts. The wolf from 'The Three Weird Pigs 'interrupts the narrative about Bill and the burglar and is informed by the narrator that he is in the wrong story.

The third story, 'Mary Had a Little Lamb Chop,' was inspired by a cartoon that Eddie had seen on television:

*E: Yeah, and 'Mary Had a Little Lamb Chop,' I thought of that at my house
as well when I was in my bed, and I thought Mary had a little lamb, but I
ate it. That was in a cartoon that I saw so I thought, 'Hey, wait a minute!
Maybe I could do almost the same thing, but with a little twist.' So I
came up with 'Mary Had a Little Lamb Chop.'*

In this story, Mary takes her lamb to school but the narrator interrupts
his storytelling due to a technicality with a date in the story. The narrator orders readers to stop reading and the wolf from the first story,
speaking in his polite pink font, also interrupts the tale.

Finally, 'F.A.T.' is moralistic tale about an annoying turtle that teases
obese people. Once a fairy casts a spell on the turtle that makes him fat,
the turtle ceases his irritating behaviour. The entire story is written in
black uppercase letters. Eddie explained that the idea for 'F.A.T' came
from a story that he had read on the Internet:

*E: I actually saw this thing on the Internet. Once there was a guy and he
became fat and no one ever heard of him again. And so I thought well
maybe I could make one of those um ... sycronyms [means acronyms] or
whatever you call them out of the word fat and then make it a story.*

INTERTEXTUALITIES

Eddie 'borrowed' ideas from literature, television, and the Internet for
the basis of his stories. He made intertextual references to *The Three
Little Pigs*, the nursery rhyme *Mary Had a Little Lamb*, a television
cartoon, and a Web-based story. When I asked Eddie about his use of
capital letters in 'F.A.T.,' he explained, 'You know in the army they
sometimes have writing like that and then they have those sycronyms
[means acronyms] so I thought, 'Hey this would look really good!''
Eddie also borrowed a common phrase from many cartoon and movie
characters. In 'Mary Had a Little Lamb Chop,' the wolf comments,
'Good-bye, cruel world!' when the narrator tells the readers that a
hunter shot the wolf.

Eddie also made connections in his stories to his own life. He
explained how 'Bill and the Burglar' was based on one of his dreams
and he included a reference to the leap year in one of his stories.

RADICAL CHANGE CHARACTERISTICS

Eddie's Analysis. When I asked if any of the picturebooks affected the
content of his book, Eddie said that he had been influenced by

Wiesner's *The Three Pigs*. Eddie responded to my question about the Radical Change characteristics in his book by describing the fonts in his stories, the intertextual connections, the interruptions and disruptions, and the interaction of characters with each other or the reader:

E: *I used alteration of stories, like I have connections to other stories, people interrupting stories, the wolf interrupts a lot like here ['Bill and the Burglar'] he's in the wrong story. And here ['Mary Had a Little Lamb Chop']... here he's interrupting this one even more.*

S: *Hmm, hmm. 'Mary Had a Little Lamb Chop.'*

E: *Yeah, goodbye cruel world.*

S: *Yes, he's interrupting.*

E: *And he says, 'Stupid narrator.' I almost should have put, 'Why you little ...' Ha, ha.*

S: *Ha, ha. That would have been good to have the narrator then respond to him.*

E: *Yeah.*

S: *Any other Radical Change characteristics?*

E: *Yeah, I had characters talking to each ... interfering with each other and I had characters interacting with the reader. Like the narrator here ['Mary Had a Little Lamb Chop'] says, [reads from story] 'Please go the next story. Are you still reading? Stop that right now! Oh, all right! I'll make up something as an ending for you.'*

During my interview with Eddie, he carefully explained the reasons he selected the font styles and colours for the wolf and the three pigs in the first story in his book:

E: *Definitely with the fonts. Like the wolf, he's all polite and everything, and you know sometimes at fancy dinners and stuff the writing is sometimes purple or pink or something, so I thought well, first I need a really fancy shmancy font, so I chose the Blackadder font. And then I thought well it's fancy, but not fancy enough because the wolf would be kind of delicate and all, so I used pink, but then when he turns into the big evil wolf, where's that ...[looks in book] – I used Latin because it's the most bold kind of font and it just stands out a lot and I made it red.*

...

E: *And I kind of chose the font colour for the pigs a bit corresponding to their attitude and their houses. Like the first weird pig, he's always kind of like yelling and stuff like that, so he's just kind of like mad but in a good way.*

S: *Hmm, hmm.*

E: *Like not insane mad, but mad mad. So I made it red. And then the second one is kind of all like cool and stuff. He's like, 'Totally you'll get indigestion dude!'*

S: *Ha, ha.*

E: *And then he makes his house out of fish, which is another reason it's [the font] blue. And it's all in that font because he's all cool and everything, and then the third little pig, he's kind of just playful and rather smart and everything, and he doesn't really stand out much in the story, so that's why his font is kind of light.*

S: *OK.*

E: *Because to the other little pigs he doesn't really stand out that much, and he hardly ever talks, he's rather shy you know, but really smart. See, that's why I got him this type of font because it just kind of looks smart with all the little curls and everything.*

S: *Hmm, hmm. That makes sense.*

E: *Yeah, and the reason I chose the narrator's font to be green is because green is just kind of a casual ... not really any mood colour just a good no mood colour, and the font because um ... narrators' fonts are something like this – in books sometimes there's a character and his font is kind of bold and then the narrator's font is kind of italic, and this is the most italic font I could get, and then I made the font itself italic.*

My Analysis. Eddie incorporated several Radical Change characteristics into his stories. He used colour symbolically to communicate meaning about the characters in his stories, and the design and placement of words in his text transmitted meaning or represented sound. In three of Eddie's stories, he included interruptions and disruptions as characters and/or narrators interact in front of or speak directly to the readers. For example, the wolf interrupts the narrator as he describes the events at the third pig's house, and when the narrator tells the wolf, 'Hey! I wasn't finished!' the wolf replies, 'I DON'T CARE! HA, HA!' 'Mary Had a Little Lamb' also abandons a linear organization as the wolf interrupts the narrator, the narrator stops telling the story because of a technicality about a date, and the narrator addresses the readers and tells them to stop reading. The narrator then creates a new narrative in front of the readers and the wolf editorializes as the narrator tells the story. Two of Eddie's stories thus contained stories within stories.

Eddie also included several interactive features in his stories. Characters and/or the narrator interact with one another and with the readers, create the story in front of the readers, and comment on the creation of the story. Further, the readers must be attentive to the multiple stories and interruptions in the book.

Eddie's stories exhibited several features of the type two Radical Change characteristic multiple verbal and visual perspectives. He included both multiple voices and multiple language forms in his stories. His text incorporated storybook language ('Once upon a time there were three weird pigs') and 'people prose' (Purves, 1994). The nature of the dialogue of the three pigs included typical conversational and colloquial language, and reflected a contemporary discourse style ('Dude, we need houses!' 'Totally, to like cook food in!'). Finally, Eddie's first story was a new perspective on existing literature and the illustrations in his stories reflected various visual perspectives.

Eddie acknowledged that he was influenced by Wiesner's *The Three Pigs*. I believe that Eddie was also influenced by *The Stinky Cheese Man and Other Fairly Stupid Tales*. He identified Scieszka's collection of fractured tales as one of his favourite books, stating that he 'liked the humour a lot' and 'all the messing up between the stories.' Eddie talked about several of the Scieszka's stories during his interview, and identified elements or aspects that he enjoyed about each tale. I believe that Eddie's book echoed Scieszka's work with respect to the title, content, discursive structures, and type of humour in the stories.

Jenatine: Profile

Jenatine was exceeding Grade 5 level provincial expectations in reading and writing. She was a perceptive ten-year-old student who contributed original and thoughtful ideas to small-group and whole-class discussions. On the questionnaire distributed at the end of project, Jenatine wrote:

Reader – I like to connect with the characters. I like characters I can build on and relate to. I read above average and I like fiction. I like quiet when I read.
Writer – Most of the time I get ideas for my writing from my dreams. I think I have original ideas. I would like to work on my spelling.

Jenatine was an active and enthusiastic participant in all of the research activities. When asked to describe which part of the study she most enjoyed, Jenatine wrote, 'I like the book poster the best because I felt I could really show what I felt about the book. At first I did not like responding but now I am glad because I can now refeel that great feeling.' One of my questions asked the students to describe what they had learned about reading picturebooks. Jenatine wrote, 'Take in the colours. Find different things in the pictures. Connect. Different types of language. Look through the page. Take another look.'

Red, Blue and Yellow

Jenatine's book, *Red, Blue and Yellow*, was nine pages in length, was written on 8½-by-11-inch paper, and had a front and back cover. The cover had four different bands of yellow, red, blue, and green drawn in with pencil crayons on the white paper. She designed endpapers out of four wavy bands of the same colours of construction paper. Page 1, 'Facts About the Characters,' provides a bit of information about each of the eleven characters in the book. For example, 'Pam: She likes talking on the phone with her friends. Is 12 years old and lives in Victoria.'

On page 2, Jenatine introduces readers to the four stories in the book, 'The Move,' 'Where are you, Mrs. Rabbit?,' 'Diamond in the Rust,' and 'It Could be a Mystery.' Jenatine emulated the structure and format of Macaulay's picturebook *Black and White* in her use of four frames and four different illustrative mediums. It is challenging to use only words to describe Jenatine's book due to its complexity and the synergy between the words and illustrations, and between the four stories.

'The Move' is about a family moving from Vancouver to Victoria. Two girls in Nova Scotia search for a missing stuffed rabbit in 'Where are you, Mrs. Rabbit?' At the beginning of 'Diamond in the Rust,' a reporter is interviewing two girls but the reporter becomes frustrated and ends the interview. These three stories are connected by the appearance of a trunk and a stuffed toy, Mrs. Rabbit. The family packs a trunk and eventually Mrs. Rabbit ends up in their house (or so it seems). In 'Where are you, Mrs. Rabbit?,' the trunk is in the girls' bedroom and Mrs. Rabbit leaves the girls in search of her identity. In 'Diamond in the Rust,' one of the girls finds Mrs. Rabbit upstairs in the attic in front of a trunk. A leprechaun named Greeny, who was unsuccessful in school and believes that she is a detective, is the character in the fourth story, 'It Could be a Mystery,' and essentially she comments on events in the other three stories. On page 6, the frames disappear and the four stories merge into one, as in *Black and White*. On the next page, Jenatine, like Macaulay, reverts to the four-frame structure and the stories end. Page 9 is blank except for a speech balloon at the bottom in which Greeny speaks to the creator of the book: 'Hey, down here. What about the dedication page?' Jenatine includes a dedication at the top of page 10, and a speech balloon at the bottom of the page with Greeny addressing the readers: 'This is the end. Bye …'

INTERTEXTUALITIES

During the interview about her book, Jenatine explained how she had included several intertextual connections in her book. She incorporated many allusions to the picturebooks used in the study, as well as to other selections of literature and film. Jenatine explains that she was greatly influenced by David Macaulay's picturebook, *Black and White*:

S: *The first question, Jenatine, is how did you come up with the ideas for your story?*

J: *Um, originally it was going to be kind of a different story but then I changed it to* Red, Blue, and Yellow *because I liked how in* Black and White *they used the four square, and I used the four square in my story through most of it, and I thought…well then for the cover page instead of black and white, I'd do the opposite colours, so I did red, blue, and yellow, and that's where I got the title and I also used the four square, and I used the green because on* Black and White, *they have the green thing, and one of my characters is a green leprechaun and she doesn't understand why we have green on the cover, but she's actually the reason that I have green on the cover.*

She also described how one of her stories, 'The Move,' was similar to one of Macaulay's four stories in *Black and White*. 'That's the simple story and I kind of took that one from the simple story from "Seeing Things" [in *Black and White*]. And I wanted it to be kind of, to be like, to have a boy in it that was – like that story was very normal, and it was the one story that you could always see throughout the book.' Jenatine explained how Greeny the leprechaun was like the character Desperate Dan who appeared in Macaulay's picturebooks *Why the Chicken Crossed the Road* and *Black and White*:

J: *Why I did Greeny, the character, is from Desperate Dan. Because he's had a bad background and that was also kind of like another series of books that I've read. It's called* Dive.

S: *Yes, I've read those books.*

J: *And they [the characters in the* Dive *trilogy] messed up, and then they try to make things better and Greeny's trying to help everybody, but she's not really helping anybody. She's just like Desperate Dan, it's like he never really tries to help anybody and stuff like that. And Desperate Dan never talks, and she only talks in speech balloons.*

Jenatine was influenced by Gordon Korman's trilogy called *Dive* (*The Danger, The Deep, The Discovery*, 2003). She also acknowledged that she borrowed ideas for her plot, characters, and illustrations from other books, including *The Stinky Cheese Man and Other Fairly Stupid Tales*. She described how the reporter who interrupted the girls was 'like the Red Hen.' Jenatine explained her reasons for cutting out pictures from magazines for the illustrations in the story 'Diamond in the Rust': 'I thought that they would be easier because I can't really draw realistic things and also from *The Stinky Cheese Man*, I thought it looked cool how they had overlapping pictures cut out in that one collage [double-page spread of 'Giant Story'].'

When Jenatine talked about page 6 of her book, she described how she incorporated ideas from *Willy the Dreamer* (Browne, 1997) and the movie, *Monsters, Inc.* (Disney Enterprises, Inc./Pixar Animation Studios, 2001):

S: *Right, and then this looks like a house, the way you put it together.*

J: *Yeah, that's right. And I drew an alien even though nobody is standing there.*

S: *Oh, you did. OK, she's talking about in the mirror you've got an alien back in there.*

J: *Even though there's not an alien there, and I kind of took that from* Willy the Dreamer. *Because in the water there's a reflection of somebody but he's not even there (this illustration does not appear in* Willy the Dreamer; *she may be referring to the image of Willy in the chair at the end of the book or Willy's reflection on the slide in* Voices in the Park*).*

S: *Oh, that's an excellent idea. See I didn't figure that out. I'm going to have to write my notes on that as well. Oh, that's good – I like that!*

J: *And this [illustration in the bottom left-hand corner] is meant to be behind the scenes because that's the scene going up in the stage lights.*

And that's why I said up here that he's really an evil scientist. And in Monsters, Inc., the movie, it's how they go behind stage. Like it changed. The kid's a robot and that story ends suddenly, and then they're like...the people they're just having coffee and stuff, and that's what that was meant to be, an interruption again.

Later on during the interview, Jenatine explained further about the links to *Monsters, Inc.*, as well as the connections to Harry Potter, *Walk Two Moons* (Creech, 1994), the novel she read during the study, and other literature.

J: Yeah, Bob's the dad, but you never really know that Bob's the dad. And like you never really know the mom's true name. Like Walk Two Moons.
S: Right, you don't know her name.
J: So you never really know his real ... true name.
S: OK, so Bob is the dad. He's an alien?
J: Yeah, he's really an alien. Right there [points to illustration].
S: So is that supposed to be his shadow?
J: Yeah, that's his shadow, but he's not standing there so you kind of have to put that together and the facts [on page 1] tell you because he's the guy from Monsters, Inc. *that's really an alien. And his true reflection ... and why I did it in the mirror is because in Harry Potter the mirror shows the true things, and so that was going to be his true reflection, he's really a space alien, not a person.*
S: I can't believe all of the things that you have incorporated in here. You've done just an outstanding job. You've made intertextual connections to other books and to movies. It's amazing.
J: And I wish I had kind of done ... if I was going to do a sequel for this I would do Mr. Rabbit from another family and how he's trying ... I think that's what she [Mrs Rabbit] was originally trying to find, and why they find her in the bathroom is because she's trying to find her true identity in the mirror.
S: Oh, ha, ha, ha.
J: And it shows his [Bob's] true identity.
S: That's right.
J: And she doesn't know, maybe she's a real human or something like that, but I didn't draw her reflection because they don't know what she is. She's still trying to figure out what she really is sort of thing, and I also used that from lots of the books that I've read. It's a girl who's often question- ing who she is and stuff and Mrs. Rabbit can't really tell what she's ques-

tioning but I didn't really ... it's hard to tell the person, the reader, all the things about the characters.

When I asked Jenatine how she came up with the ideas for her stories, she explained that she first made a family tree to connect the characters. She explained how she had 'read a series over the summer and it was a story, and it was how each generation, and they were all connected by magic, and so I wanted to connect it, but using that same thing with a trunk.' Near the end of the interview Jenatine expressed regret over not including a family tree in the book to assist readers in understanding the connections among the characters. 'But I couldn't figure it out [drawing the family tree] on the computer – how to get it for my endpapers because that was what I was going to do, because then you could find these characters and figure out their stories but I couldn't figure out how to do it.'

One final connection Jenatine talked about was a life-to-text connection – a belief of some young children that they can converse with their stuffed animals. On the sheet with facts about the characters, Jenatine wrote that Kate, a five-year-old girl, could translate for Mrs. Rabbit. Jenatine explained: 'And why I did that is because Kate – when you're little you often think that stuffies can talk and so you can apparently hear what they are saying, so Kate can translate for you because she can speak rabbit.'

RADICAL CHANGE CHARACTERISTICS

Jenatine's Analysis. Jenatine was influenced by several picturebooks used in the study. She identified several Radical Change characteristics in her book: 'I used the four square, I used an interrupting page, where this page back here ... it's blank, you think that it's going to be four squares again, this page where it all comes together it looks like it has just been put in between the two four-square pages. I used different kinds of fonts, it was different layers.' She used different mediums for the illustrations: pencil crayons, a fine-tip black marker, pictures cut out from magazines, and coloured paper, cut out and glued. Jenatine remarked, 'I actually tried to isolate the characters and I think I did that by doing the fonts and the different kinds of mediums I used.' She explained her symbolic use of colour and choice of illustrative medium: 'And then with this one ['It Could Be a Mystery'] I did green paper. The green story is this leprechaun girl.' Jenatine used a fine-tip black felt marker for the illustrations for 'Where are you, Mrs. Rabbit?' but she only coloured Mrs. Rabbit. She explained her illustrative choices for 'Diamond in the Rust': 'And then that one, it was the coloured font in weird fonts with diamonds on it because that's the newest generation. They're the youngest kids, and that's why there's … that's why it's so bright, and it's like wonky and stuff.' Jenatine also included a rainbow in 'The Move' to communicate meaning: 'And this … you can kind of tell it's the end because there's the rainbow there, and they've moved and everything's happy for them.'

Jenatine talked about the interruptions she included in her book, such as Greeny commenting on the other stories and asking about the dedication page, the reporter interrupting the story with her question, and the 'behind the scenes' illustration like in *Monsters Inc.*, when the four stories merge into one. Jenatine explained Greeny's role in the book: 'It doesn't really tell you that she's a leprechaun except for up there, and she makes comments about all of the characters, so she's saying, "Ahh her hair is so lovely," to that lady [the reporter]. "That sky is beautiful." "I wish I was up there," for the next page where you see the sky.' Jenatine knew that readers could read her book in a number ways because of the mosaic narratives and the nonlinear structure of the text:

S: *As a reader, does it matter which one of these you start at?*
J: *Um, I don't think so. It helps to start there ['The Move'], no, but then it doesn't really. I think 'Where are you, Miss Rabbit?' would be the easiest one to start, because that's the only story that I really … it was done when I started it, that was the only story I knew what was going to happen, and all the other stories just kind of happened as I went.*

Ms. H. had the students self-evaluate their stories. One of the questions on the form asked the students to identify the Radical Change characteristics included in their stories. Jenatine noted the 'speech bubbles' (multiple sets of words) and 'story book language' (multiple language forms) she used in her book.

My Analysis. Jenatine incorporated into her stories many of the Radical Change characteristics that she had learned about throughout the research project. She used colour symbolically to communicate meaning – green paper for the leprechaun story, the rainbow – and chose a different font and colour for each story. The design or placement of words transmitted meaning in Jenatine's book. For example, for the title 'It Could be a Mystery,' the words 'could' and 'be' were placed under a magnifying glass that enlarged the size of the words. On page 3 she used a black think cloud, like the one Willems uses in *Don't Let the Pigeon Drive the Bus* (2003), to communicate the character's thoughts in 'Diamond in the Rust' (I had read Willems book to the students). Synergy existed among the four individual stories in *Red, Blue and Yellow,* and between each story and its illustrative medium, such as the magazine pictures for 'Diamond in the Rust.'

Each narrative in Jenatine's book was linear and sequential, but her use of four frames generated a verbal and visual layering of stories within stories. The format of the book created interruptions and disruptions in the reading of each narrative. Jenatine's use of four frames as an organizational structure resulted in a multilayered and nonlinear reading experience. Indeed, her story was polysequential in nature because of the four discontinuous narratives (Douglas Yellowlees, 2001).

The reader is the observer of the interactivity among the characters and stories in *Red, Blue and Yellow.* The nonlinear organization and format, the polysequential nature of the work, the multiple layers of meaning, and the multiple narratives in both text and illustrations all require a considerable degree of interactivity from the reader. Dresang writes that 'radically changed forms and formats demand a greater degree of attentiveness and interaction ... children must decide whether to "point and click" here or there with their eyes and their minds' (1999, p. 114). The hypertextual format of the book requires readers to make decisions about which textual and/or illustrative path to follow. Other interactive features in *Red, Blue and Yellow* include multiple texts, Greeny's voice commenting on the story and addressing readers, and Mrs. Rabbit looking directly at readers (much like Wiesner's illustration of one pig in *The Three Pigs*) on page 3 and saying, 'Sh... sh...'

Jenatine's book included multiple voices and multiple language forms, including the storybook language in 'The Move,' conversation, and colloquial language. She depicted front, side, and back visual perspectives in her illustrations. Finally, although 'The Move' has a clear ending, the other three the stories in *Red, Blue and Yellow* have indeterminate endings.

Bert: Profile

Bert was meeting provincial grade level expectations in reading and writing. He was a confident and well-spoken student who was very conscientious about all aspects of his schoolwork. On the end-of-project questionnaire, Bert described himself as a reader and a writer:

Reader – I think that I'm a good reader because I've finished 12 Redwall books since halfway through August. I enjoy reading Brian Jacques series called Redwall. When I read I imagine the scene that's happening in the book.
Writer – I think that I'm an above average writer. When I write I sort of connect subjects together. I really enjoy writing adventure stories.

Bert demonstrated interest in and enthusiasm for every activity he completed during the study. In answer to the question, 'What did you learn by being in the research project?' Bert wrote: 'When I was reading picturebooks, I learned that taking your time and really looking hard is important because you find stuff that the average reader wouldn't see.' When asked to identify the aspect of the research project that he most enjoyed, Bert explained that 'I enjoyed writing my story the most because I got to use my mind the most! I got to let my creative side go wild!'

The Three Little Spoons and the Big Bad Cow

Bert used letter-sized paper to create his thirteen-page book that included six full-page colour illustrations. A unique version and parody of the traditional story of *The Three Little Pigs, The Three Little Spoons and the Big Bad Cow* is actually a movie being filmed as the reader reads it. The director interrupts the narration of the story/the filming of the movie on several occasions. The actors also interact with one another and with the director as the story/movie unfolds.

The three spoons, Ross, George, and Charles, are graduates of Kellogg's University. They build their houses out of Honeycomb, Frosted Flakes, and Sugar Crisp cereals. One day, as Ross is watching his favourite video, *Lord of the Spoons*, someone knocks at his door. Ross peers out of the window and is horrified to discover that it's the Big Bad Cow! Ross's house becomes a soggy mess when the Big Bad Cow soaks it with her milk. Ross runs as fast 'as his stubby handle could take him' to George's house to warn his cutlery brother of the impending danger. However, the Big Bad Cow is speedy, and before Ross can warn George, the evil bovine releases a spray of milk that pins Ross to a tree. The Big Bad Cow then soaks George's Frosted Flakes house. George scampers to the refuge of Charles's Sugar Crisp house, but the Big Bad Cow arrives and threatens the two spoons: 'Little Spoons. Little Spoons. Let me in or I'll soak and I'll soak your house down!' George just laughs at the threat and the Big Bad Cow sprays her milk at his house but to no avail – the stickiness of the Sugar Crisp cereal holds the house together. George devises a scheme that tricks the Big Bad Cow into believing that she has defeated the spoons, so she leaves 'to pester some other cutlery.'

INTERTEXTUALITIES

When I asked Bert where he got the ideas for his story, he explained:

B: *Well, when I started just writing, I just didn't want to do the basic old pigs and the wolf, so I did the ... I thought of spoons and then how they interact with the cereal, and how cows, they make the milk to go in the cereal. So that's why I put the Big Bad Cow, and to put some more Radical Change in I made interruptions, sort of like in the movie, and every time I was just interacting with things that interact with spoons and stuff, like cereal, Kellogg's, and then Lord of the Spoon, like I sort of got that idea from 'Lord of the Pants.'*

'Lord of the Pants,' a spoof of *Lord of the Rings*, is available on the Internet. One morning during the study, one of the boys in 5A came to school with the text of 'Lord of the Pants.' The text circulated among the students and they all enjoyed the parodic appropriation.

Bert not only included intertextual connections to products, a movie, an Internet text, and a story, but he also explained how he 'borrowed' ideas from a nursery rhyme: 'and instead of the dish ran away with the spoon, I thought it'd be cool if there's a different character, and then I thought of how the cow puts milk into cereal, so then that's how I got the cow idea.' Bert's story also included the names of well-known actors Leonardo DiCaprio and Julia Roberts.

Although he did not identify the intertextual connection to the song 'Monster Mash' (Pickett, 1962) during the interview about his book, Bert included this reference when the Big Bad Cow sprayed milk on one of the cereal houses: 'The Big Bad Cow splurted out her soya milk (which is her favourite milk to use) but to her surprise she did the Mash! It was the Monster Mash!' The director interrupted the actors at this point in the story/movie and complained about the spontaneous outburst.

RADICAL CHANGE CHARACTERISTICS

Bert's Analysis. When I asked Bert to describe the Radical Change characteristics in his story, he explained how he had decided to use different font styles and colours for the text:

B: *I did all the different fonts and different colours because at first I was thinking of just printing it in black and using different fonts, but it didn't look that good. So I started changing the fonts and the colours. So everyone has a different colour of font.*

Other Radical Change characteristics identified by Bert included interruptions, intertextual connections, and an unresolved ending:

B: *And I did a few interruptions and a lot more talking from the characters.*
S: *Yes. Interruptions in the story.*
B: *And I put, like, famous actors to make it sort of funny. Like they are intertextual connections. But I guess my story is an intertextual connection too because it's like* The Three Little Pigs, *right?*
S: *Yes, that's right. So you've got intertextual connections.*
B: *And at the end ... it's not an ending ... because we're not supposed to figure it out.*

Bert explained how he had learned about using different typographic styles and colours from the literature he read during the study: 'Well, basically it was just the fonts and the colours.' He also mentioned how he had used an idea from *The Stinky Cheese Man and Other Fairly Stupid Tales*: 'And the interruptions ... I got that idea from *The Stinky Cheese Man* because there's lots of interruptions in that book.'

My Analysis. The Three Little Spoons and the Big Bad Cow exhibited a number of Radical Change characteristics. Although Bert used different font styles and colours for the characters in his book, unlike Eddie and Jenatine he did not explain his reasons for selecting particular typographic techniques. I believe Bert selected red for the director's text because the Little Red Hen in *The Stinky Cheese Man* speaks in a red font and she, like the director in Bert's story, often interrupts other characters. Two other examples of Bert's text design communicating meaning were when the Big Bad Cow whispered (in a small-size font) to herself, 'Why don't I flood this house through the chimney?' and when the director (in large, uppercase letters) yelled at the actors.

The interruptions by the director and the actors and the story-within-story structure contributed to the nonlinearity of Bert's book. He incorporated several interactive features into his story, such as characters interacting with one another, characters creating the story in front of readers, and characters commenting on the story as it was being created. *The Three Little Spoons and the Big Bad Cow* requires attentive reading due to the multiple stories, disruptions, and intertextual connections.

With respect to multiple perspectives, Bert included various voices – the narrator, the director, and the actors – and his story presented a new perspective on existing literature. Bert used multiple language forms in his story including storybook language –'One fine day there were three little spoons and their names were Ross, George and Charles' – and people prose. Charles, the third spoon, speaks 'street,' like Eddie's three weird pigs. When Charles opens the door to greet George, he exclaims, 'Wazzzzzzzzzzzup, George, ma' man. How's it goin', dude?'

Finally, the ending of Bert's story remains somewhat unresolved. After the words, 'The End,' the text continues: 'Hey, we're not done yet! Come on you guys! Ya' there? Uh guys, stop playin' with me. I know you're there. GRRRRRRRRRRRR ... What's the use? Fine! It's the end of the story! THE END.' During his interview about his story, Bert commented, 'it's not an ending ... because we're not supposed to figure it out.' When I asked who was saying this last part in the book, he replied, 'Anyone who's in the movie could be saying that.'

Overall Analysis of the Grade 5 Students' Stories/Books

Type One Radical Change – Changing Forms and Formats

GRAPHICS IN NEW FORMS AND FORMATS

All of the students in 5A and 5C and all but one student in 5B used typography in their stories to communicate meaning or sound. Eleven students in 5A, fifteen students in 5B and eight students in 5C used different colours for their various fonts. Matt, who borrowed the plot structure of *Why the Chicken Crossed the Road* to create his book, *Runaway Snowboard*, explained his choices of fonts when describing the Radical Change characteristics in his book:

Matt: So it was nonlinear, nonsequential, um, intertextual connections, two or more stories, and what? I've got it written down in my book – maybe I should get it. Oh yeah, different fonts.
S: You do use different fonts for the different stories.
Matt: Yeah.
S: All right, good. Why did you use that font for Matt's story [the main character in his story]? Did you pick the fonts for a reason?
Matt: Yeah, the first one is just normal, whenever I'm writing a story that's just normal I'll use Comic Sans. And then I used Yukon font for the snowboard because it's kind of all over the place and it's kind of messy [there is a runaway snowboard in his story].
S: Oh, OK.
Matt: That's what the font is. And Matt is kind of like worrisome, losing his snowboard.

Eight students in 5A, seven in 5B, and two in 5C used colour symbolically to convey mood, or a character's personality or emotions, or various narratives. Although thirty-four of the fifty-seven students (one student in 5C did not write a story) used different colours for the fonts in their stories, about half of them explained how they had purposefully selected the various colours to convey meaning. Finally, eight students in 5A, four in 5B, and seven in 5C superimposed text on an illustration so they appeared simultaneously as picture and words in their books.

Jenny employed colour and typographic elements to communicate meaning in her story, *The Origin of the Three Blind Mice*, a multilayered tale of three blind mice searching for houses. The pessimistic Mouse Three has dark grey fur and a rather stoic-looking grey font while Mouse Two the optimist has a flowing orange font. Mouse One's speech is sprinkled with 'dudes' and 'likes' in a green, rather 'typical' textbook font. In several of the speech balloons, Jenny has written the text is in capital letters to communicate the emotions of the characters. Finally, on several pages she has placed text over a picture to create simultaneity.

WORDS AND PICTURES REACHING NEW LEVELS OF SYNERGY

Several students created sophisticated illustrations to accompany their texts, but I do not believe that any of their work exemplifies Dresang's definition of graphic synergy, in which words and pictures cannot be separated (as in *Black and White* and *The Stinky Cheese Man and Other Fairly Stupid Tales*). The work of three students in 5A and one in 5C demonstrated synergy among varying illustrative styles. Jenatine's book included synergy among the four individual stories and between each story and its illustrative medium.

NONLINEAR AND NONSEQUENTIAL ORGANIZATION AND FORMAT

In varying ways, seventeen students in 5A, twelve in 5B, and ten in 5C used a nonlinear organization and format for their stories. The events in or the organization of the narratives of all of the girls and six of the boys in 5A lacked a logical or chronological order. However, only four students in 5B and five in 5C wrote stories that had polysequential organizations. Amber explained some of the challenges in reading her comic-book-style book, *The No Name Story*, because of its nonlinearity and multiple stories:

Amber: *In one of my stories, I'll make something happen and then you'll go see something else happen, and then something else will happen on the next page, but that same thing will still be going on. Just when you flip the page something else will be going on, and then finally like four or five pages later you get back to the same thing.*

Zoe used the visual structure of a four-slice pizza for her book, *Pizza for Dinner*. A different story is told in each slice of pizza and readers need to rotate the book to read the four stories:

S: *So, you said different fonts and different colours of fonts. OK, how about when somebody reads your story, how can they read it? Like do you have to read ... do you have to start here [I point at one particular story]?*

Zoe: *No. You can ... like the way, how I kind of planned for people to read it ... I mean people can read it however they want, right.*

Textual or illustrative disruptions or interruptions were evident in the stories of seventeen students in 5A twelve in 5B, and ten in 5C. During my interview with Michelle about her book, *The Stinky Cheese*

Man, she explained how she had learned about including interruptions in her work:

Michelle: Um, well, first I came up with the idea for the story from, what was that story called? The Stinky Cheese Man. I got it from that book, but I just decided – I thought it would be really cool to make it so there were, like, a lot of interruptions and to make another character, Stinky Pickle Man.

S: Ha, ha.

Michelle: Ha, ha, and yeah, it just like … it kind of made the story better. And if I didn't read all those other books, like the picturebooks and stuff, and then I probably wouldn't have known to do like the interruptions and stuff.

In Alyssa's book, *The Untold Story*, the main characters are four captains (Kirk, Picard, Sisco, and Janeway) from various Star Trek television programs: *Star Trek*; *Star Trek: The Next Generation*; *Star Trek: Deep Space Nine*; and *Star Trek: Voyager* (see Pantaleo 2007b for a detailed discussion of Alyssa's work). Each page in Alyssa's book has four quadrants, framed in black, with a white margin between each quadrant. As *The Untold Story* begins, each of the four main characters is hanging from a physical structure. They conversationally address the readers and tell them that they will convey the events that led to their current quandaries. On the second page, the story slips back in time to when the characters have graduated from Zephrim Cockren High. Each narrative strand then proceeds in a linear manner, but the format Alyssa used results in four discontinuous series of events. The four narrations are interdependent and synergistic, but the use of the four frames creates a disrupted or interrupted reading experience that is polysequential in nature.

Multiple Layers of Meaning. Stories within stories were employed to create a multilayered reading experience in the stories of fourteen students in 5A and eight in both 5B and 5C. Only some of the children's work exhibited synergy among the multiple stories (ten students in 5A, three in 5B, and two in 5C). Alyssa's four main characters independently tell readers about the events that led to their current predicaments. The four narratives and the structural format of the book generate a multilayered reading and viewing experience (verbal and visual layering of stories). For her book, *Confused*, Jessy borrowed ideas from the plot structure of *Shortcut*: events and characters in her book's five chapters were interconnected. Jessy explained, 'Well, I really liked the book *Shortcut*, where one thing linked to another. I thought that was really cool how it happened and I thought I could do a few things like that.'

According to Dresang, visual layering of stories can include pictures within pictures, stories bordering other stories, or stories that are 'embedded in large illustrations, or weave in and out of the main text' (1999, p. 22). Six students in 5A, one in 5B, and two in 5C included visual layering in their work as multiple stories bordered each other.

Interactive Formats. One of the most prevalent interactive format features in the work of the Grade 5 students (sixteen in 5A, eighteen in 5B, and twelve in 5C) was the interaction of the character(s) or narrator with readers. For example, on the cover of Maddie's book, *The Three Dudish Bears*, the characters interact both with one another and with the narrator:

S: *OK, so that's why he's asking that. And then what about this [referring to one of the speech bubbles on the cover]?*
Maddie: *[Reads from the cover] 'Shut up you two. This is the cover picture, and look at the camera.' Because they're taking a picture with a camera for the cover, and um, I have them all have different eye colours. The dad has green, the baby has blue.*
S: *So the mother is talking to the other two bears?*
Maddie: *Yeah. Tony is the dad ... he's like a dude, and so the baby wants to be like him, and it says on the cover, 'The Three Bears,' but he put the word 'dudish' into it, and he's [the narrator] like [reads from the cover], 'Tony you messed up the title. I worked hard on that!' and it's the narrator speaking.*
S: *OK, so the narrator is telling him hey, I worked hard on the cover, and Tony's sticking in the word dudish.*
Maddie: *Right.*

The other dominant interactive feature in the Grade 5 stories/books, was the use of multiple stories, disruptions, and/or intertextual connections that demanded reader attentiveness. This device was evident in the work of seventeen students in both 5A and 5B, and fifteen students in 5C. For example, on the first page of Shazia's book, *What? Hello!*, she includes a visual intertextual connection to *Shortcut*. As the four symbols in the graphic are meaningful to the two stories in her book, the visual is both intertextual and intra-textual in nature:

Shazia: And then this part was from Shortcut.
S: All right – she's talking about the part on page one [of her book] in the centre. OK, now how's that from Shortcut?
Shazia: On the bridge.
S: From the bridge. Right, the crest and all of the items that mean some-thing. So then what do those [symbols in her circle] mean?
Shazia: So this is a question mark.
S: OK, the question mark.
Shazia: The spaceship.
S: The spaceship.
Shazia: The earth. And then this is her teddy bear, you have to look really closely, it's hard to see.

Amber described an intertextual connection in her book, *The No Name Story*, to *Who's Afraid of the Big Bad Book?*:

S: Anything else you want to explain about your story?
Amber: You know in Beware of the Storybook Wolves *book [Child, 2000]?*
S: Yes.
Amber: You know how in the second one [Who's Afraid of the Big Bad Book?] *where he [Herb] draws moustaches and stuff on it? I took that idea because they're [characters in her book] looking at a book and they don't like it, so they scribble all over it and mess it up.*
S: So that's what's going on here? Well, I'm glad you told me that, because I wasn't sure what you were doing here.
Amber: Yeah, they [the characters] were looking at the book – this [illustra-tion] was before the book looked like this, and that's why I wrote, 'After the book looked like this.'

Like many of the Grade 5 students, Ray included interruptions as a device in his story. Ray's chicken character is similar to the interrupting Red Hen in Scieszka's *The Stinky Cheese Man and Other Fairly Stupid Tales*. The yellow chicken on Ray's book cover informs readers, 'Sorry we couldn't think of a name for our story!' and then proceeds to interrupt the telling of the three narratives in the book with ideas for the title:

S: So, what radical change characteristics did your story include?
Ray: Um, three stories within one.
S: Right.
Ray: Um, like the idea of characters talking to the reader.
S: Hmm, hmm. Like in The Stinky Cheese Man, *right?*
Ray: Yeah, the chicken always talks to you. She interrupts the stories.

Eleven students in 5A, and one in both 5B and 5C included parallel stories in their work. Further, one girl in both 5B and 5C told a manifold narrative (Trites, 1994) entirely through illustrations. In Maddie's book, for example, the three bears leave their original story and enter the storyboards of *Why the Chicken Crossed the Road* and *Shortcut*. She explained, 'I took ideas from the stories that we've read and then, I ... like they're in the story worlds like *The Three Pigs*.' Ray also had three simultaneous narratives in his book. When I asked him where he got the idea, he replied, 'Um from *Black and White*. I really liked the four stories, but I tried something different. And so I just thought of three, and I couldn't think of a fourth story, so I made it three.' One of the narratives in Nicky's story, *Rapunzel's Story*, was told entirely through illustrations. Nicky conveyed the brown bird's story through its actions and facial expressions, as well as the image symbols above its head (! and ?).

Some of the other features the students included in their work were characters interacting with one another (eighteen students), hypertextual-type text (thirteen students), the necessity of moving back and forth between text and pictures (eight students), and texts requiring the reading of more than one set of words (sixteen students). Sammy's book, *Hey ... Don't Let the Dragon Drive the Race Car!*, was inspired by *Don't Let the Pigeon Drive the Bus!* by Willems, and included characters interacting with one another and with the narrator:

Sammy: This narrator also talks to the readers.
S: Right. And he talks to the characters, right?
Sammy; Yeah, and also he's like a character. He's not just a person who's just going blah, blah, blah – he's actually part of the story, and he's talking to you, and he's talking to everybody.

A total of nineteen students inserted a voice (or voices) that commented on their stories. For example, Shazia wrote two stories that took place simultaneously on each page in her book, *Hello! What?*, but at the bottom of each page the narrator commented about the characters ('Boy, she sure talks a lot!') or the stories ('Notice anything about these two stories?'). ·

Type Two Radical Change – Changing Perspectives

MULTIPLE PERSPECTIVES, VISUAL AND VERBAL
Eleven students in 5A, four students in 5B, and six students in 5C included the device of multiple voices in their stories and books. Multiple language forms were evident in the work of eleven students in 5A, thirteen students in 5B, and eight students in 5C. The stories of seven students in 5A, five students in 5B, and six students in 5C provided new perspectives on existing literature, a feature that I added to this particular Radical Change characteristic. Kudo explained how he decided to create a modern version of *Goldilocks and the Three Bears*: 'Well, some … like, lots of people tell that Goldilocks, you know, sat on the chair and it broke, and then so I just thought, or I'm like, instead of beds, like, nice beds and porridge and just like the fairytale, I decided to do like a modern version, like with jello. And then there were beanbag chairs, and then there were air mattresses, and then she sat on the beanbag chair and it broke.'

Multiple visual perspectives were evident in the illustrations in the books of seven students in 5A, one girl in 5B, and three students in 5C. Front, side, back, and top-down perspectives were all depicted in the illustrations of these children's work. For example, as well as using front and side views in their illustrations, Fritz included a top-down view of a cruise ship and some lifeboats on the ocean, and Zoe included several top-down views of pizza.

Type Three Radical Change – Changing Boundaries

UNRESOLVED ENDINGS
The endings of the texts of nine students in 5A, four students in 5B, and one girl in 5C were unresolved and open to reader interpretation. When I asked Sammy if she had explained a certain aspect at the end of her story to readers, she replied confidently, 'No, I didn't. I have no explaining about anything in the story. You have to figure it out by yourself.' Fritz was another student who chose an unresolved ending for his book, *Weirdoes*:

S: *So, what about the end? You've got the end and you've a question mark.*
Now why did you do that?
Fritz: *Is it really the end or does it go on, dum, dum, da, you can even use a*
drum roll or anything like that.
S: *Ha, ha. So you've got the Radical Change characteristic of an unresolved*
ending. Like, is it the end or is it not the end?
Fritz: *Exactly. Maybe it's the end but maybe not!*

Group and Gender Similarities and Differences

My study data revealed a number of similarities and differences both
in the stories produced in the three classes and between the genders of
the students. A single Radical Change feature was evident in the
stories of all but one of the students: the design or placement of words
on a page to represent sounds or transmit meaning. In many instances
the students used fonts as images (Kress, 2003a). During the class discussion about *The Three Pigs*, the students talked about Wiesner's
choice of typography and shared their opinions on their own favourite
fonts. We also discussed the significance of Browne's font selections for
the four characters in *Voices in the Park*, and the multiple fonts in *Starry
Messenger*, *The Stinky Cheese Man and Other Fairly Stupid Tales*, *Beware of
the Storybook Wolves*, *Who's Afraid of the Big Bad Book?*, and *Black and
White*. Other books that I brought into the classroom for the students
to read also exhibited the use of this design feature. Meaning was
communicated by and represented through 'the visuality of writing'
(p. 151) in the literature the students read and in their own work. All
students could easily manipulate typography by using the font menus
on their word processing programs. Two girls in 5A completed comic-
book-style stories, but they still varied the typography design of their
handwritten texts.

Other features that were evident in over three-quarters of the twenty
students' stories in 5A included: nonlinear organization and format;
multiple stories, disruptions, and/or intertextual connections; and
character and/or narrator interaction with readers. The last two features listed above were most in evidence in the stories written by 5B
and 5C. Overall, the students in 5A incorporated significantly more
Radical Change features in their work than the students in either 5B or
5C. The stories of the 5A girls exhibited the most Radical Change features, an average of 15.2 features per girl, and the work completed by
the 5C boys exhibited the fewest number of Radical Change features,
an average of 5.7 features per boy. The girls in 5B and the boys in 5A

included a similar number of features in their stories (10.6 features per girl in 5B, and 10.1 features per boy in 5A).

The girls in 5A incorporated almost twice as many interactive format features into their work as their male peers and the students in the other two classes. Overall, interactive format features accounted for approximately 40 per cent of the total number of Radical Change features in the stories of the girls in 5A and approximately one-third of the total number of Radical Change features in the stories of the 5B and 5C boys. Appendix K illustrates the breakdown by gender of specific Radical Change characteristics used in the stories written by each Grade 5 class. A few notable findings follow.

The girls in each Grade 5 class included more Radical Change features in their stories/books than the boys in the classes. In 5A, only two features were used more by the boys than the girls: multiple language forms in a book, and new perspective(s) on existing literature. The interactive feature of multiple stories, disruptions, and/or intertextual connections was more evident in the boys' stories in both 5B and 5C than in the girls' work in those classes. Compared to the work of their female classmates, the boys' stories in 5C contained slightly more examples of characters interacting with each other in front of readers. The stories completed by the boys in 5A exhibited the most features of Type Two Radical Change, multiple visual and verbal perspectives, and the work of the girls in 5A exhibited the least amount of features of this particular characteristic. The girls in 5B and 5C also included several multiple visual and verbal perspectives in their stories/books.

Why did the students in 5A incorporate many more Radical Change features into their stories than the students in 5B and 5C? Why did the eleven girls in 5A include more Radical Change features in their stories than any other group of students? And why did the girls in each class incorporate more Radical Change features into their work than the boys? Although I do not have definitive answers to these questions, I believe that my findings reflect a number of interrelated factors. As a group, the students in 5A were more confident about and creative in their thinking, and more willing to take risks in their writing and in general than the children in 5B and 5C. Interestingly, I believe that we were more explicit in our teaching about Radical Change theory to the students in 5B and 5C, and unlike the students in 5B and 5C, the children in 5A had no examples of student work to look at when it came time for them create their stories.

A few gender-specific differences in the students' stories emerged from my data analysis. The girls may have been more willing to take risks in their writing, or wanted to challenge themselves by including numerous features in their work. They may also have included more Radical Change characteristics in their written work to exceed expectations or to 'please' Ms H. and myself. Perhaps the girls derived more pleasure or satisfaction from breaking many of the conventions or 'rules' associated with traditional narrative writing. However, Blair and Sanford (2004) described how the boys in their research often 'morphed' traditional school writing activities to include visual, interactive, humorous, and pop culture elements. The picturebooks that were read during my research and the nature of the writing assignment provided the Grade 5 boys with the knowledge and opportunity to create books that were consistent with several of the boys' literacy behaviours and preferences found in the research by Blair and Sanford, including contravention of traditional narrative conventions.

Other researchers have also reported gender differences in students' writing. Guzzetti, Young, Gritsavage, Fyfe, and Hardenbrook (2002) noted that 'writing as a gendered social practice' (p. 80) emerged as one of the themes from their analyses of studies on writing and gender. They describe several studies that found gender differences with respect to both the content and form of note writing, 'choice of author voice, topic and genre,' and the depiction of male and female characters (pp. 81–2). As Peterson noted in her review of the research on the influence of gender on writing, marked differences have been found 'in much of the research examining boys' and girls' writing in primary through middle grades' (2006, p. 314). Since prior research has revealed gender differences in student writing, perhaps it was not surprising that some disparities existed between the Grade 5 girls and boys with respect to the number of Radical Change features incorporated in their stories. However, the openness of the writing assignment requirements did not impose gender expectations or constraints, as Peterson has found in past research.

It is important to note that my data analysis also revealed differences within each gender. One of the biggest differences was the fact that the girls and the boys in 5A incorporated significantly more Radical Change features in their stories compared to their same-gendered peers in the other two classes. A combination of individual, social, and contextual factors may account for the differences between the number of Radical Change features incorporated in the stories of the girls and boys within and across the three Grade 5 classes. Numerous factors associated with individual identity, including the students' own gender ideologies, their beliefs about writing, and their self-efficacies, must be considered when interpreting the findings. Further, much research has revealed how the writing of both genders is influenced by the social context, including the purposes and interactions that sur- round students' writing (Peterson, 2006). Thus, multiple theoretical lenses are required to understand the complexity of gender and writing in classrooms.

The Intertextual Nature of Texts and the Classroom Community

During the course of my study, the students were exposed to a variety of literary styles, encouraged to discuss how stories are constructed, and learned to recognize the literary concepts that are elements of story structure. These lessons gave the students a vocabulary and set of skills they were then able to apply to their own writing. Meek has written that 'the most important single lesson that children learn from texts is *the nature and variety of written discourse*, the different ways that language lets a writer tell, and the many and different ways a reader reads' (1988, p. 21). The many lessons that the students learned throughout my research affected both the content and the form of the signs they included in their stories. For example, several of the chil- dren purposefully created books with nonlinear reading paths. Kress wrote about how readers are socialized into particular forms of reading: 'So a reading path is nearly as much a matter of the social as it is of the semiotic' (2003b, p. 160). During the studies, the students read several books with nonlinear narratives and learned how the mediated telling of events by an author is a construction, and the chronology of events is often varied in some way for a particular effect (Holquist, 1990, p. 113). The students used their knowledge of litera- ture, writing, imagery, and Radical Change characteristics to produce the particular signs – the visual and verbal texts – in their books. 'The making of signs, outwardly as articulation or inwardly as interpreta- tion, complex or simple, large or small, in the socially shaped environ- ments of everyday lives, is the process of semiosis' (Kress, 2003b, p. 44). The students were able both to participate in 'some existing liter- acy and make meanings within it,' and 'able to transform and actively produce it' (Lankshear & Knobel, 2003, p. 11).

   Most of the stories the children wrote during the research were 'writerly texts' (Barthes, 1975) that required gap-filling by readers (Iser, 1978). Their work demonstrated how they had extended their schemata or cognitive representations of various story elements and structures and indeed, the Grade 5 students capably incorporated

Radical Change characteristics into their texts. The children, who had little, if any previous experience in writing print texts with such diverse semiotic systems, confidently approached and completed their assignment and were both cognitively and affectively engaged with their writing. According to Barthes (1975), 'jouissance' is associated with texts that disrupt readers' assumptions; they provide the pleasure of non-conformity as they create discomfort and impose 'a state of loss' and fragmentation (p. 14). During both the writing of and the interviews about their stories, the students communicated enjoyment in their non-conforming texts: most of the Grade 5 children thought their work was amusing and entertaining indeed.

The literature I used in the research was framed by other texts with respect to content, language, style, and genre. As Chandler has noted, 'Each text exists within a vast "society of texts" in various genres and media: no text is an island entire of itself' (2002, p. 201). The Grade 5 students, like the texts they read, were a plurality of other texts. Resonating with the research discussed in chapter 1 on how students draw upon other texts when writing their own texts (Beach, Appleman, & Dorsey, 1990; Cairney, 1990, 1992; Lancia, 1997), my own research shows that the Grade 5 students drew upon the contents, conventions, and formats of the books they read during the study when they created their own stories. They also made intertextual links to other cultural texts (famous actors, characters, or events from other books or movies, songs, sayings, Internet sites, or brand names), and to each other's stories.

The students' membership in a particular 'social/textual community' (Kress, 2003b, p. 159) also affected their use of and conversations about the signs in their writing. The students' experiences during the research projects created a particular type of 'literacy club' (Smith, 1988) with specific values and knowledge about, among other things, the structural, discursive, linguistic, literary, and visual features of literature with Radical Change characteristics. The Grade 5 children learned and used the metalanguage of Radical Change. They acquired a discourse, a language to talk about selections of literature and their own writing (and movies, television shows, art work, video games, and Internet sites) that displayed Radical Change characteristics. The students' writing was embedded in a specific context of social interaction and activity that was generated due to their engagements with particular kinds of texts. Much as other research findings have demonstrated (Bloome & Egan-Robertson, 1993; Oyler & Barry, 1996), the social nature of intertextuality was most evident in the research classrooms.

6 Contemporary Picturebooks and Collateral Learning

Contextualizing Narrative Structures

The process of narrative or storying is a way of making sense of human experience. Hardy has suggested that narrative is a 'primary act of mind' (1975, p. 4), a way of thinking, and that we remember much of our experience in and knowledge of the world in the form of story (Rosen, 1986). Children come to school with various oral story-telling traditions and they draw upon their oral narrative experiences when they encounter written stories. Through multiple experiences with oral and written stories, readers construct schemata or cognitive representations of story structures, elements, and genres. McCabe has found that variation in storytelling 'within a culture is as remarkable as variation between cultures' (1997, p. 455). McCabe's research indicates that many European North American children come to school 'equipped for the kind of stories they hear in school,' which have a 'clear beginning, middle and end' and 'contain a clear temporal sequence of events that matches some sequence of events in the real world' (p. 456). However, not all children are familiar with linear and sequential narratives; researchers who have examined children's oral narrative forms have found significant differences in how storytellers construct their stories. For example, McCabe reports that European North American 'children tend to talk about one important thing at a time' (p. 456), 'Japanese children living in America tend to tell concise stories that are cohesive collections of several experiences they have had' (p. 457), and 'African-American children usually plot numerous sequences of events within the context of the individual experiences combined' (p. 460). Adults who work with children need to 'recognize, appreciate, and value cultural differences in storytelling style' (p. 462), and understand that the European North American linear narrative structure of beginning, middle, and end is only one discursive narrative structure. Children need to experience multiple types of narrative structures in both print and digital texts.

The literature discussed in this book characterizes a growing number of picturebooks and novels, as well as movies, television programs, computer software programs (including hypertext fictions), and video games that offer readers and viewers a range of storytelling styles and narrative forms and formats. Johnson wrote that, 'Multiple threading is the most acclaimed structural convention of modern television programming' (2005, p. 65). In his study of the effects of popular culture, Johnson notes that the narrative complexity of television shows and films has increased so that viewers need to hold multiple threads in their consciousness like a 'kind of mental calisthenics' (p. 129). Students are immersed in a plurality of texts in their lives, and educators need to respond by acknowledging students' out-of-school experiences with texts that have multiple reading, writing, and viewing pathways. These alternate discursive structures may in fact be more familiar to some children in our schools than the European North American linear narrative structure, and for other students, these variant structures can augment their structural schemata. According to structural theory, literary understanding consists of an internalized grammar of story structure and knowledge about the ways that stories work (literary competences) (Culler, 1980). Individuals extend their repertoires of literary and life experiences by reading and listening to stories, repertoires that they can access when listening to or reading other stories, viewing movies, shows, or dramatic productions, engaging in conversations, or writing.

Some curricular documents continue to privilege a European North American traditional narrative structure with a linear beginning, middle, and end. A case in point are the *BC Performance Standards: Reading Revised Edition* (BC Ministry of Education, 2002a) and *BC Performance Standards: Writing Revised Edition* (BC Ministry of Education, 2002b). A chart in the reading standards document describes the *'general characteristics of reading material suitable for most students in March–April Grade 1'* and organizes the characteristics into four headings: language, ideas and organization, graphics, and format (BC Ministry of Education, 2002a, p. 18). In the section on ideas and organization, one of the features of 'suitable' texts is a 'sequence [that] is clear and predictable; stories are usually sequenced using time order' (p. 18). Thus, a linear, sequential narrative structure is identified as being most appropriate for Grade 1 students.

Although the government does not mandate the above British Columbia ministry documents, they are used extensively by classroom teachers in the province. The introduction to the reading document describes the development and goals of the standards as a resource to 'support ongoing instruction and assessment ... [that] supports a criterion-referenced approach to evaluation and enables teachers, students, and parents to compare student performance to provincial standards' (BC Ministry of Education, 2002a, p. 1). The BC performance standards explain and provide examples of student work in four levels of achievement (not yet within expectations, meets expectations at a minimal level, fully meets expectations, exceeds expectations) for areas of learning in reading and writing connected to the language arts curriculum. Grade 5 student reading achievement is evaluated in reading literature and reading for information, and student writing achievement is evaluated for personal impromptu writing, writing to communicate ideas and information, and literary writing.

According to the Grade 5 reading standards document, 'The study of literature is at the heart of English language arts' (BC Ministry of Education, 2002a, p. 135). A chart describes the *general characteristics of literature suitable for most students in March-April of Grade 5*' and organizes the characteristics into three headings: language and ideas; organization and graphics; and format (p. 138). With respect to narrative structure and trajectory, four of the ten characteristics of organization and graphics are most relevant:

- plots are generally straightforward, but are beginning to feature some twists and surprises;
- narratives generally follow simple time order; may be some foreshadowing, but no flashbacks;
- in stories and novels, the problem is solved; there is rarely any ambiguity in the ending; and
- selections often feature a clear message. (p. 138)

In varying respects, the narrative structures of the picturebooks the Grade 5 (and Grade 1) students read, responded to, and discussed during their participation in my research extended and often contradicted the characteristics listed above. The Grade 5 students most capably read, responded to, discussed and interpreted the picture-books with non-linear chronology that included multiple and interrelated stories and ambiguity in text and illustrations. These writerly texts (Barthes, 1975) demanded that the students take an active role in the creation of meaning and participate in co-authoring the stories, required a high degree of reader attentiveness and concentration (Dresang 1999), and developed students' abilities in comprehending text both inferentially and critically. Instead of reading literature with linear clarity and organization as suggested by the curriculum document, the Grade 5 students were reading texts with multiple pathways, varying interpretations, and sophisticated challenges to meaning creation. Clearly, the students were developing the repertoire of 'skilled and experienced' readers (Coles & Hall, 2001, p. 111).

Kress (2003b) has written about how readers are socialized into particular forms of reading, that the reading path is as much social as semiotic. Like McCabe, I believe that researchers and teachers, as well as curriculum developers, need to expand their 'existing definition[s] of a good story' (1997, p. 470). The narrative heterogeneity of the picturebooks not only contributed to the students' schemata of and strategies for reading print texts, but it helped them to develop an understanding of structures, conventions, and literary devices, and to apply this knowledge as readers and writers. The cognitive flexibility to make connections about diverse choices, to feel comfortable with ambiguity, and, ultimately, to find the experience meaningful is learning that will be useful well beyond their reading of these texts.

When evaluating Grade 5 student achievement in writing, the performance standards focus on meaning, style, form, and conventions (BC Ministry of Education, 2002b, p. 11). Form, the aspect pertinent to my focus, is described as 'attention to the "rules" of the particular form of writing' (p. 11) and includes the following features: beginning, middle, and end; sequence; characters; setting; and dialogue (p. 212). The characteristics of the four levels of achievement that focus on narrative structure and trajectory in stories follow:

NOT YET WITHIN EXPECTATIONS
- may be very brief, without a clear beginning, middle, and end
- includes some action and events, but these are not developed into a complete story
- beginning and ending may be missing, abrupt, or illogical

MEETS EXPECTATIONS (MINIMAL LEVEL)
- includes a logically sequenced beginning, middle, and end; may wander in places
- focuses on action; may seem to be a retelling of a familiar story, television program, or movie
- beginning introduces the situation; there is a conclusion, but it may be rather sudden or fail to tie up the story middle and end

FULLY MEETS EXPECTATIONS
- includes a logically sequenced beginning, middle, and end
- focuses more on action than on character or meaning
- beginning establishes interest and introduces the characters; the ending attempts to tie up the story, but may be somewhat weak

EXCEEDING EXPECTATIONS
- develops logically from beginning, to middle, to end; some story elements (e.g., plot, setting, character, message) are well developed
- may be focused around a theme, relationship, or idea; often attempts to create a mood
- reveals the 'story problem' in an engaging beginning; conclusion is believable but usually predictable. (pp. 212–13)

Undoubtedly the written texts the Grade 5 students created as a culminating activity were much more complex than the criteria suggested by the BC performance standards. The students wrote and illustrated stories that contradicted some of the characteristics for meeting fully or exceeding the performance standards' expectations for writing, and they were encouraged to create stories that included forms, structures, and conventions that were 'not yet within expectations' or that minimally met expectations for writing. Not surprisingly, my analysis of the students' work revealed that they were influenced by the picturebooks and other literature that they read, responded to, and discussed throughout the research. Further, the students drew upon their reservoirs of literary and life experiences and adopted and adapted signs from other texts that they had read, viewed, or discussed both inside and outside of the classroom context. Indeed, readers and writers can be described as 'intertexts': other texts 'lurk' inside them and shape meanings, whether they are 'conscious of this or not' (Scholes, 1982, p. 145).

Collateral Learning

The collection of picturebooks used in my research afforded the students with highly enjoyable reading experiences and gave them valuable insights into how literature works from the point of view of both the reader and writer. The literature I used in the research provided private reading lessons (Meek, 1988) that enriched the development of students' literary competences (Culler, 1980) and that extended their understandings of textual structures, forms, and devices that they could then include in the creation of their own texts. Texts such as these provide the kinds of reading experiences that develop readers' abilities to critically examine, deconstruct, and construct an array of texts and representational forms (Anstey, 2002). Texts with Radical Change characteristics and metafictive devices often demand attentiveness to information conveyed in the nontextual features, acquisition of multiple sources of information, analysis of information, and associative processing (Sutherland-Smith, 2002), the same skills required by Web literacy. The similarities between the literature I used in my studies and Sutherland-Smith's description of what Web-based texts offer are striking. Web-based literature 'permits nonlinear strategies of thinking; allows nonhierarchical strategies; offers nonsequential strategies; requires visual literacy skills to understand multimedia components; is interactive, with the reader able to add, change, or move text; and enables a blurring of the relationship between reader and writer' (pp. 664–5).

Students do need to learn the pragmatics of and conventions associated with reading, writing, and viewing various types of texts, but there is more to literature than 'learning the rules.' Children also need to understand how and why authors and illustrators subvert the rules 'for how things work around here' (Meek, 1988, p. 18), and to appreciate and contextualize the 'breaking of the rules' within sociocultural contexts. Students are at a disadvantage if they read and write texts that include only the narrative structures such as those described in the performance standards. They should have opportunities to read, view, discuss, and create print and digital texts in school that reflect changing ways of communicating and representing in their world.

By reading, discussing, and writing about the picturebooks and creating their own books and stories, the children in Grades 1 and 5 were given the opportunity to experience and experiment with fictional models of being human in a postmodern and complex world, a world with a lack of tidy endings where it isn't always 'necessary to think in a straight line to make sense' (Macaulay 1991, p. 419). It is fundamental for educators to develop their repertoires and expand their understanding of the range of contemporary texts available to students. Teachers must broaden their knowledge of and use of the metalanguage needed to teach with and about multimodal texts. By challenging our students with narratives that reflect the complexity and diversity of their communities and that demand particular cognitive skills for engagement, we offer them a richer and wider world than one in which narratives must have straightforward beginnings, middles, and ends. By expanding children's literary experiences, the potential exists to facilitate the kind of 'collateral learning' (Dewey, 1938) that will assist students as they navigate in our multimedia world with its ever-increasing diversity of symbolic representations. According to Dewey,

> Perhaps the greatest of all pedagogical fallacies is the notion that a person learns only that particular thing he is studying at the time. Collateral learning in the way of formation of enduring attitudes, of likes and dislikes, may be and often is much more important than the spelling lesson or lesson in geography or history that is learned. For these attitudes are fundamentally what count in the future. (1938, p. 48)

Dewey's concept of collateral learning went well beyond a focus on subject matter and the teaching of specific knowledge. He described the school as a social environment where learners could grow into what Giarelli calls 'self-directed members of a learning community' (2001, p. 286). The latter has implications for the relationships and connections important for learning both inside and outside of school.

Research that examines students' interpretive practices of an ever-growing range of symbolic representations in our culture (Mackey, 2003) should include further exploration of children's textual engagements with literature with Radical Change characteristics and metafictive devices. Anstey (2002) and Coles and Hall (2001) believe that postmodern picturebooks provide experiences for students to engage with many understandings that are indicative of the new literacies. We need to continue to explore how children and adolescents respond to, interpret, and create various narrative structures and discursive and illustrative devices in texts, and how students' experiences with these contemporary texts influence their literary competences, literacy, and language abilities.

Although most children have wide exposure to visual images through books, television, video games, movies, and the Internet, they still need to be explicitly taught visual literacy skills in order for them to develop the critical thinking skills required to put these images into context, to understand the meaning of the images, and to determine the effects of the images on themselves as viewers and readers. Illustrators combine many visual elements and techniques to create their desired effects in picturebooks. Layout, borders, colour, illustrative media, shapes and sizes of elements, patterns, lines, frames, perspective, typography, and representational characteristics are just some aspects of the artwork that students can learn about in order to enrich their understanding of and responses to picturebooks. Research (e.g., Day, 1996; Kiefer, 1995; Styles & Arzipe, 2001) has indicated the importance of implementing specific instructional strategies to teach students how to view, comprehend, and discuss the meaning-making systems in visual images.

The limited research on immigrant children's responses to and interpretations of visual images in contemporary picturebooks has shown that despite different cultural backgrounds, these students were emotionally engaged and reached deep levels of meaning. Although elements and techniques of the non-verbal semiotics were not the focus of my research, the oral contributions of the boys and girls in Ms P.'s Grade 1 class who were immigrants to Canada demonstrated their engagement with and comprehension of the artwork in the picturebooks during the small-group read-aloud sessions. The students did not hesitate to pose questions, to wonder, to make suggestions, or to offer their opinions and interpretations. However, further studies are needed to specifically examine how students of varying ages and backgrounds respond to and interpret the artwork and design of picturebooks, as well as to explore their understanding of the ecological relationship between words and pictures (Lewis, 2001).

A further recommendation would be to examine the role of the teacher in critically exploring the artwork in picturebooks with her or his students. It is important to investigate the role of teacher influence on students' transactions with contemporary picturebooks. Teachers generally play some type of role in mediating students' experiences with literature and a wealth of research has documented how the nature of the classroom interpretive community (Fish, 1980), of which the teacher is the most influential member, influences children's and adolescents' responses to and understanding of literature.

We also need to continue to explore how students engage with and create texts with nontraditional designs (The New London Group, 1996). Outside of school many students interact with or access print and digital texts that embody Radical Change characteristics and metafictive devices, and that consequently offer multiple reading and writing pathways (e.g., MSN messaging, blogging, video and computer games). Students should also have opportunities in school to read, view, discuss, and create texts that reflect changing ways of communicating and representing in their world.

Appendix A:
List of Metafictive Devices

a) 'Overly obtrusive narrators who directly address readers and comment on their own narrations' (McCallum, 1996, p. 397) (Anstey, 2002; Georgakopoulou, 1991; Lodge; 1992; Nikolajeva & Scott, 2001; Stephens & Watson, 1994; Waugh, 1984);

b) polyphonic narratives or multiple narrators or character focalisers (McCallum, 1996; Stephens & Watson, 1994);

c) manifold or multiple narratives (Goldstone, 1998; McCallum, 1996; Stephens & Watson, 1994; Trites, 1994; Waugh, 1984) or multistranded narratives (i.e. 'two or more interconnected narrative strands differentiated by shifts in temporal and spatial relationships, and/or shifts in narrative point of view' McCallum, 1996, p. 406);

d) narrative framing devices (e.g., stories within stories, 'Chinese-box structures,' and 'characters reading about their own fictional lives ... self-consuming worlds or mutually contradictory situations ... a nesting of narrators' Waugh, 1984, p. 22 & 30);

e) disruptions of traditional time and space relationships in the narrative(s) (Georgakopoulou, 1991; Goldstone, 1998; Lodge, 1992; McCallum, 1996; Stephens & Watson, 1994; Waugh, 1984);

f) nonlinear and nonsequential plots including narrative discontinuities (Goldstone, 1998; McCallum, 1996; Stephens & Watson, 1994; Waugh, 1984);

g) intertextuality (Anstey, 2002; McCallum, 1996; Nikolajeva & Scott, 2001; Waugh, 1984);

h) 'parodic appropriations of other texts, genres and discourses' (Stephens & Watson, 1994, p. 44) (Lodge, 1992; McCallum, 1996; Waugh, 1984);

i) typographic experimentation (McCallum, 1996; Stephens & Watson, 1994; Waugh, 1984);

j) 'mixing of genres, discourse styles, modes of narration and speech representation' (McCallum, 1996, p. 397), including 'people prose' (Goldstone, 1998; Stephens & Watson, 1994; Waugh, 1984);

k) 'situations where characters and narrators change places, or shift from one plane of being to another' (Stephens & Watson, 1994, p. 44);

l) 'a pastiche of illustrative styles' (Anstey, 2002, p. 447) or literary pastiche (Waugh, 1984);

m) 'new and unusual design and layout, which challenge the reader's perception of how to read a book' (Anstey, 2002, p. 447);

n) excess (i.e. 'testing limits – linguistic, literary, social, conceptual, ethical, narrative' Lewis, 1990, p. 144);

o) illustrative framing, including mise-en-abyme (i.e. 'a text – visual or verbal – embedded within another text as its miniature replica' Nikolajeva & Scott, 2001, p. 226);

p) description of the creative process making readers 'conscious of the literary and artistic devices used in the story's creation' (Goldstone, 1998, p. 50) (Georgakopoulou, 1991; McCallum, 1996; Waugh, 1984);

q) 'indeterminacy in written or illustrative text, plot, character or setting' (Anstey, 2002, p. 447) (Goldstone, 1998; Lewis, 1990; McCallum, 1996); and

r) 'availability of multiple readings and meanings for a variety of audiences' (Anstey, 2002, p. 447) (McCallum, 1996; Nikolajeva & Scott, 2001; Stephens & Watson, 1994).

Appendix B:
Sample of Picturebooks That Exhibit Radical Change Characteristics and/or Metafictive Devices

Banks, K. (1998). *And if the moon could talk*. New York: Farrar, Straus & Giroux.

Banyai, I. (1995). *Re-zoom*. New York: Puffin Books.

Banyai, I. (1995). *Zoom*. New York: Puffin Books.

Brett, J. (1990). *Berlioz the bear*. New York: Putnam.

Brett, J. (1992). *Trouble with trolls*. New York: Scholastic.

Brett, J. (2002). *Who's that knocking on Christmas Eve?* New York: G.P. Putnam's Sons.

Browne, A. (1979). *Bear hunt*. London: Hamish Hamilton.

Browne, A. (1986). *The piggybook*. New York: Knopf.

Browne, A. (1990). *The tunnel*. New York: Knopf.

Browne, A. (1997). *Willy the dreamer*. Cambridge, MA: Candlewick Press.

Browne, A. (1998). *Voices in the park*. London: Picture Corgi Books.

Browne, A. (2004). *Into the forest*. Cambridge, MA: Candlewick Press.

Burningham, J. (1977). *Come away from the water, Shirley*. New York: Harper.

Burningham, J. (1978). *Time to get out of the bath, Shirley*. New York: Harper.

Burningham, J. (1984). *Granpa*. London: Jonathan Cape.

Bunting, E. (1991). *Fly away home*. New York: Clarion Books.

Bunting, E. (1994). *Smoky night*. San Diego: Harcourt Brace.

Cannon, J. (1993). *Stellaluna*. San Diego: Harcourt Brace.

Cecil, R. (2004). *One dark and stormy night*. New York: Henry Holt and Company.

Child, L. (2000). *Beware of the storybook wolves*. New York: Scholastic.

Child, L. (2002). *Who's afraid of the big bad book?* New York: Hyperion.

Cole, J. (1993). *The Magic School Bus in the solar system*. Richmond Hill, ON: Scholastic Canada.

Coy, J. (2003). *Two old potatoes and me*. New York: Knopf.

Crew, G. (2003). *The viewer*. Vancouver, BC: Simply Read Books.

De Brunhoff, L. (2003). *Babar's museum of art*. New York: Harry N Abrams.

Duke, K. (1992). *Aunt Isabel tells a good one*. New York: Puffin Books.

Duke, K. (1996). *Aunt Isabel makes trouble*. New York: Puffin Books.

French, J. (2002). *Diary of a wombat*. Toronto: HarperCollins.

Gaiman, N. (1997). *The day I swapped my dad for two goldfish*. Clarkson, GA: White Wolf Publishing.

Gaiman, N. (2003). *There were wolves in the walls*. New York: HarperCollins.

Gilman, P. (1992). *Something from nothing*. Richmond Hill, ON: Scholastic Canada.

Goble, P. (1990). *Iktomi and the ducks: A Plains Indian story*. New York: Orchard Books.

Gosling, G. (2003). *The top secret files of Mother Goose*. Vancouver, BC: Walrus Books.

Gravett, E. (2005). *Wolves*. London: Macmillan.

Gravett, E. (2006). *Meerkat mail*. London: Macmillan.

Grey, M. (2006). *The adventures of the dish and the spoon*. New York: Knopf.

Harrison, T. (1997). *Don't dig so deep, Nicholas!* Toronto: Owl Books.

Hebert, M. F. (2005). *Where in the world*. Montreal: Smith, Bonappetit & Son.

Henkes, K. (1996). *Lilly's purple plastic purse*. New York: Greenwillow.

Heo, Y. (1994). *One afternoon*. New York: Orchard Books.

Hodges, M. (1984). *St. George and the dragon*. New York: Little, Brown.

Hutchins, P. (1969). *Rosie's walk*. London: Bodley Head Press.

Jackson, S. (1998). *The old woman and the wave*. New York: DK.

Jeffers, O. (2006). *The incredible book eating boy*. London: HarperCollins.

Jonas, A. (1983). *Round trip*. New York: Greenwillow Books.

Joyce, W. (1990). *A day with Wilbur Robinson*. New York: HarperCollins.

Keller, L. (2003). *Arnie the doughnut*. New York: Henry Holt and Company.

Kitamura, S. (1997). *Lily takes a walk*. London: Happy Cat Books.

Lehman, B. (2004). *The red book*. New York: Houghton Mifflin.

Lendler, I., & Martin, W. (2005). *An undone fairy tale*. New York: Simon & Schuster.

Lorbiecki, M. (1998). *Sister Anne's hands*. New York: Dial Books.

Lyon, G. (1996). *A day at damp camp*. New York: Orchard Books.

Macaulay, D. (1990). *Black and white*. Boston: Houghton Mifflin.

Macaulay, D. (1995). *Shortcut*. Boston: Houghton Mifflin.

Marsden, J. (2003). *The rabbits*. Vancouver, BC: Simply Read Books.

Martin, J. B. (1998). *Snowflake Bentley*. New York: Scholastic.

McGovern, A. (1997). *The lady in the box*. New York: Turtle Books.

Meddaugh. S. (1992). *Martha speaks*. Boston: Houghton Mifflin.

Meddaugh, S. (1996). *Martha blah blah*. Boston: Houghton Mifflin.

O'Malley, K. (2006). *Once upon a cool motorcycle dude*. New York: Walker & Company.

Petach, H. (1995). *Goldilocks and the three hares*. New York: Putnam & Grosset.

Priceman, M. (1999). *Emeline at the circus*. New York: Knopf.

Raschka, C. (1992). *Charlie Parker played be bop*. New York: Orchard Books.

Raschka, C. (1993). *Yo! Yes?* New York: Orchard Books.

Rathmann, P. (1995). *Officer Buckle and Gloria*. New York: Putnam.

Scieszka, J. (1992). *The Stinky Cheese Man and other fairly stupid tales*. New York: Viking.

Sis, P. (1996). *Starry messenger: Galileo Galilei*. New York: Farrar, Straus & Giroux.

Sis, P. (2000). *Madlenka*. New York: Farrar, Straus & Giroux.

Sis, P. (2002). *Madlenka's dog*. New York: Farrar, Straus & Giroux.

Sis, P. (2003). *The tree of life*. Toronto: Groundwood Books.

Stevens, J., & Stevens Crummel, S. (2001). *And the dish ran away with the spoon*. New York: Harcourt.

Stevenson, J. (2004). *No laughing, no smiling, no giggling*. New York: Frances Foster Books.

Tan, S. (2003). *The red tree*. Vancouver, BC: Simply Read Books.

Tan, S. (2004). *The lost thing*. Vancouver, BC: Simply Read Books.

Teague, M. (2002). *Dear Mrs. LaRue: Letters from obedience school*. New York: Scholastic.

Teague, M. (2004). *Detective La Rue: Letters from the investigation*. New York: Scholastic.

Van Allsburg, C. (1995). *Bad day at Riverbend*. Boston: Houghton Mifflin.

Vere, E. (2006). *The get away*. New York: Puffin Books.

Whatley, B. (2001). *Wait! No paint!* New York: HarperCollins.

Wiesner, D. (1991). *Tuesday*. New York: Clarion Books.

Wiesner, D. (2001). *The three pigs*. New York: Clarion Books.

Wiesner, D. (2006). *Flotsam*. New York: Clarion Books.

Willems, M. (2003). *Don't let the pigeon drive the bus!* New York: Hyperion.

Willems, M. (2004a). *Knuffle Bunny: A cautionary tale*. New York: Hyperion.

Willems, M. (2004b). *The pigeon finds a hot dog!* New York: Hyperion.

Willems, M. (2006). *Don't let the pigeon stay up late!* New York: Hyperion.

Willems, M. (2007). *Knuffle Bunny too: A case of mistaken identity*. New York: Hyperion.

Wong, J., & Roberts, D. (2007). *The dumpster diver*. Cambridge, MA: Candlewick Press.

Appendix C:
Picturebook and Novel Annotations

Picturebooks

Banyai, I. (1995). *Re-zoom*. New York: Puffin Books.
Banyai, I. (1995). *Zoom*. New York: Puffin Books.
  In Banyai's wordless picturebooks, each page is part of the next succeeding
  scene. Black verso pages contribute to the visual effect of an imaginary
  camera pulling back from each scene. Both books deal with place, time,
  and perspective, and have philosophical messages.
Bateman, R. (1998). *Safari*. Toronto: Penguin Studio.
  The book features Bateman's paintings of African animals, informational
  text boxes about each creature, and narratives about Bateman's encounters
  with several of the animals.
Browne, A. (1997). *Willy the dreamer*. Cambridge, MA: Candlewick Press.
  Willy, a zoomorphic character, dreams of many things including fame,
  adventure, heroism, destitution, the past, and the future. The book is filled
  with visual intertextualities.
Browne, A. (1998). *Voices in the park*. London: Picture Corgi Books.
  The book is organized into four voices. Each zoomorphic character tells his
  or her version of the events that occurred in a park one day when the four
  characters met.
Child, L. (2000). *Beware of the storybook wolves*. New York: Scholastic.
  When Herb's mother neglects to take the bedtime storybook out of his
  room one night, two wolves leave their stories and threaten to devour him.
  Herb seeks assistance from other storybook characters to deal with the
  long-toothed visitors.
Child, L. (2002). *Who's afraid of the big bad book?* New York: Hyperion.
  One night Herb falls asleep with a book of fairy tales on his chest. When
  he awakens, Herb discovers that he has fallen into the book. Herb encoun-

ters many disgruntled storybook characters because he has tampered with the book, defaced characters, and removed or altered various artefacts from their stories.

Demi. (1990). *The empty pot*. New York: Henry Holt.
In this Chinese folktale, an Emperor announces that the next heir to the throne will be the child who grows the best flowers from the seeds that he distributes to the children. Ping is greatly disappointed when his seed does not sprout and he must go to the Emperor with an empty pot.

Gilman, P. (1992). *Something from nothing*. Richmond Hill, ON: Scholastic Canada.
An adaptation of a traditional Jewish tale, the book tells the story of Joseph's growth as he wears out the items his grandfather makes for him. A second parallel narrative, told entirely through illustrations, tells the story of the mice who live under the floorboards of the grandfather's house.

Lyon, G. (1996). *A day at damp camp*. New York: Orchard Books.
Although the narrative is told mainly through the illustrations, twenty-seven pairs of rhyming words assist in conveying the story of a summer camp adventure and the developing friendship of two girls. The double-page spreads with text have six words and three rectangles nested inside of one another.

Macaulay, D. (1987). *Why the chicken crossed the road*. Boston: Houghton Mifflin.
In this cause and effect story, readers learn why the chicken crossed the road. Macaulay's circuitous answer to an old joke includes multiple narratives, characters, and intratextualities.

Macaulay, D. (1990). *Black and white*. Boston: Houghton Mifflin.
Four parallel yet synergistic stories are told in a unique manner. Each double-page spread is divided into four sections so that the four narratives about trains, cows, parents, children, a dog, and a thief unfold simultaneously.

Macaulay, D. (1995). *Shortcut*. Boston: Houghton Mifflin.
In nine chapters and an epilogue, Macaulay relates the story of Albert, the melon farmer, and June, his horse. The story details the consequences of the actions of June and Albert on their weekly trip to the market.

Martin, J.B. (1998). *Snowflake Bentley*. Boston: Houghton Mifflin.
A biography of William Bentley, a self-taught scientist who wanted to capture the beauty of snowflakes, that tells how he learned to photograph individual snowflakes in order to study their intricate and unique formations.

Scieszka, J. (1989). *The true story of the three little pigs*. New York. Scholastic.
A. Wolf narrates his version of the traditional tale, and explains how the

events that unfolded were due to a 'misunderstanding.' Indeed, he was framed!

Scieszka, J. (1992). *The Stinky Cheese Man and other fairly stupid tales*. New York: Viking.

Most conventions associated with the publisher's peritext are violated in this collection of fractured fairy tales.

Sis, P. (1996). *Starry messenger: Galileo Galilei*. New York: Farrar, Straus & Giroux.

This book details the life of Galileo. The text is augmented by handwritten messages taken from Galileo's own works and other primary documents. Detailed and sophisticated illustrations provide further layers of information.

Wiesner, D. (1991). *Tuesday*. New York: Clarion Books.

Wiesner's wordless picturebook portrays the adventures of a group of frogs that becomes airborne when their lily pads mysteriously become miniature flying carpets.

Wiesner, D. (2001). *The three pigs*. New York: Clarion Books.

After the three pigs exit their original tale and fly on a storyboard airplane, they enter other selections from literature and alter those stories as well. In the end, the pigs reconstruct the ending to their own story.

Novels

Creech, S. (1996). *Walk two moons*. New York: HarperCollins.

Sal learns much about herself and her family during a road trip with her eccentric and loving grandparents. On their journey Sal tells her grandparents stories about her friend, Phoebe. Beneath these narratives is Sal's own story. This realistic and multilayered novel contains stories within stories, time switches, and colourful characters.

Di Camillo, K. (2003). *The tale of Despereaux*. Cambridge, MA: Candlewick Press.

The first of four books in the novel tells the story of Despereaux Tilling, a mouse. His love for Princess Pea causes him to be banished to the rat-filled dungeon. The second book is about Roscuro, a rat who loves light and soup. The third book is about a peasant girl named Miggery Sow, and the fourth book returns to the dungeon and connects the lives of the book's characters.

Fleischman, S. (1997). *Seedfolks*. New York: HarperTrophy.

A girl clears a small space in a vacant and garbage-filled lot and plants some bean seeds. Others follow her lead and the resulting neighbourhood

garden transforms a group of strangers. Thirteen very different voices tell
their stories of how the garden affected them and others in the neighbourhood.

Konigsburg, E.L. (1996). *The view from Saturday*. New York: Atheneum.
A teacher invites four precocious sixth-grade students to form a team to
compete in the school's academic bowl. Ethan, Julian, Nadia, and Noah
become the 'Souls.' Each character's individual story is told as the Souls
prepare for and participate in competitions.

Sachar, L. (1998). *Holes*. New York: Farrar, Straus & Giroux.
In this multilayered novel, Stanley Yelnats is unjustly sent to Camp Green
Lake. The warden makes the boys at the detention centre dig a five-feet-
wide and five-feet-deep hole each day. A series of events results in
Stanley's eventual release from Camp Green Lake and from the curse that
has plagued generations of the Yelnats family.

Van Draanen, P. (2001). *Flipped*. New York: Alfred A. Knopf.
Bryce and Julianna each tell their story in alternating chapters in this
romantic comedy of errors. The plot contains a series of missed opportunities, misunderstandings, and misinterpretations. The two main characters
learn much about themselves and others through their experiences.

Appendix D:
Favourite Picturebooks of 5A Students[1]

Title	# of Students		Reasons		
	F	M		F	M
Shortcut	01	01	1. humorous	01	00
			2. element of surprise	01	00
			3. intratextual connections	00	01
			4. overall structure	00	01
			5. multiple stories	00	00
			6. reader interactivity required to make connections among stories	00	00
Why the Chicken Crossed the Road	02	00	1. intratextual connections	02	00
			2. story structure	01	00
			3. reworking of familiar concept	01	00
			4. illustrations – content	01	00
			5. liked characters	00	00
Black and White	01	01	1. puzzle nature of the book	01	00
			2. multiple stories – intratextual nature of book	01	01
			3. flexibility of format – read many ways	01	00
			4. illustration style	01	00
			5. overall format and structure	00	01
			6. liked a particular story	00	00
Voices in the Park	02	01	1. intertextual connections with Browne's other books	01	00
			2. overall structure and format	01	00
			3. illustrations – content, details	01	01
			4. fonts – significance	01	00
			5. story content/messages	00	01
			6. other intertextual connections	00	00
			7. intratextual connection of hats	00	00

Title	# of Students		Reasons		
	F	M		F	M
The Starry Messenger	03	00	1. gained knowledge or information	03	00
			2. synergy between text and illustrations	01	00
			3. illustrations – content	02	00
			4. overall format	01	00
			5. relate to previous experiences	01	00
Re-zoom	00	04	1. overall format and structure	00	04
			2. novel or unique	00	01
			3. flexibility of format – read backwards	00	01
			4. intratextual nature (book within a book)	00	01
			5. black pages	00	00
			6. indeterminacy	00	00
			7. detail of illustration	00	02
Zoom	02	02	1. overall structure – zooming	02	02
			2. novel or unique	01	02
			3. flexibility of format – read backwards	01	01
			4. intratextual nature (book within a book)	00	00
			5. black pages	00	00
			6. indeterminacy	01	00
			7. detail of illustration	00	00
The Three Pigs	03	06	1. illustration style	03	03
			2. synergy between text and illustrations	01	01
			3. reworking of familiar story (unique version)	01	05
			4. characters interact with one other (characters leave their stories)	01	05
			5. multiple stories – stories within stories	01	01
			6. contradiction between text and illustrations	01	04
			7. multiple visual perspectives	01	01
			8. humorous	01	03
			9. looking for intratextual connections	00	00
			10. characters interact with reader	01	01
			11. intertextual nature	00	00
			12. typographic elements	00	00
			13. language forms	00	00
			14. construct story in front of reader	00	01

Title	# of Students		Reasons	F	M
	F	M			
The Stinky Cheese Man	09	05	1. humorous	07	04
			2. reworking of familiar story – fractured nature of story	07	04
			3. relate to previous experiences (familiarity)	03	00
			4. multiple stories	03	00
			5. typographical elements	01	01
			6. characters interacting with the reader	03	02
			7. fondness for particular characters/stories	02	01
			8. peritextual information	04	01
			9. intertextual connections	01	01
			10. style of illustrations	04	00
			11. construct story in front of readers	01	00
			12. characters interact with each other	01	03
			13. interruptions and disruptions	04	00
			14. intratextualities	00	01
			15. format	00	00

[1]5 students (4 girls and 1 boy) selected 1 title, 8 students (3 girls and 5 boys) selected 2 titles, 6 students (3 girls and 3 boys) selected 3 titles, and 1 girl selected 4 titles.

Appendix E:
Favourite Picturebooks of 5B Students[1]

	# of Students				
Title	F	M	Reasons	F	M
Zoom	00	00	1. overall structure – zooming	00	00
			2. novel or unique	00	00
			3. flexibility of format – read backwards	00	00
			4. intratextual nature (book within a book)	00	00
			5. black pages	00	00
			6. indeterminacy	00	00
			7. detail of illustration	00	00
Why the Chicken Crossed the Road	00	01	1. intratextual connections	00	00
			2. story structure	00	01
			3. reworking of familiar concept	00	00
			4. illustrations – content	00	00
			5. liked characters	00	01
Beware of the Storybook Wolves	00	00	1. intertextual nature	00	00
			2. characters interacting with one another	00	00
			3. humorous	00	00
			4. illustration style	00	00
			5. synergy between text and illustrations	00	00
Re-zoom	00	02	1. overall format and structure	00	02
			2. novel or unique	00	00
			3. flexibility of format – read backwards	00	01
			4. intratextual nature (book within a book)	00	01
			5. black pages	00	00
			6. indeterminacy	00	00
			7. detail of illustration	00	00

Title	# of Students		Reasons		
	F	M		F	M
Shortcut	01	01	1. humorous	00	00
			2. element of surprise	00	00
			3. intratextual connections	00	01
			4. overall structure	00	00
			5. multiple stories	01	01
			6. reader interactivity required to make connections among stories	01	01
Voices in the Park	03	02	1. intertextual connections with Browne's other books	00	00
			2. overall structure and format	03	01
			3. illustrations – content, details	02	02
			4. fonts – significance	01	01
			5. story content/messages	00	00
			6. other intertextual connections	01	01
			7. intratextual connection of hats	00	00
Black and White	03	02	1. puzzle nature of the book	00	00
			2. multiple stories – intratextual nature of book	01	02
			3. flexibility of format – read many ways	02	00
			4. illustration style	01	01
			5. overall format and structure	02	01
			6. liked a particular story	00	01
The Stinky Cheese Man	02	04	1. humorous	01	03
			2. reworking of familiar story – fractured nature of story	02	03
			3. relate to previous experiences (familiarity)	00	00
			4. multiple stories	01	01
			5. typographical elements	00	00
			6. characters interacting with the reader	00	01
			7. fondness for particular characters/stories	00	01
			8. peritextual information	00	01
			9. intertextual connections	02	01
			10. style of illustrations	04	02
			11. construct story in front of readers	00	00
			12. characters interact with each other	00	00
			13. interruptions and disruptions	00	01
			14. intratextualities	00	00
			15. format	00	00

Title	# of Students F	M	Reasons	F	M
Who's Afraid of the Big Bad Book?	06	04	1. intertextual nature	02	01
			2. characters interacting with one another	02	01
			3. illustration style	06	03
			4. gatefold	01	01
			5. pages upside down, hole in book	00	02
			6. visual layering	01	00
			7. typographic elements	02	01
			8. fractured nature of story and character depiction (Goldilocks not sweet)	03	00
			9. mise-en-abyme	01	00
			10. humorous	01	00
			11. metafictive nature of book	02	00
			12. synergy between text and illustrations	01	00
			13. reader interactivity	00	00
The Three Pigs	05	07	1. illustration style	04	03
			2. synergy between text and illustrations	03	02
			3. reworking of familiar story (unique version)	03	05
			4. characters interact with one other (characters leave their stories)	05	04
			5. multiple stories – stories within stories	00	02
			6. contradiction between text and illustrations	02	01
			7. multiple visual perspectives	00	00
			8. humorous	02	04
			9. looking for intratextual connections	00	00
			10. characters interact with reader	01	01
			11. intertextual nature	01	03
			12. typographic elements	02	01
			13. language forms	00	00
			14. construct story in front of reader	00	00

[1]15 children (5 girls and 10 boys) identified 2 favourites, 3 children (2 girls and 1 boy) identified 3 favourites, 1 girl identified 4 favourites.

Appendix F:
Favourite Picturebooks of 5C Students[1]

Title	# of Students		Reasons		
	F	M		F	M
Why the Chicken Crossed the Road	00	00	1. intratextual connections	00	00
			2. story structure	00	00
			3. reworking of familiar concept	00	00
			4. illustrations – content	00	00
			5. liked characters	00	00
Re-zoom	01	00	1. overall format and structure	01	00
			2. novel or unique	01	00
			3. flexibility of format – read backwards	00	00
			4. intratextual nature (book within a book)	00	00
			5. black pages	00	00
			6. indeterminacy	00	00
			7. detail of illustration	00	00
Zoom	00	01	1. overall structure – zooming	00	01
			2. novel or unique	00	00
			3. flexibility of format – read backwards	00	01
			4. intratextual nature (book within a book)	00	00
			5. black pages	00	00
			6. indeterminacy	00	00
			7. detail of illustration	00	00
Shortcut	01	00	1. humorous	01	00
			2. element of surprise	00	00
			3. intratextual connections	01	00
			4. overall structure	00	00
			5. multiple stories	00	01
			6. reader interactivity required to make connections among stories	01	00

Title	# of Students		Reasons	F	M
	F	M			
Voices in the Park	00	02	1. intertextual connections with Browne's other books	00	00
			2. overall structure and format	00	02
			3. illustrations – content, details	00	01
			4. fonts – significance	00	01
			5. story content/messages	00	00
			6. other intertextual connections	00	01
			7. intratextual connection of hats	00	01
Black and White	00	03	1. puzzle nature of the book	00	00
			2. multiple stories – intratextual nature of book	00	02
			3. flexibility of format – read many ways	00	01
			4. illustration style	00	01
			5. overall format and structure	00	02
			6. liked a particular story	00	00
Beware of the Storybook Wolves	04	01	1. intertextual nature	03	00
			2. characters interacting with one another	00	01
			3. humorous	02	01
			4. illustration style	04	00
			5. synergy between text and illustrations	00	00
The Stinky Cheese Man	00	09	1. humorous	00	08
			2. reworking of familiar story – fractured nature of story	00	09
			3. relate to previous experiences (familiarity)	00	00
			4. multiple stories	00	03
			5. typographical elements	00	00
			6. characters interacting with the reader	00	00
			7. fondness for particular characters/stories	00	01
			8. peritextual information	00	01
			9. intertextual connections	00	02
			10. style of illustrations	00	03
			11. construct story in front of readers	00	00
			12. characters interact with each other	00	00
			13. interruptions and disruptions	00	01
			14. intratextualities	00	00
			15. format	00	01

| Title | # of Students | | Reasons | F | M |
	F	M			
The Three Pigs	02	08	1. illustration style	01	04
			2. synergy between text and illustrations	00	03
			3. reworking of familiar story (unique version)	01	06
			4. characters interact with one other (characters leave their stories)	01	06
			5. multiple stories – stories within stories	00	02
			6. contradiction between text and illustrations	00	01
			7. multiple visual perspectives	01	00
			8. humorous	00	02
			9. looking for intratextual connections	00	00
			10. characters interact with reader	00	00
			11. intertextual nature	00	00
			12. typographic elements	00	02
			13. language forms	01	00
			14. construct story in front of reader	01	02
Who's Afraid of the Big Bad Book?	06	04	1. intertextual nature	03	00
			2. characters interacting with one another	00	01
			3. illustration style	06	01
			4. gatefold	01	02
			5. pages upside down, hole in book	02	02
			6. visual layering	00	00
			7. typographic elements	00	02
			8. fractured nature of story and character depiction (Goldilocks not sweet)	03	00
			9. mise-en-abyme	01	00
			10. humorous	03	01
			11. metafictive nature of book	02	00
			12. synergy between text and illustrations	01	01
			13. reader interactivity	00	01

[1] 2 boys selected 1 favourite, 13 children (7 girls and 6 boys) selected 2 favourites, 3 boys selected 3 favourites, 1 boy selected 5 favourites.

Appendix G:
Picturebooks 5A Students Found Challenging[1]

Title	# of Students		Reasons		
	F	M		F	M
Re-zoom	01	00	1. illustrations – content – gaps	01	00
			2. uncertain of significance of black pages	00	00
Shortcut	01	00	1. plot trajectory	01	00
			2. did not notice all of the visual connections	00	00
			3. chapter format	00	00
			4. reliance on the visual connections	00	00
The Three Pigs	00	01	1. surprised by version of story	00	01
The Stinky Cheese Man	01	01	1. nonlinearity of overall structure	01	01
			2. fractured nature of stories	01	00
			3. interruptions and disruptions	00	01
			4. typographical issues	00	00
			5. multiple stories	00	00
Zoom	02	00	1. illustrations – content – gaps	01	00
			2. overall structure of zooming out	01	00
The Starry Messenger	04	04	1. historical content in text	02	02
			2. handwriting font	02	02
			3. visual layering of information	01	00
			4. lack of background knowledge	01	01
			5. changing setting in book	01	00
			6. overall structure	01	00
			7. content of illustrations	01	01
			8. confusing	00	01
			9. gaps between two texts (narrative and script)	00	01

Title	# of Students		Reasons		
	F	M		F	M
Black and White	07	05	1. overall structure and format	07	05
			2. making intratextual connections between the stories	06	04
			3. illustrations – content puzzling	01	00
			4. not engaging	00	00

[1]13 students (6 girls and 7 boys) selected 1 title and 7 students (5 girls and 2 boys) selected 2 titles.

Appendix H:
Picture Books 5B Students Found Challenging[1]

Title	# of Students		Reasons		
	F	M		F	M
Re-zoom	00	02	1. illustrations – content – gaps	00	02
			2. uncertain of significance of black pages	00	01
Shortcut	00	01	1. plot trajectory	01	00
			2. did not notice all of the visual connections	00	01
			3. chapter format	00	00
			4. reliance on the visual connections	00	00
Who's Afraid of the Big Bad Book?	01	00	1. multiple text on pages – what to read first	01	00
			2. upside down text	01	00
Black and White	02	05	1. overall structure and format	02	04
			2. making intratextual connections between the stories	02	04
			3. illustrations – content puzzling	00	00
			4. not engaging	01	00
Why the Chicken Crossed the Road	05	03	1. story structure	05	02
			2. numerous illustrations	01	01
			3. title and story content unconnected	01	01
			4. lack of familiarity with books with RC characteristics	01	01

[1] 19 students identified 1 title.

Appendix I:
Picturebooks 5C Students Found
Challenging[1]

Title	# of Students		Reasons		
	F	M		F	M
Shortcut	02	03	1. plot trajectory	01	02
			2. did not notice all of the visual connections	00	00
			3. chapter format	01	01
			4. reliance on the visual connections	02	01
The Stinky Cheese Man	02	00	1. nonlinearity of overall structure	00	00
			2. fractured nature of stories	01	00
			3. interruptions and disruptions	00	00
			4. typographical issues	02	00
			5. multiple stories	01	00
Why the Chicken Crossed the Road	03	01	1. story structure	03	01
			2. numerous illustrations	01	00
			3. title and story content unconnected	00	01
			4. lack of familiarity with books with RC characteristics	00	00
Black and White	03	09	1. overall structure and format	03	09
			2. making intratextual connections between the stories	00	06
			3. illustrations – content puzzling	00	00
			4. not engaging	00	00

[1] 14 students (4 girls and 10 boys) selected 1 title, 4 students (3 girls and 1 boy) selected 2 titles.

Appendix J:
Radical Change Characteristics in
Three Students' Stories/Books

Radical Change Characteristics	Eddie	Jenatine	Bert
Type 1 – Changing Forms and Formats			
a) **Graphics in new forms and formats** (Dresang, 1999, p. 82)			
• colour may be used symbolically to communicate meanings (colour may take the place of words)	X	X	X
• the design or placement of words on a page represents sounds or transmits meaning	X	X	X
• text is superimposed 'on a picture appearing simultaneously as both words and picture'		X	
b) **Words and pictures reaching new levels of synergy** (pp. 89–93)			
• words become pictures and pictures become words		X	
• synergy among varying illustrative styles or types of art		X	
c) **Nonlinear organization and format** (pp. 116–118, 233–234)			
• disruptions or interruptions in the story or stories	X	X	X
• not a linear beginning, middle and end	X	X	X
d) **Nonsequential organization and format** (pp. 116–118, 232–234)			
• one thing does not follow another in chronological, causal, or logical order (i.e. lack of consecutiveness or continuity)	X	X	X
e) **Multiple layers of meaning (multilayered reading experience)** (pp. 22, 116–118)			
• verbal layering of story – literary devices of time switches, and stories within stories	X	X	X
• synergy among multiple stories*		X	X
• visual layering of story		X	

Radical Change Characteristics (*continued*)	Eddie	Jenatine	Bert
f) Interactive formats (pp. 22–4, 114–16)			
• characters interacting with one another	X	X	X
• character(s) or narrator interact with reader	X	X	
• characters create story in front of reader	X		X
• character(s)/voice(s) comment on story, 'creating story around the story'	X	X	X
• readers must be attentive because of multiple stories, disruptions, intertextual connections	X	X	
• reader interactivity – hypertextual nature of text		X	
• readers must move back and forth between text and pictures		X	
• second narrative told entirely through illustrations		X	
• parallel stories with words		X	
• 'pattern of reading more than one set of words,' cartoon bubbles		X	

Type 2 – Changing Perspectives

	Eddie	Jenatine	Bert
a) Multiple perspectives, visual and verbal (pp. 126–130, 138–140)			
• multiple voices in one book	X	X	X
• multiple language forms used in book	X	X	X
• new perspective(s) on existing literature*	X		X
• multiple visual perspectives	X	X	

Type 3 – Changing Boundaries

	Eddie	Jenatine	Bert
a) Unresolved endings (pp. 232–233)		X	X

* Radical Change features that I added to Dresang's list.

Appendix K:
Overall Analysis of Grade 5 Students'
Stories

Radical Change Characteristics	5A		5B		5C	
	F/11	M/09	F/08	M/11	F/07	M/11

Type 1 – Changing Forms and Formats

a) Graphics in new forms and formats (Dresang, 1999, p. 82)

• colour may be used symbolically to communicate meanings (colour may take the place of words)	06	02	05	02	02	00
• the design or placement of words on a page represents sounds or transmits meaning	11	09	08	10	07	11
• text is superimposed 'on a picture appearing simultaneously as both words and picture'	08	00	04	00	05	02

b) Words and pictures reaching new levels of synergy (pp. 89–93)

• words become pictures and pictures become words	00	00	00	00	00	00
• synergy among varying illustrative styles or types of art	02	01	00	00	01	00

c) Nonlinear organization and format (pp. 116–118, 233–234)

• disruptions or interruptions in the story or stories	11	06	05	07	05	05
• not a linear beginning, middle and end	11	06	02	04	05	02

d) Nonsequential organization and format (pp. 116–118, 232–234)

• one thing does not follow another in chronological, causal, or logical order (i.e. lack of consecutiveness or continuity)	11	06	02	02	03	02

Radical Change Characteristics (*continued*)	5A		5B		5C	
	F/11	M/09	F/08	M/11	F/07	M/11

Type 1 – Changing Forms and Formats (*continued*)

e) Multiple layers of meaning (multilayered reading experience) (pp. 22, 116–118)

	5A		5B		5C	
• verbal layering of story – literary devices of time switches, and stories within stories	08	06	04	04	04	04
• synergy among multiple stories*	06	04	03	00	02	00
• visual layering of story	05	01	01	01	02	00

f) Interactive formats (pp. 22–24, 114–116)

	5A		5B		5C	
• characters interacting with one another	07	03	02	03	02	04
• character(s) or narrator interact with reader	10	06	08	10	05	07
• characters create story in front of reader	05	03	02	01	00	01
• character(s)/voice(s) comment on story, 'creating story around the story'	06	04	06	03	01	03
• readers must be attentive because of multiple stories and/or disruptions and/or intertextual connections	11	06	01	11	05	10
• reader interactivity – hypertextual nature of text	07	01	01	00	04	00
• readers must move back and forth between text and pictures	07	00	00	00	01	00
• second narrative told entirely through illustrations	00	00	01	00	01	00
• parallel stories with words	07	04	01	00	01	00
• 'pattern of reading more than one set of words,' cartoon bubbles	07	00	02	01	04	02

Type 2 – Changing Perspectives

a) Multiple perspectives, visual and verbal (pp. 126–130, 138–140)

	5A		5B		5C	
• multiple voices in one book	08	02	02	02	03	03
• multiple language forms used in book	03	08	06	07	04	04
• new perspective(s) on existing literature*	01	06	04	01	04	02
• multiple visual perspectives	04	03	01	00	02	01

Type 3 – Changing Boundaries

a) Unresolved endings (pp. 232–233)

	5A		5B		5C	
	05	04	02	02	01	00

*Radical Change features that I added to Dresang's list.

References

Agosto, D. (1999). One and inseparable: Interdependent storytelling in picture storybooks. *Children's Literature in Education, 30* (4), 267–80.

Allen, G. (2000). *Intertextuality*. New York: Routledge.

Allington, R. (2001). *What really matters for struggling readers: Designing research-based programs*. New York: Addison-Wesley.

Allington, R. (2002). What I've learned about effective reading instruction from a decade of studying exemplary elementary classroom teachers. *Phi Delta Kappan, 83* (10), 740–7.

Almasi, J. (1995). The nature of fourth-graders' sociocognitive conflicts in peer-led and teacher-led discussions of literature. *Reading Research Quarterly, 30* (3), 314–51.

Almasi, J., O'Flahavan, J., & Arya, P. (2001). A comparative analysis of student and teacher development in more or less proficient discussions of literature. *Reading Research Quarterly, 36* (2), 96–120.

Almasi, J., Garas, K., Cho, H., Ma, W., Shanahan, L., & Augustino, A. (2004, December). The impact of peer discussion on social, cognitive, and affective growth in literacy. Paper presented at the 54th annual meeting of the National Reading Conference, San Antonio, TX.

Anfara, V., Brown, K., & Mangione, T. (2002). Qualitative analysis on stage: Making the research process more public. *Educational Researcher, 31* (7), 28–38.

Anstey, M. (2002). 'It's not all black and white': Postmodern picture books and new literacies. *Journal of Adolescent and Adult Literacy, 45* (6), 444–57.

Arizpe, E., & Styles, M. (2003). *Children reading pictures: Interpreting visual texts*. London: RoutledgeFalmer.

Bader, B. (1976). *American picturebooks from* Noah's ark *to* The beast within. New York: Macmillan.

Bakhtin, M.M. (1981). *The dialogic imagination*. Austin: University of Texas Press.

Barnes, D. (1976). *From communication to curriculum* (1st ed.). Harmondsworth, England: Penguin.

Barnes, D. (1992). *From communication to curriculum* (2nd ed.). Portsmouth, NH: Boynton/Cook Publishers.

Barone, D. (1990). The written responses of young children: Beyond comprehension to story understanding. *The New Advocate, 3* (1), 49–56.

Barrentine, S. J. (1996). Engaging with reading through interactive read-alouds. *The Reading Teacher, 50* (1), 36–43.

Barthes, R. (1970, trans. 1974). *S/Z: An essay*. New York: Hill & Wang.

Barthes, R. (1975). *The pleasure of the text*. London: Jonathan Cape.

Barthes, R. (1977). *Image-music-text*. London: Fontana.

Barton, D. (2007). *An introduction to the ecology of unwritten language* (2nd ed.). Oxford: Blackwell.

Barton, D., & Hamilton, M. (2000). Literacy practices. In D. Barton, M. Hamilton, & R. Ivanic (Eds.), *Situated literacies: Reading and writing in context* (pp. 7–15). London: Routledge.

Battle, J. (1995). Collaborative story talk in a bilingual kindergarten. In N. Roser & M. Martinez (Eds.), *Book talk and beyond: Children and teachers respond to literature* (pp. 157–67). Newark, DE: International Reading Association.

Baumann, J., & Bergeron, B. (1993). Story mapping instruction using children's literature: Effects on first-graders' comprehension of central narrative elements. *Journal of Reading Behavior, 25,* 407–37.

Beach, R. (1993). *A teacher's introduction to reader-response theories*. Urbana, IL: National Council of Teachers of English.

Beach, R., Appleman, D., & Dorsey, S. (1990). Adolescents' use of intertextual links to understand literature. In R. Beach & S. Hynds (Eds.), *Developing discourse practices in adolescence and adulthood* (pp. 224–45). Norwood, NJ: Albex Publishing Corporation.

Berk, L., & Winsler, A. (1995). *Scaffolding children's learning: Vygotsky and early childhood education*. Washington, DC: National Association for the Education of Young Children.

Blair, H., & Sanford, K. (2004). Morphing literacy: Boys reshaping their school-based literacy practices. *Language Arts, 81* (6), 452–60.

Bloome, D., & Egan-Robertson, A. (1993). The social construction of intertextuality in classroom reading and writing lessons. *Reading Research Quarterly, 28* (4), 305–32.

British Columbia Ministry of Education. (2002a). *BC performance standards: Reading revised edition*. Victoria, BC: Author.

British Columbia Ministry of Education. (2002b). *BC performance standards: Writing revised edition*. Victoria, BC: Author.

Britton, J. (1968). Response to literature. In J. R. Squire (Ed.), *Response to literature: The Dartmouth seminar papers* (pp. 3–10). Champaign, IL: National Council of Teachers of English.

Cairney, T. (1990). Intertextuality: Infectious echoes from the past. *The Reading Teacher, 43* (7), 478–84.

Cairney, T. (1992). Fostering and building students' intertextual histories. *Language Arts, 69* (7), 502–7.

Caroff, S., & Moje, E. (1992/1993). A conversation with David Wiesner: 1992 Caldecott Medal winner. *The Reading Teacher, 46* (4), 284–9.

Cassady, J. (1998). Wordless picture books: No-risk tools for inclusive middle-age classrooms. *Journal of Adolescent & Adult Literacy, 41* (6), 428–33.

Coles, M., & Hall, C. (2001). Breaking the line: New literacies, postmodernism and the teaching of printed texts. *Reading: Literacy and Language, 35* (3), 111–14.

Colledge, M. (2005). Baby Bear or Mrs. Bear? Young English Bengali-speaking children's responses to narrative picture books at school. *Literacy, 39* (1), 24–30.

Columbia/Tri Star Studios. (2000). *Timecode*. Hollywood: Columbia/Tri Star Studios.

Commeyras, M., & Sumner, G. (1996). Literature discussions based on student-posed questions. *The Reading Teacher, 50* (3), 262–5.

Copenhaver, J. (2001). Running out of time: Rushed read-alouds in a primary classroom. *Language Arts, 79* (2), 148–58.

Coulthard, K. (2003). 'The words to say it': Young bilingual learners responding to visual texts. In E. Arizpe & M. Styles (Eds.), *Children reading pictures: Interpreting visual texts* (pp. 164–90). London: Routledge.

Crawford, P., & Hade, D. (2000). Inside the picture, outside the frame: Semiotics and the reading of wordless picture books. *Journal of Research in Childhood Education, 15* (1), 66–80.

Cuddon, J. A. (1999). *The Penguin dictionary of literary terms and literary theory* (4th ed.). New York: Penguin.

Culler, J. (1980). Literary competence. In J. Tompkins (Ed.), *Reader-response criticism: From formalism to post-structuralism* (pp. 101–17). Baltimore: Johns Hopkins University Press.

Dawes, L. (2001). Talking about language. In P. Goodwin (Ed.), *The articulate* classroom: *Talking and learning in the primary classroom* (pp. 125–32). London: David Fulton.

Day, K. S. (1996). The challenge of style in reading picturebooks. *Children's Literature in Education, 27* (3), 153–66.

Dentith, S. (2000). *Parody.* New York: Routledge.

Dewey, J. (1938). *Experience and education.* New York: Touchstone.

Dewey, J. (1966). *Democracy and education.* New York: First Press.

Disney Enterprises, Inc./Pixar Animation Studios. (2001). *Monsters, Inc.* Burbank: Disney Enterprises, Inc./Pixar Animation Studios.

Doonan, J. (1993). *Looking at pictures in picture books.* Stroud, Glos.: Thimble Press.

Doonan, J. (1999). Drawing out ideas: A second decade of the work of Anthony Browne. *The Lion and the Unicorn, 23* (1), 30–56.

Douglas Yellowlees, J. (2001). *The end of books – or the books without end? Reading interactive narratives.* Ann Arbor: University of Michigan Press.

Dresang, E. (1999). *Radical change: Books for youth in a digital age.* New York: The H. W. Wilson Company.

Dresang, E. (2005). Radical change. In K. Fisher, S. Erdelez, & L. McKechnie, L. (Eds.), *Theories of information behavior: A researcher's guide* (pp. 298–302). Medford, NJ: Information Today.

Duke, N., & Pearson, P.D. (2002). Effective practices for developing reading comprehension. In A.E. Farstrup & S.J. Samuels (Eds.), *What research has to say about reading instruction* (2nd ed., pp. 205–42). Newark, DE: International Reading Association.

Dyson, A.H. (2001). Introduction … and a warning. *The Elementary School Journal, 101* (4), 379–83.

Eeds, M., & Wells, M. (1989). Grand conversations: An exploration of meaning construction in literature response groups. *Research in the Teaching of English, 23* (1), 4–29.

Eisner, E. (1997). The promise and perils of alternative forms of data representation. *Educational Researcher, 26* (6), 4–10.

Ellis, D., & Preston, F. (1984). Enhancing beginning reading using wordless picture books in a cross-age tutoring program. *The Reading Teacher, 37* (8), 692–8.

Evans, K. (1996). Creating spaces for equity? The role of positioning in peer-led literature discussions. *Language Arts, 73* (3), 194–202.

Evans, K. (2002). Fifth-grade students'·perceptions of how they experience literature discussion groups. *Reading Research Quarterly, 37* (1), 46–69.

Fairclough, N. (1992). Intertextuality in critical discourse. *Linguistics and Education, 4,* 269–293.

Fish, S. (1980). Interpreting the Variorum. In J. Tompkins (Ed.), *Reader-response criticism: From formalism to post-structuralism* (pp. 164–84). Baltimore: Johns Hopkins University Press.

Fish, S. (1994). Is there a text in the class? In D. Richter (Ed.), *Falling into theory: Conflicting views on reading literature* (pp. 226–37). New York: St. Martin's Press.

Fisher, K., Erdelez, S., & McKechnie, L. (Eds.). (2005). *Theories of information behavior: A researcher's guide.* Medford, NJ: Information Today.

Flately, J., & Rutland, A. (1986). Using wordless picture books to teach linguistically/culturally different students. *The Reading Teacher, 40* (3), 276–81.

Galda, L., Ash, G., & Cullinan, B. (2000). Children's literature. In M. Kamil, P. Mosenthal, P. D. Pearson, & R. Barr (Eds.), *Handbook of reading research* (Vol. 3, pp. 361–79). Mahwah, NJ: Lawrence Erlbaum Associates.

Galda, L., & Cullinan, B. (2002). *Literature and the child* (5th ed.). Belmont, CA: Wadsworth/Thomson Learning.

Gardner, H. (1993). *Frames of mind: The theory in practice.* New York: Basic Books.

Gardner, H. (1995). Reflections on multiple intelligences: Myths and messages. *Phi Delta Kappan, 77* (3), 200–9.

Genette, G. (1982). *Palimpsestes.* Paris: Seuil.

Giarelli, J. (2001). The education of *Eros* and collateral learning in teacher education. In S. Rice (Ed.), *Philosophy of education society yearbook 2001,* (pp. 285–7). Champaign, IL: Philosophy of Education Society Publications.

Gitelman, H. (1990). Using wordless picture books with disabled readers. *The Reading Teacher, 43* (7), 525.

Glaser, B., & Straus, A. (1967). *The discovery of grounded theory: Strategies for qualitative research.* Chicago: Aldine.

Golden, J. (1990). *The narrative symbol in childhood literature: Explorations in the construction of text.* Berlin: Mouton.

Goldstone, B. (1998). Ordering the chaos: Teaching metafictive characteristics of children's books. *Journal of Children's Literature, 24* (2), 48–55.

Goldstone, B. (2001/2002). Whaz up with our books? Changing picture book codes and teaching implications. *The Reading Teacher, 55* (4), 362–70.

Graham, J. (1990). *Pictures on the page.* Sheffield, UK: The National Association for the Teaching of English.

Guralnik, D. (Ed.). (1976). *Webster's new world dictionary of the American language* (2nd ed.). New York: William Collins and World Publishing.

Guzzetti, B., Young, J., Gritsavage, M., Fyfe, L., & Hardenbrook, M. (2002). *Reading, writing, and talking gender in literacy learning.* Newark, DE: International Reading Association.

Halliday, M. (1969). Relevant models of language. *Educational Review*, 21 (3), 26–37.

Hardy, B. (1975). *Tellers and listeners: The narrative imagination*. Dover, NH: Longwood.

Hickman, J. (1981). A new perspective on response to literature: Research in an elementary setting. *Research in the Teaching of English, 15* (4), 343–54.

Hickman, J. (1983). Everything considered: Response to literature in an elementary school setting. *Journal of Research and Development in Education, 16* (3), 8–13.

Hickman, J. (1984). Research currents: Researching children's response to literature. *Language Arts, 61* (3), 278–84.

Holquist, M. (1990). *Dialogism: Bakhtin and his world*. New York: Routledge.

Hunt, P. (1991). *Criticisms, theory and children's literature*. Oxford: Blackwell.

Hutcheon, L. (1985). *A theory of parody: The teachings of twentieth-century art forms*. London: Methuen.

Hynds, S. (1992). Challenging questions in the teaching of literature. In J.A. Langer (Ed.), *Literature instruction: A focus on student response* (pp. 78–100). Urbana, IL: National Council of Teachers of English.

Iser, W. (1978). *The act of reading*. Baltimore: Johns Hopkins University Press.

Iser, W. (1980). The reading process: A phenomenological approach. In J. Tompkins (Ed.), *Reader-response criticism: From formalism to post-structuralism* (pp. 50–69). Baltimore: Johns Hopkins University Press.

Jewell, T., & Pratt, D. (1999). Literature discussions in the primary grades: Children's thoughtful discourse about books and what teachers can do to make it happen. *The Reading Teacher, 52* (8), 842–50.

Johnson, S. (2005). *Everything bad is good for you: How today's popular culture is actually making us smarter*. New York: Riverhead Books.

Johnston, P. (2004). *Choice words: How our language affects children's learning*. Portland, ME: Stenhouse Publishers.

Kauffman, G., Short, K., Crawford, K., Kahn, L., & Kaser, S. (1996). Examining the roles of teachers and students in literature circles across classroom contexts. In D. Leu, C. Kinzer, & K. Hinchman (Eds.), *Literacies for the 21st century: Forty-fifth yearbook of the National Reading Conference* (Vol. 45, pp. 373–84). Chicago: National Reading Conference.

Keep, C., McLaughlin, T., & Parmar, R. (2002, May 15). *Intertextuality*. Retrieved from http://www.iath.virginia.edu/elab/hfl0278.html.

Kiefer, B. (1993). Children's responses to picture books: A developmental perspective. In K. Holland, R. Hungerford, & S. Ernst (Eds.), *Journeying: Children responding to literature* (pp. 267–83). Portsmouth, NH: Heinemann.

Kiefer, B. (1995). *The potential of picturebooks: From visual literacy to aesthetic understanding*. Englewood Cliffs, NJ: Prentice-Hall.

Klein, M. (1977). *Talk in the language arts classroom*. Urbana, IL: National Council of Teachers of English.

Kress, G. (2003a). Interpretation or design: From the world told to the world shown. In M. Styles & E. Bearne (Eds.), *Art, narrative and childhood* (pp. 137-153). Stoke-on-Trent: Trentham Books.

Kress, G. (2003b). *Literacy in the new media age*. London: Routledge.

Kristeva, J. (1980). *Desire in language: A semiotic approach to literature and art*. New York: Columbia University Press.

Labbo, L. (1996). Beyond storytime: A sociopsychological perspective on young children's opportunities for literacy development during story extension time. *Journal of Literacy Research, 28* (3), 405–28.

Lancia, P. (1997). Literary borrowing: The effects of literature on children's writing. *The Reading Teacher, 50* (6), 470–5.

Lankshear, C., & Knobel, M. (2003). *New literacies: Changing knowledge and classroom learning*. Philadelphia: Open University Press.

Leal, D. (1993). The power of literary peer-group discussions: How children collaboratively negotiate meaning. *The Reading Teacher, 47* (2), 114–21.

Lewis, D. (1990). The constructedness of texts: Picture books and the metafictive. *Signal, 62*, 131–46.

Lewis, D. (2001). *Reading contemporary picture books: Picturing text*. New York: RoutledgeFalmer.

Lodge, D. (1992). *The art of fiction*. London: Penguin Books.

Lukens, R. (1999). *A critical handbook of children's literature* (6th ed.). New York: Addison-Wesley.

Macaulay, D. (1991). Caldecott acceptance speech. *Horn Book, 67* (4), 410–21.

Mackey, M. (1990). Metafiction for beginners: Allan Ahlberg's *Ten in a bed*. *Children's Literature in Education, 21* (3), 179–87.

Mackey, M. (2003). At play on the borders of the diegetic: Story boundaries and narrative interpretation. *Journal of Literacy Research, 35* (1), 591–632.

Maloch, B. (2002). Scaffolding student talk: One teacher's role in literature discussion groups. *Reading Research Quarterly, 37* (1), 94–112.

Maloch, B. (2004). One teacher's journey: Transitioning into literature discussion groups. *Language Arts, 81* (4), 312–22.

Many, J., & Wiseman, D. (1992). The effect of teaching approach on third-grade students' responses to literature. *Journal of Reading Behavior, 24* (3), 265–87.

McCabe, A. (1997). Cultural background and storytelling: A review and implications for schooling. *The Elementary School Journal, 97* (5), 453–73.

McCallum, R. (1996). Metafictions and experimental work. In P. Hunt (Ed.), *International companion encyclopedia of children's literature* (pp. 397–409). New York: Routledge.

McClay, J. (2000). 'Wait a second ...': Negotiating complex narratives in *Black and white*. *Children's Literature in Education, 31* (2), 91–106.

McGee, L. (1992). An exploration of meaning construction in first graders' grand conversations. In C. K. Kinzer & D. J. Leu (Eds.), *Literacy research, theory and practice: Views from many perspectives: Forty-first yearbook of the National Reading Conference* (pp. 177–86). Chicago: National Reading Conference.

McGillis, R. (1996). *The nimble reader: Literary theory and children's literature.* New York: Twayne.

McRobbie, C., & Tobin, K. (1997). A social constructivist perspective on learning environments. *International Journal of Science Education, 19* (2), 193–208.

Marantz, K. (1977). The picture book as art object: A call for balanced reviewing. *Wilson Library Bulletin, 52* (2), 148–51.

Marshall, J.D. (1987). The effects of writing on students' understanding of literary texts. *Research in the Teaching of English, 21* (1), 30–62.

Marshall, J. (2000). Research on response to literature. In M. Kamil, P. Mosenthal, P. D. Pearson, & R. Barr (Eds.), *Handbook of reading research* (Vol. 3, pp. 381–402). Mahwah, NJ: Lawrence Erlbaum Associates.

Martinez, M., & Roser, N. (2003). Children's responses to literature. In J. Flood, D. Lapp, J. Squire, & J. Jensen (Eds.) *Handbook of research on teaching the English language arts* (2nd ed., pp. 799–813). Mahwah, NJ: Lawrence Erlbaum Associates.

Meek, M. (1988). *How texts teach what readers learn.* Stroud, Glos.: Thimble Press.

Mercer, N. (1995). *The guided construction of knowledge: Talk amongst teachers and learners.* Clevedon, UK: Multilingual Matters.

Mercer, N. (2000). *Words and minds: How we use language to think together.* London: Routledge.

Mitchell, W.J.T. (1994). *Picture theory: Essays on verbal and visual representations.* Chicago: University of Chicago Press.

Morrow, L.M. (1987). The effect of small group story reading on children's questions and comments. In S. McCormick & J. Zutell (Eds.), *Cognitive and social perspectives for literacy research and instruction: Thirty-seventh yearbook of the National Reading Conference* (pp. 77–86). Chicago: National Reading Conference.

Morrow, L.M. (1988). Young children's responses to one-to-one story readings in school settings. *Reading Research Quarterly, 23* (1), 89–107.

Morrow, L.M., & Gambrell, L. (2000). Literature-based reading instruction. In M. Kamil, P. Mosenthal, P.D. Pearson, & R. Barr (Eds.), *Handbook of reading research* (Vol. 3, pp. 563–86). Mahwah, NJ: Lawrence Erlbaum Associates.

Morrow, L.M., & Smith, J.K. (1990). The effects of group size on interactive storybook reading. *Reading Research Quarterly, 25* (2), 214–31.

The New London Group. (1996). A pedagogy of multiliteracies: Designing social futures. *Harvard Educational Review, 66* (1), 60–92.

Nikolajeva, M. (1998). Exit children's literature? *The Lion and the Unicorn, 22* (2), 221–36.

Nikolajeva, M., & Scott, C. (2000). The dynamics of picturebook communication. *Children's Literature in Education, 31* (4), 225–39.

Nikolajeva, M., & Scott, C. (2001). *How picturebooks work.* New York: Garland Publishing.

Nodelman, P. (1988). *Words about pictures: The narrative art of children's picture books.* Athens: University of Georgia Press.

Nodelman, P. (1996). *The pleasures of children's literature* (2nd ed.). New York: Longman.

Nodelman, P., & Reimer, M. (2003). *The pleasures of children's literature* (3rd ed.). Boston: Allyn and Bacon.

Oyler, C., & Barry, A. (1996). Intertextual connections in read-alouds of information books. *Language Arts, 73* (5), 324–9.

Pantaleo, S. (1995). The influence of teacher practice on student response to literature. *Journal of Children's Literature, 21* (1), 38–47.

*Pantaleo, S. (2002). Grade 1 students meet David Wiesner's three pigs. *Journal of Children's Literature, 28* (2), 72–84.

*Pantaleo, S. (2003a). 'Godzilla lives in New York': Grade 1 students and the peritextual features of picture books. *Journal of Children's Literature, 29* (2), 66–77.

*Pantaleo, S. (2003b). The art of playful parody: Exploring David Wiesner's *Tuesday. The Dragon Lode, 22* (1), 42–50.

*Pantaleo, S. (2004a). Young children and radical change characteristics in picture books. *The Reading Teacher, 58* (2), 178–87.

*Pantaleo, S. (2004b). Young children interpret the metafictive in Anthony Browne's *Voices in the park. Journal of Early Childhood Literacy, 4* (2), 211–33.

*Pantaleo, S. (2004c). Exploring Grade 1 students' textual connections. *Journal of Research in Childhood Education, 18* (3), 211–25.

*Pantaleo, S. (2004d). The long, long way: Young children explore the fabula and syuzhet of *Shortcut. Children's Literature in Education: An International Quarterly, 35* (1), 1–20.

Pantaleo, S. (2005a). 'Reading' young children's visual texts. *Early Childhood Research & Practice* [On-line serial] 7 (1). Available http://ecrp.uiuc.edu/v7n1/pantaleo.html.

*Pantaleo, S. (2005b). Young children engage with the metafictive in picture books. *Australian Journal of Language and Literacy, 28* (1), 19–37.

*Pantaleo, S. (2006a). Readers and writers as intertexts: Exploring the intertextualities in student writing. *Australian Journal of Language and Literacy, 29* (2), 163–81.

Pantaleo, S. (2006b). Postmodernism, metafiction and *Who's afraid of the big bad book? The Journal of Children's Literature Studies, 3* (1), 26–39.

*Pantaleo, S. (2007a). 'How could that be?': Reading Banyai's *Zoom* and *Re-Zoom. Language Arts, 84* (3), 222–3.

*Pantaleo, S. (2007b). Writing texts with radical change characteristics. *Literacy, 41* (1), 16–25.

Pantaleo, S. (2007c). Scieszka's subversive little red hen: Aka 'One annoying chicken.' *Journal of Children's Literature, 33* (1), 22–32.

Pantaleo, S. (2007d). 'Everything comes from seeing things': Narrative and illustrative play in *Black and white. Children's Literature in Education: An International Quarterly, 38* (1), 45–58.

*Pantaleo, S. (2007e). Exploring the metafictive in elementary students' writing. *Changing English, 14* (1), 61–76.

*Pantaleo, S. (2007f). Interthinking: Young children using language as a tool to think collectively during interactive read-alouds. *Early Childhood Education Journal, 34* (6), 439–47.

Pantaleo, S. (2007g). Scieszka's *The stinky cheese man*: A tossed salad of parodic re-versions. *Children's Literature in Education: An International Quarterly, 38* (4), 277–95.

*Pantaleo, S., & Luce-Kapler, R. (2006). Collateral learning, changing texts and the curriculum. *English in Australia, 41* (2), 51–60.

Peterson, S. (2006). Influence of gender on writing development. In C. MacArthur, S. Graham, & J. Fitzgerald (Eds.), *Handbook of writing research* (pp. 311–23). New York: Guilford Press.

Pickett, B. (1962). *Monster mash.* Hollywood: Homewood Studios.

Purves, A. (1973). *Literature education in ten countries: An empirical study.* New York: Halsted.

Purves, A. (1974). People prose. In R. Fox (Ed.), *Images in language, media and mind* (pp. 3–27). Urbana, IL: National Council of Teachers of English.

Purves, A.C., & Rippere, V. (1968). *Elements of writing about a literary work: A study of response to literature.* Research Report No. 9. Urbana, IL: National Council of Teachers of English.

Purves, A., Rogers, T., & Soter, A. (1990). *How porcupines make love II: Teaching a response-centered curriculum.* New York: Longman.

Rose, M. (1993). *Parody: Ancient, modern and post-modern.* Cambridge: Cambridge University Press.

Rosen, H. (1986). The importance of story. *Language Arts, 63* (3), 226–37.

Rosenblatt, L. (1976). *Literature as exploration* (4th ed.). New York: The Modern Language Association of America.

Rosenblatt, L. (1978). *The reader, the text, the poem: The transactional theory of the literary work.* Carbondale: Southern Illinois University Press.

Rosenblatt, L. (1981). The readers' contribution in the literary experience. *The English Quarterly, 14* (1), 3–12.

Rosenblatt, L. (1985). Viewpoints: Transaction versus interaction – a terminological rescue operation. *Research in the Teaching of English, 19* (1), 96–107.

Rosenblatt, L. (1986). The aesthetic transaction. *Journal of Aesthetic Education, 20* (4), 122–7.

Rosenblatt, L. (1988). The literary transaction. In P. Demers (Ed.), *The creating word* (pp. 66–85). Edmonton: University of Alberta Press.

Rosenblatt, L. (1991). Literary theory. In J. Flood, J. Jensen, D. Lapp & J. Squire (Eds.), *Handbook of research on teaching the English Language Arts* (pp. 57–62). New York: Macmillan.

Rosenblatt, L. (1994). The transactional theory of reading and writing. In R. Ruddell, M. Ruddell, & H. Singer (Eds.), *Theoretical models and processes of reading* (4th, ed., pp. 1057–92). Newark, DE: International Reading Association.

Roser, N., & Martinez, M. (1985). Roles adults play in preschoolers' response to literature. *Language Arts, 62* (5), 485–90.

Roukes, N. (1997). *Humor in art: A celebration of visual wit.* Worcester, MA: Davis Publications.

Ryan, M., & Anstey, M. (2003). Identity and text: Developing self-conscious readers. *Australian Journal of Language and Literacy, 26* (1), 9–22.

Schwandt, T. (1998). Constructivist, interpretivist approaches to human inquiry. In N. Denzin & Y. Lincoln (Eds.), *The landscape of qualitative research: Theories and issues* (pp. 221–59). Thousand Oaks, CA: Sage Publications.

Schwarcz, J. (1982). *Ways of the illustrator: Visual communication in children's literature.* Chicago: American Library Association.

Schwarcz, J., & Schwarcz, C. (1991). *The picture book comes of age.* Chicago: American Library Association.

Short, K., Kauffman, G., Kaser, S., Kahn, L., & Crawford, K. (1999). Teacher watching: Examining teacher talk in literature circles. *Language Arts, 76* (5), 377–85.

Siegel, M. (1995). More than words: The generative power of transmediation for learning. *Canadian Journal of Education, 20* (4), 455–75.

Silvey, A. (2001). Pigs in space. *School Library Journal, 47* (1), 48–50.

Sinclair, J., & Coulthard, M. (1975). *Towards an analysis of discourse: The English used by teachers and pupils.* London: Oxford University Press.

Sipe, L. (1998). How picture books work: A semiotically framed theory of text-picture relationships. *Children's Literature in Education, 29* (2), 97–108.

Sipe, L. (2000a). The construction of literary understanding by first and second graders in oral response to picture storybook read-alouds. *Reading Research Quarterly, 35* (2), 252–75.

Sipe, L. (2000b). 'Those two gingerbread boys could be brothers': How children use intertextual connections during storybook readalouds. *Children's Literature in Education, 31* (2), 73–90.

Sipe, L. (2001). A palimpsest of stories: Young children's construction of intertextual links among fairytale variants. *Reading Research and Instruction, 40* (4), 333–51.

Sipe, L., & Bauer, J. (2001). Urban kindergartners' literary understanding of picture storybooks. *The New Advocate, 14* (4), 329–42.

Smith, F. (1988). *Joining the literacy club: Further essays into education.* Portsmouth, NH: Heinemann.

Spiro, R., Coulson, R., Feltovich, P., & Anderson, D. (2004). Cognitive flexibility theory: Advanced knowledge acquisition in ill-structured domains. In R. Ruddell & N. Unrau (Eds.), *Theoretical models and processes of reading* (5th ed., pp. 640–53). Newark, DE: International Reading Association.

Squire, J.R. (1990). Research on reader response and the national literature initiative. In M. Hayhoe & S. Parker (Eds.), *Reading and response* (pp. 13–24). Philadelphia: Open University Press.

Stephens, J. (1992). *Language and ideology in children's literature.* New York: Longman.

Stephens, J., & Watson, K. (Eds). (1994). *From picture book to literary theory.* Sydney, AU: St Clair Press.

Stevenson, D. (1995). *Zoom.* [Review of the book *Zoom*]. *The Bulletin of the Center for Children's Books, 48* (6), 189–90.

Still, J., & Worton, M. (1990). Introduction. In M. Worton & J. Still (Eds.), *Intertextuality: Theories and practices* (pp. 1–44). Manchester: Manchester University Press.

Styles, M., & Arizpe, E. (2001). A gorilla with 'grandpa's eyes': How children interpret visual texts – a case study of Anthony Browne's *Zoo. Children's Literature in Education, 32* (4), 261–81.

Sutherland-Smith, W. (2002). Weaving the literacy Web: Changes in reading from page to screen. *The Reading Teacher*, 55 (7), 662–9.

Taylor, B., Peterson, D., Pearson, P.D., & Rodriguez, M. (2002). Looking inside classrooms: Reflecting on the 'how' as well as the 'what' in effective reading instruction. *The Reading Teacher*, 56 (3), 270–9.

Teale, W. (2003). Reading aloud to children as a classroom instructional activity: Insights from research and practice. In A. van Kleeck, S. Stahl, & E. Bauer (Eds.), *On reading books to children: Parents and teachers* (pp. 114–39). Mahwah, NJ: Lawrence Erlbaum Associates.

Thomson, J. (1984). Wolfgang Iser's 'The act of reading' and the teaching of literature. *English in Australia*, 70, 18–30.

Tompkins, J.P. (Ed.). (1980). *Reader response criticism: From formalism to poststructuralism*. Baltimore: Johns Hopkins University Press.

Torr, J. (2004). Talking about picture books: The influence of maternal education on four-year-old children's talk with mothers and pre-school teachers. *Journal of Early Childhood Literacy*, 4 (2), 181–210.

Trites, R. S. (1994). Manifold narratives: Metafiction and ideology in picture books. *Children's Literature in Education*, 25(4), 225–42.

Villaume, S., & Worden, T. (1993). Developing literate voices: The challenge of whole language. *Language Arts*, 70 (6), 462–8.

Vygotsky, L. (1978). *Mind in society*. Cambridge: Harvard University Press.

Vygotsky, L. (1981). The genesis of higher mental functions. In J. Wertsch (Ed. & Trans.), *The concept of activity in Soviet psychology* (pp. 144–88). Armonk, NY: Sharpe. (Original work published 1960).

Walsh, M. (2000). Text-related variables in narrative picture books: Children's response to visual and verbal texts. *The Australian Journal of Language and Literacy*, 23 (2), 139–56.

Walsh, M. (2003). 'Reading' pictures: What do they reveal? Young children's reading of visual texts. *Reading: Literacy and Language*, 37 (3), 123–30.

Wasik, B., & Bond, M. (2001). Beyond the pages of a book: Interactive book reading and language development in preschool classrooms. *Journal of Educational Psychology*, 93 (2), 243–50.

Waugh, P. (1984). *Metafiction: The theory and practice of self-conscious fiction*. New York: Methuen.

Wells, G. (1986). *The meaning makers: Children learning language and using language to learn*. Portsmouth, NH: Heinemann.

Wiesner, D. (1992). Caldecott acceptance speech. *The Horn Book*, 68 (4), 416–22.

Wiesner, D. (2002). The 2002 Caldecott medal acceptance speech. *Journal of Youth Services in Libraires*, 15 (4), 14–16.

Yaden, D., Rowe, D., & MacGillivray, L. (2000). Emergent literacy: A matter (polyphony) of perspectives. In M. Kamil, P. Mosenthal, P.D. Pearson, & R. Barr (Eds.), *Handbook of reading research* (Vol.3, pp. 425–54). Mahwah, NJ: Lawrence Erlbaum Associates.

Yearwood, S. (2002). Popular postmodernism for young adult readers: *Walk two moons*, *Holes* and *Monster*. *The ALAN Review*, *29* (3), 50–3.

Yenawine, P. (2005). Thoughts on visual literacy. In J. Flood, S. Brice Heath & D. Lapp (Eds.). *Research on teaching literacy through the communicative and visual arts* (pp. 845–6). Mahwah, NJ: Lawrence Erlbaum Associates.

Children's Literature References

Banyai, I. (1995). *Re-zoom*. New York: Puffin Books.

Banyai, I. (1995). *Zoom*. New York: Puffin Books.

Bateman, R. (1998). *Safari*. Toronto: Penguin Studio.

Browne, A. (1977). *A walk in the park*. London: Julia MacRae Books.

Browne, A. (1984). *Willy the wimp*. London: Julia MacRae Books.

Browne, A. (1997). *Willy the dreamer*. Cambridge, MA: Candlewick Press.

Browne, A. (1998). *Voices in the park*. London: Picture Corgi Books.

Child, L. (2000). *Beware of the storybook wolves*. New York: Scholastic.

Child, L. (2002). *Who's afraid of the big bad book?* New York: Hyperion.

Creech, S. (1994). *Walk two moons*. New York: HarperCollins.

Demi. (1990). *The empty pot*. New York: Henry Holt and Company.

Di Camillo, K. (2003). *The tale of Despereaux*. Cambridge, MA: Candlewick Press.

Fleischman, S. (1997). *Seedfolks*. New York: HarperTrophy.

Gilman, P. (1992). *Something from nothing*. Richmond Hill, ON: Scholastic Canada.

Konigsburg, E. L. (1996). *The view from Saturday*. New York: Atheneum.

Korman, G. (2003). *The danger*. New York: Scholastic.

Korman, G. (2003). *The deep*. New York: Scholastic.

Korman, G. (2003). *The discovery*. New York: Scholastic.

Lyon, G. (1996). *A day at damp camp*. New York: Orchard Books.

Macaulay, D. (1987). *Why the chicken crossed the road*. Boston: Houghton Mifflin.

Macaulay, D. (1990). *Black and white*. Boston: Houghton Mifflin.

Macaulay, D. (1995). *Shortcut*. Boston: Houghton Mifflin.

Martin, J. B. (1998). *Snowflake Bentley*. Boston: Houghton Mifflin.

Rylant, C. (1985). *Every living thing*. New York: Macmillan.

Sachar, L. (1998). *Holes*. New York: Farrar, Straus & Giroux.

Scieszka, J. (1989). *The true story of the three little pigs*. New York. Scholastic.

Scieszka, J. (1992). *The Stinky Cheese Man and other fairly stupid tales*. New York: Viking.

Seuss, Dr. (1970). *Bartholomew and the oobleck*. New York: Random House.

Sis, P. (1996). *Starry messenger: Galileo Galilei*. New York: Farrar, Straus & Giroux.

Van Draanen, P. (2001). *Flipped*. New York: Alfred A. Knopf.

Wiesner, D. (1991). *Tuesday*. New York: Clarion Books.

Wiesner, D. (2001). *The three pigs*. New York: Clarion Books.

Willems, M. (2003). *Don't let the pigeon drive the bus!* New York: Hyperion.

Author Index

McCallum, R., 4, 10, 12, 16, 63, 91, 93, 100
McClay, J., 12
McGee, L., 12, 27–28
McGillis, R., 77, 91
McKechnie, L., 17
McLaughlin, T., 70
McRobbie, C., 25
Meek, M., 7, 9, 67, 91, 99, 100, 103, 138, 151, 179
Mercer, N., 5, 24, 25, 101, 102
Mitchell, W.J.T., 9
Moje, E., 77, 79, 85, 88
Morrow, L.M., 26, 27, 29, 103

The New London Group, 189
Nikolajeva, M., 8, 9, 11, 12, 16, 18, 57, 71
Nodelman, P., 8, 51, 71, 149

Oyler, C., 30, 104, 180

Pantaleo, S., 16, 26, 35, 37, 38–39, 123, 141, 143, 147–148
Pearson, P.D., 35, 103, 118
Parmar, R., 70
Peterson, D., 35, 103
Peterson, S., 178, 179
Pratt, D., 27
Purves, A.C., 14, 21, 26, 50, 157

Reimer, M., 149
Rippere, V., 21
Rodriguez, M., 35, 103
Rose, M., 77, 78
Rosen, H., 181
Rosenblatt, L., 21, 22–23, 29, 67, 77
Roser, N., 25, 103
Roukes, N., 79
Rowe, D., 25

Ryan, M., 102

Sanford, K., 178
Schwandt, T., 24
Schwarcz, J., 8–9
Scieszka, J. See *The Stinky Cheese Man and Other Fairly Stupid Tales*
Scott, C., 8, 9, 12, 18, 57, 71
Shanahan, L., 29
Short, K., 27
Silvey, A., 14, 15
Sinclair, J., 37
Sipe, L., 8, 9, 12, 18, 26, 27, 28, 43, 71
Sis, P., See *Starry Messenger*
Smith, F., 30, 180,
Smith, J.K., 26
Spiro, R., 100, 138
Squire, J.R., 21–22
Stephens, J., 11–12, 70, 77, 78
Stevenson, D., 124
Still, J., 29, 71
Straus, A., 113
Styles, M., 8, 9, 139, 149, 188
Sumner, G., 12, 27
Sutherland-Smith, W., 186

Taylor, B., 35, 103
Teale, W., 25
Thomson, J., 23, 138
Tobin, K., 24
Tompkins, J.P., 22
Torr, J., 103
Trites, R.S., 11–12, 16, 63, 174

Villaume, S., 26, 27
Vygotsky, L., 24, 102

Walsh, M., 9, 28, 139
Wasik, B., 26
Watson, K., 11–12, 70, 77, 78, 91

Waugh, P., 3, 4, 11, 77, 91, 138
Wells, M., 26, 27
Wiesner, D., 75–76, 77, 89. See also
  The Three Pigs; *Tuesday*
Winsler, A., 24, 102
Wiseman, D., 12, 26, 27

Worden, T., 26, 27
Worton, M., 29, 71

Yearwood, S., 10
Yenawine, P., 139
Young, J., 178

Subject Index

illustrations: careful reading of, 148–149; contradicting text, 13, 46, 116; as evolving, 129; interpretation of, 74, 188; metafictive devices in, 12, 43, 55, 144; as visual links, 93, 96–97, 147, 162–163. *See also* mise-en-abyme; recurring images; visual layering; wordless picturebooks
illustrative media, mixing of, 15, 118, 121, 144, 146, 162–163
imagetext, 9
imagination: of authors, 10, 15, 75, 79, 143; of readers, 126, 139, 146
immigrant children, 28, 188
indeterminacy, 15, 55, 57, 93, 164
information behaviour, 17
interactivity, 17, 19–20, 60–63; in the digital world, 16, 186; in students' stories, 156–157, 164, 168, 172, 177; in *The Stinky Cheese Man and Other Fairly Stupid Tales*, 142–143; in *The Three Pigs*, 48–52; in *Voices in the Park*, 60–63. *See also* reading aloud
interdependent storytelling, 8
interruptions, 149; in Grade 5 students' stories, 153, 154, 155, 156, 157, 162, 163, 164, 165, 167, 168, 170–171, 173–174; in *The Stinky Cheese Man and Other Fairly Stupid Tales*, 143; in *The Three Pigs*, 19, 51, 118; in *Voices in the Park*, 56, 60
interpretation, 22–24, 28, 105; by Grade 1 students, 43–45, 66; and intertextuality, 71; and parody, 78. *See also* readers, as co-authors
intertextuality, 28, 57, 70–72, 102, 104, 179–180; in Eddie's stories, 154; in Jenatine's stories, 159–162;

in other Grade 5 students' stories, 166–167, 168, 172–173, 180; in *Re-zoom*, 124–125; social nature of, 29–31; in *The Stinky Cheese Man and Other Fairly Stupid Tales*, 141; in *The Three Little Spoons and the Big Bad Cow*, 166–167; in *The Three Pigs*, 13–14, 48–49; in *Willy the Dreamer*, 69–70, 72–75, 108–109. *See also* parody
interthinking, 24, 101, 103. *See also* exploratory talk
intratextuality: in *Re-zoom* and *Zoom*, 123–124, 126; in *Shortcut*, 93–94, 95, 96–98; social nature of, 29–31; in *The Three Pigs*, 13, 48–50; in *Voices in the Park*, 56, 57–61; in *Willy the Dreamer*, 109
'It Could be a Mystery,' 158–159, 162–163

Jenatine, stories by, 157–164

language forms, 20, 50–51. *See also* nursery rhyme language; people prose; pop-culture prose; storybook language
layout features, 15, 188; and meaning, 18. *See also features of stories by name*
linear narrative, 182–185
literacy, 26, 30, 31, 33–34, 102, 103, 152, 180. *See also* visual literacy

'Mary Had a Little Lamb Chop,' 153–154
meaning: construction of, 21, 22, 23–24, 67; multiple layers of, 47–48, 57–60
metafiction: and the child reader,

99–101; and postmodernism, 16; in *Shortcut*, 92–99; techniques of, 11–15, 99, 103; in *Willy the Dreamer*, 72–75; in *Re-zoom* and *Zoom*, 138–139
mise-en-abyme, 124, 144, 145
Monsters, Inc., 161
mosaic narrative, 52
'The Move,' 158, 159, 163
multilayered reading, 19, 93, 171–172
multiple perspectives, 20, 50, 53, 63–64, 164. *See also* multiple voices; narrators; *Re-zoom*; *The Three Little Spoons and the Big Bad Cow*; *Zoom*
multiple stories: in Grade 5 students' stories, 171–172. See also *Black and White*; Eddie, stories by; parallel stories; *Red, Blue, and Yellow*; *Re-zoom*; *Shortcut*; *The Three Little Spoons and the Big Bad Cow*; *The Three Pigs*; *Voices in the Park*; *Zoom*
multiple voices, 20, 50, 53, 56, 175. See also *The Three Little Spoons and the Big Bad Cow*; *Voices in the Park*

narrative devices, 6, 30–31, 63, 100; in context, 181–185. *See also* linear narrative; multiple perspectives; multiple stories; parallel stories
narrators: in Eddie's stories, 155, 156–157; interactivity of, 142, 154, 172, 174–175; multiple, 53
nonlinear text, 19; in Grade 5 students' stories, 163–164, 168, 170–175, 179; in *Shortcut*, 92–99,

121–122; in *The Three Pigs*, 46–47, 48–50; in *Voices in the Park*, 56–57. *See also* Web-based literature
nursery rhyme language, 20
nursery rhymes: in *The Three Little Spoons and the Big Bad Cow*, 166; in *The Three Pigs*, 13, 48–49. *See also* fairy tales

omissions, in text, 23. *See also* indeterminacy; interruptions
oral responses. *See* group talk; peer-led discussions; *and stories by name*

palimpsest, 71–72
parody: in literature, 77–79, 91; and postmodernism, 78; in *The Three Little Spoons and the Big Bad Cow*, 165–168; in *The Three Pigs*, 13, 15; in *Tuesday*, 77; in *Willy the Dreamer*, 69. *See also* visual parody
parallel stories, 8, 19, 145, 174. *See also* four-frame format
peer-led discussions, 29, 109–110
people prose, 14–15, 50–51, 157, 168. *See also* pop-culture prose
peritextual features, 104, 115–116. *See also by feature term*
perspectives. *See* multiple perspectives
plot trajectory, 19, 46–47. *See also* nonlinear text
polyphonic narratives, 57–80
pop-culture prose, 153
postmodernism: features of, 10–11; and metafiction, 16, 100
prediction, 14, 19–20, 23–24, 28; by Grade 1 students, 39–40, 42, 47,

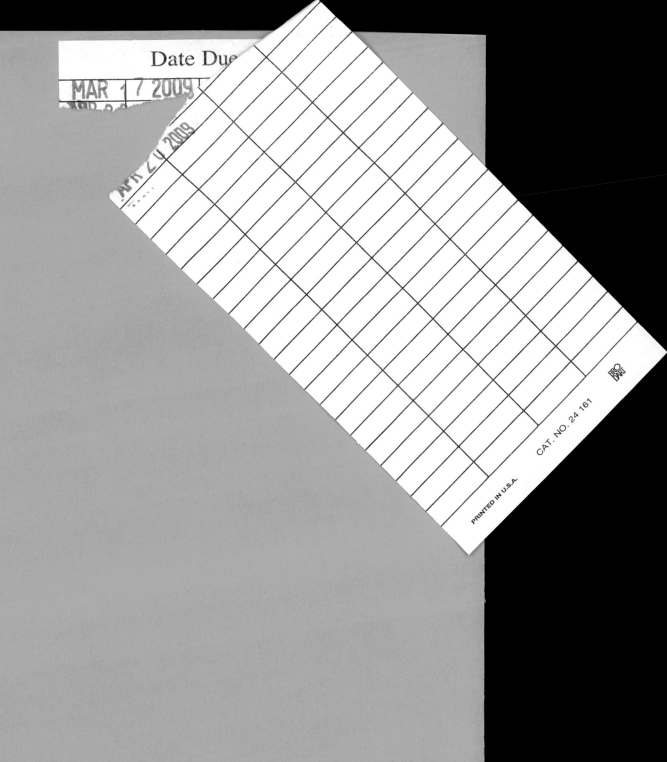